ESSENTIALS OF SUBFILE PROGRAMMING
AND ADVANCED TOPICS IN RPG IV

PHIL LEVINSON

A Division of
DUKE COMMUNICATIONS INTERNATIONAL
221 E. 29th Street • Loveland, CO 80538
(800) 621-1544 • (970) 663-4700 • www.29thStreetPress.com

29th Street PRESS

Library of Congress Cataloging-in-Publication Data

Levinson, Phil, 1947-
    Essentials of subfile programming and advanced topics in RPG IV
/ by Phil Levinson.
    p. cm.
    Includes index.
    ISBN 1-58304-051-X
    1. IBM AS/400 (Computer)—Programming. 2. RPG (Computer program
language) I. Title.
    QA76.8.I25919 L49 1999
    005.2'42—dc21

                                                99-6493
                                                CIP

 Published by 29th Street Press
DUKE COMMUNICATIONS INTERNATIONAL
Loveland, Colorado

Copyright © 1999 by Phil Levinson

This book was printed and bound in Canada.

ISBN 1-58304-051-X

2001 2000 1999 WL 10 9 8 7 6 5 4 3 2 1

To my loving bride, Janice,
and our two bundles of joy,
Jeremy and Joshua.

Acknowledgments

Many people made this textbook possible, among them Bryon Escobar and the Cooper Bussmann IT team, who provided me with resources and real-world experiences; Dean Frank Thoendal and Vice President Dan Steadman of Jefferson College, who provided confidence and support; my students, who inspired me to continue to develop this material and identified where improvements were needed; my fellow faculty members, who carried an extra load to allow me the time to complete the manuscript, and my family, who made time whenever it was needed. This textbook also would not exist without the guidance and assistance of Veronica Patterson, Dawn Cyr, and the other editors and staff of 29th Street Press.

Table of Contents at a Glance

Table of Contents

Welcome to the World of Subfiles

Many courses for AS/400 programmers stop short of teaching you subfile programming. Subfiles are the AS/400 tool that supports displaying lists of data on the screen, and in today's increasingly screen-based world, you must understand and be able to use them. In fact, every list that you have seen the AS/400 display has been created using the same programming techniques that you will learn in these chapters.

This text introduces you to subfiles and leads you through the process of creating and debugging subfile programs. As new subfile concepts are presented, you will develop and expand the same programs to meet expanded specifications. This approach mirrors the real world in which new specifications continually add to the complexity of interactive programs. You will program interactive displays that help users find the data they need and update records as required. You will learn several techniques for designing screens that help make user displays intuitive and easy to use. In a later chapter, you'll learn to use two tools — journaling and commitment control — that will protect your database's integrity when programs let records be changed.

The two ongoing sets of exercises in this text take you through the process of developing an inventory display screen and a purchase order line display screen with data maintenance capabilities. To get the most from this book, work through all segments of the continued exercises, as well as through the additional bookstore order system project that follows Chapters 5 and 7.

Chapters 8 and 9 introduce Integrated Language Environment (ILE) tools for RPG. These include bound calls, multiple modules in a program, creating and using service programs, using procedures, and prototyping.

Other advanced topics include using such file-oriented elements as record format level identifiers, the OVRDBF (Override with Database File) and OPNQRYF(Open Query File) CL commands, file and record locks, and file security; mining the file-information and program-status data structures for information; handling errors via the *PSSR subroutine, the INFSR keyword, and the Input/Output operation error indicator; and using data queues for program-to-program communication.

Don't neglect the appendices! Appendix A explores the programming standards you'll meet in most IS departments and takes you beyond them into issues of programming style. Appendix B introduces debugging tools and techniques to support your programming skills. Finally, Appendix C gives you invaluable training in using Screen Design Aid (SDA).

When you interview for a job as an AS/400 programmer, you will be asked about your knowledge of subfiles and other advanced RPG topics. Once you complete this text, its exercises, and the additional bookstore order system project, you'll have a head start on your first programming position or — if you're already a programmer — additional professional development that will count in your department and your company.

Section I

Essentials of Subfile Programming

Today more than ever, programs and systems are screen-based. Section 1 (Chapters 1 through 7) of *Essentials of Subfile Programming and Advanced Topics in RPG IV* focuses on screen-based, interactive programs, and especially on the use of subfiles. Subfiles are an AS/400 tool used to display lists of data on the screen. In fact, every list that you've seen the AS/400 display can be created with the programming techniques presented in Section 1.

As an AS/400 programmer, you must understand and be able to use subfiles. Chapter 1 introduces subfiles by taking you through the development of simple subfile display screens. You'll learn to create subfile records, subfile control records, and footer records, as well as to write the RPG code to load, display, and clear a subfile, and to manage the no-records case.

Chapter 2 shows you how to modify programs to accept user options for deleting and changing records. You'll learn to use the READC (Read the Next Changed Record) operation, create pop-up windows, and write display-file and RPG code for interactive file maintenance (Add, Delete, and Change options).

Chapter 3 introduces three methods for loading subfiles with multipage lists. You will learn one method that loads all records, one that lets a subfile grow, and one that loads a single page at a time.

Chapter 4 examines the issues of programming subfiles for which the amount of display data requires multiple lines per record. When you finish Chapter 4, you will be able to describe and use the SFLDROP (Subfile Drop) and SFLFOLD (Subfile Fold) keywords, the SFLPAG (Subfile Page) keyword, and the SFLCSRRRN (Subfile Cursor Relative Record Number) keyword. You will also learn to place a blank row between records and to add Input, Output, or Both fields to the header records.

Chapter 5 explores ways to locate records and load the desired data into the subfile. You will learn programming techniques to load records from the correct position in a physical file via a selection screen and also via a selection field in the header record. You will also learn techniques for locating records based on various fields, loading the subfile from different logical files, creating a display file, and writing a program with more than one subfile.

Chapter 6 presents ways to make the system more user friendly, including changing data in list mode, adding user prompts, and including Help screens. This chapter helps you develop subfiles that let users change the data on the screen. You learn to use hidden fields, create prompts for fields, and add Help at field and screen levels.

Finally, Chapter 7 explores using subfiles in windows to provide advanced prompting features for users. You will learn to create subfiles in windows from which users can make selections using the prompt option and using the point-and-shoot feature.

In addition to the inventory maintenance and purchase order exercises that run throughout the chapters, a subfile project for a bookstore system is presented in two parts, following Chapters 5 and 7.

One of the first questions that you can expect when you interview for a job as an AS/400 programmer will be about your knowledge of subfiles. Completing Section 1's carefully developed coverage of subfiles will let you answer with confidence that you have a good working knowledge of this essential AS/400 tool.

Chapter 1

Introduction to Subfiles

Chapter Overview

Chapter 1 introduces you to the basic concept of a subfile, including

- the purpose, design, and creation of a subfile record
- the purpose, design, and creation of a subfile control record
- the purpose, design, and creation of a footer record
- the RPG code to
  - clear a subfile
  - load a subfile
  - display a subfile
  - manage the no-records case

What Is a Subfile?

A **subfile** is a special type of AS/400 display-file record. It is designed to hold a column-based list of data and to display that list in a column format. A subfile is a data file, with data-file attributes such as

- a record name and record structure
- fields with field structures and other field attributes
- records that contain data, much like records in a physical file (You can add, update, and use these records for input to an RPG program in ways that are similar to the same processes on a physical file.)

A subfile differs from other physical files in the following ways:

- It is temporary, existing only until the RPG program that creates and owns it ends.
- Within a subfile, each field's description also identifies its screen location and its display attributes, much like the description of a field in a simple interactive screen.

Subfile is an appropriate term in that we often load a subset of the records from a physical file into it. Subfiles' real use is in user screens that show multiple records at one time (in a list or spreadsheet-like layout of data).

Although AS/400 screens are actually built with a different technology, AS/400 "Work with" screens provide examples of the look and feel of subfile-based screens. For example, the WRKOBJPDM (Work with Objects Using PDM) screen shown in Figure 1.1 presents several elements:

Figure 1.1
Work with Objects Using
PDM Screen

```
                       Work with Objects Using PDM

  Library . . . . .   A300C1_STD       Position to . . . . . . . . _____
                                       Position to type  . . . . . _____

  Type options, press Enter.
    2=Change        3=Copy         4=Delete     5=Display     7=Rename
    8=Display description           9=Save      10=Restore    11=Move ...

  Opt   Object      Type      Attribute   Text
   _    OPB140ABAK  *FILE     PF-DTA      CONTRACT COPY REQUEST FILE
   _    OPB524P     *FILE     PF-DTA
   _    QCLSRC      *FILE     PF-SRC
   _    QCMDSRC     *FILE     PF-SRC
   _    QDDSSRC     *FILE     PF-SRC
   _    QRPGSRC     *FILE     PF-SRC
   _    SEPTFILL    *FILE     PF-DTA      September fill rates
   _    STD         *FILE     PF-SRC      ORIGINAL COPIES OF STD SOURCE
                                                                      More...
  Parameters or command
  ===>

  F3=Exit          F4=Prompt          F5=Refresh         F6=Create
  F9=Retrieve      F10=Command entry  F23=More options   F24=More Keys
```

- The header area at the top of the screen contains general information, options, column headings, and some input/output fields that let the user control the displayed data, such as which library is displayed and where in the library the listing is positioned.
- An area in the center of the screen lists a set of objects — in this case, eight at a time.
- Just above the list of objects, the user is offered a selection of options via which the user can act upon one or more of the listed objects.
- Function keys, defined on lines 22 and 23, provide control of global functions.
- The Page down key displays the next eight objects, and the Page up key displays the previous eight objects.

In subfile processing, the data to be displayed is loaded into records in the subfile and displayed on the screen. An RPG program loads the records, turns over control to the display screen with an EXFMT (Execute Format) operation, receives user input via the function keys — the Enter key and the Page up and Page down keys — and then responds appropriately.

The source code that describes the display file can contain a large number of records — each describing a different screen, overlay, or window. A simple subfile screen, such as the WRKOBJPDM screen, would actually require the following three separate records in the source code that defines the display file.

The **subfile record** describes the subfile record layout. The subfile record declares

- each field's name
- each field's definition
   ○ Field width, type, number of decimals, and other attributes can be explicitly included in the specification.
   ○ Field definitions can be adopted by reference to a field definition in a physical file.

- the location of the first record of the file on the screen (The area above this line can be used for the screen header data, which is usually included in the subfile control record definition.)

The **subfile control record** contains

- control data for the subfile record, including
  - the number of records the subfile can contain (SFLSIZ)
  - the number of rows that can be displayed on the screen at one time (SFLPAG)
  - a control to display the subfile (SFLDSP)
  - a control to display the control record itself, which may contain the header information (SFLDSPCTL)
  - a control to clear (remove) all records from the subfile (SFLCLR)
  - other special subfile controls that we explore in later chapters (e.g., overlay)
- the screen heading display, which defines what is to be displayed at the top of the screen above the subfile's columnar list area (Like a typical display, it can include text and variables with their locations and edit codes. This area would include the screen heading, user identification, date and time identification of user options (e.g., 4=Delete), and headings for the columns.)

The **footer record** is not necessary to create a subfile display. However, standard screen designs typically provide the definition of the function keys at the bottom of the screen.

- Everything that is displayed below the subfile on the screen must be defined in this record.
- Do not include any part of the footer on line 24, which is reserved as the default message line.

The Computers Are US Inventory Project

To demonstrate subfile programming, let's develop a simple inventory system for the fictional company Computers Are US to store and display inventory data.

- The system will store inventory data in the physical file INVPF.
- The data in the file identifies inventory currently in stock.
- Each record in the file represents a specific product, including product number, product description, quantity on hand (the number of items in stock), cost (the purchase cost for a single item), the specific warehouse in which the product is stored, and the product's physical location in the warehouse.
- The system will display the data on the screen shown in Figure 1.2.
- Inventory data is shown on a multirecord (subfile) screen.
- The first eight records appear on the screen.
- The extended cost (computed as quantity times cost) is computed and displayed.

Figure 1.2
Computers Are US
Inventory List Screen

```
  USERID                       COMPUTERS ARE US INV SYS              12/18/98
                                WORK WITH INVENTORY LISTS

  PART NUMBER   DESCRIPTION                        QNTY       COST    EXTENDED

  A123          Computer x486                        21   1,301.15   27,324.15
  A124          Computer Pent                       215   2,100.16  451,534.40
  A125          Printer - Laser                      81     974.21   78,911.01
  A213          Printer - Ink Jet                    15     457.15    6,857.25
  A214          Printer - Dot Matrix                 21     251.14    5,273.94
  A215          Scanner - Hand                       15     127.19    1,907.85
  A216          Scanner - Flat Bed                    5     421.15    2,105.75
  A319          CD-ROM                                6     115.96      695.76


  ========================================================================
  F3=Exit Subsystem
```

In later chapters, we will expand this system to maintain as well as display the data in this file.

We will load this data from the first eight records of INVPF. The file definition is shown in Figure 1.3.

Figure 1.3
File INVPF

```
*...1....+....2....+....3....+....4....+....5....+....6....7....8
A                                          UNIQUE
A          R INVPFR
A            INPN           11A            TEXT('PART NUMBER')
A            INDESC         30A            TEXT('DESCRIPTION')
A            INQOH          5S  0          TEXT('QUANTITY ON HAND')
A            INUCST         6S  2          TEXT('UNIT COST')
A            INWH           3A             TEXT('WAREHOUSE STORED IN')
A            INWHL          5A             TEXT('WAREHOUSE LOCATION')
A          K INPN
```

And, of course, we have some data in our physical file, as is shown in Table 1.1.

Table 1.1
Physical File Data

INPN	INDESC	INQOH	INUCST	INWH	INWHL
A123	Computer x486	21	1301.15	DLS	15A
A124	Computer Pent	215	2100.16	FTW	219
A125	Printer — Laser	81	974.21	DLS	X19
A213	Printer — Ink Jet	15	457.15	FTW	319
A214	Printer — Dot Matrix	21	251.14	FTW	320
A215	Scanner — Hand	15	127.19	DLS	X21
A216	Scanner — Flat Bed	5	421.15	DLS	X22
A319	CD-ROM	6	115.96	FTW	315
A320	4x CD-ROM	6	215.96	FTW	316

Creating the Subfile Record Description for the Computers Are US Inventory System

The **subfile record** must define the fields for the five columns shown in Figure 1.2. The subfile record is shown in Figure 1.4. It defines the fields of a single row: row 8. This is the first row of the subfile.

```
*...1....+....2....+....3....+....4....+....5....+....6

A* Subfile example DDS
A* Member Name: INVD011C
A* Member Type: DSPF
A* By PHIL LEVINSON 9/3/98
A*********************************************
A                                    PRINT
A                                    CF03(03)
A*********************************************
A**    subfile record - DSP01
A
A          R DSP01                   SFL
A            D1PN        11A  0  8  2
A            D1DESC      30A  0  8 15
A            D1QOH        5Y 00  8 47EDTCDE(1)
A            D1UCST       6Y 20  8 55EDTCDE(1)
A            D1LTOT       8Y 20  8 65EDTCDE(1)
A*********************************************
```

Figure 1.4

Subfile Record Definition for Computers Are US Inventory System

The example in Figure 1.4 contains definitions at the file and record level. Keywords used before the first record begins are called file-level keywords. File-level keywords are in effect for all of the records in the file. In this example, both PRINT (Print) and CF03(03) are file-level keywords.

Keywords used within a record but before the first field definition are called record-level keywords; they apply to that record and all the fields of that record, but not to other records (unless also declared in the other records). In the example in Figure 1.4, SFL (Subfile) is a record-level keyword.

Keywords used in a field definition, either on the same line as the field or on subsequent lines (but before the definition of the next field), apply to that single field only and are called field-level keywords. In the example in Figure 1.4, EDTCDE (Edit Code) is a field-level keyword.

Record DSP01 describes the subfile. The record-level keyword SFL indicates that this record describes a subfile. In many ways, this record resembles a physical-file description because it describes fields and their definitions. However, it also describes the location of the fields on the screen display (e.g., row 8, column 2).

The subfile record also describes each field's usage. In our example, all the fields are output only (O), which means that the program can load the data and display it on the screen, but the user cannot alter the screen value. Fields that are input (I) only, let users make entries, but they cannot display data the program loads. Fields capable of both input and output (B) let the program load data that can then be displayed and updated on the screen.

This subfile contains five fields, and columns are displayed beginning on row 8 (note the 8 in every field's row position). The designated usage of all fields is currently output (O), but later we introduce subfile fields with input (I) and with both (B) capabilities.

Using SDA with Subfiles

Screen Design Aid (SDA) is a great tool for creating, editing, and testing screen designs. It can be used effectively on subfile records, subfile control records, and simple records, such as our footer record.

To change the header layout or controls, work with the control record (DSP02). When you are working with a subfile control record, SDA displays that record and a layout of the subfile itself so that you can get an idea about how the entire screen will look.

To change the column layouts or attributes of a field in the subfile, work with the subfile record (DSP01). The header record is also displayed.

For more about SDA, see Appendix C.

Creating the Subfile Control Record Description for Computers Are US

The subfile DSP01 described in Figure 1.4 requires a control record in the same display file. The control record DSP02 (shown in Figure 1.5) contains the necessary keywords to define and control the subfile, as well as screen-heading information. The subfile control record (DSP02) must be entered into the same member as the subfile record that it controls (DSP01). The subfile control record description always immediately follows the subfile record description. The subfile control record controls the processing of the subfile DSP01 as indicated by the record-level keyword SFLCTL (Subfile Control), which must be followed by the name of the subfile record that it controls, in our case, SFLCTL(DSP01).

Figure 1.5

Subfile Control Record
for Computers Are US

```
*...1....+....2....+....3....+....4....+....5....+....6
A***********************************************
A*** SUBFILE CONTROL RECORD DSP02   ***
A
A           R DSP02                 SFLCTL(DSP01)
A
A*** S U B F I L E   C O N T R O L S  ***
A
A                                   SFLSIZ(08)
A                                   SFLPAG(08)
A                                   OVERLAY
A  50                               SFLDSP
A  50                               SFLDSPCTL
A N50                               SFLCLR
A
A*** S C R E E N     H E A D E R   *****
A
A                                   1 31'COMPUTERS ARE US INV SYS'
A                                   2 31'Work with Inventory lists'
A                                   1  2USER
A                                   1 71DATE
A                                      EDTCDE(Y)
A                                   6  2'Part Number'
A                                   6 15'Description'
A                                   6 47'Qnty'
A                                   6 55'Cost'
A                                   6 65'Extended'
A***********************************************
```

Although this is a single record, I've inserted comments to divide the record into two sections:

1. The subfile control section contains the subfile control commands.
2. The screen-header section contains the screen heading definition of the first six rows of the screen.

Subfile Control Keywords

Let's examine each of the subfile control keywords introduced in Figure 1.5

```
*...1....+....2....+....3....+....4....+....5....+....6

A                              SFLSIZ(Ø8)
A                              SFLPAG(Ø8)
A                              OVERLAY
```

SFLSIZ (Subfile Size) declares the number of records the subfile can contain. This number cannot exceed 9999. For the moment, we will keep the number of records low enough for all records to be displayed on a single screen.

SFLPAG (Subfile Page) declares the number of records to be displayed on the screen at one time. The number cannot exceed SFLSIZ.

OVERLAY (Overlay) lets the header and subfile be displayed on a screen that already contains other records — as long as the other records are on different areas of the display. This applies to our design because we want to display the function key definitions at the bottom of the screen, on rows 22 and 23. The OVERLAY keyword on this subfile control record lets us write the footer record with the function key definitions to the bottom of the display screen and then write the header and subfile display to the top and middle of the screen, "overlaying" and replacing any previous records in that geographic area.

To compute the area overlayed, we must consider that the header occupies rows 1 through 6 and that the subfile occupies up to eight rows, starting at row 8 and ending at row 15. Therefore, when we overlay the subfile control and subfile records onto the screen, they replace any records with geography overlapping any of the rows between 1 and 15.

Our RPG program uses indicator 50 (any number from 1 to 99 can be used) to turn on/off three subfile controls. The three keywords used in these subfile controls nearly always appear together, and SFLCLR (Subfile Clear) must have the opposite indicator value (N50 vs 50), as shown below.

```
*...1....+....2....+....3....+....4....+....5....+....6

A   5Ø                         SFLDSP
A   5Ø                         SFLDSPCTL
A  N5Ø                         SFLCLR
```

When indicator 50 is *ON and the RPG program WRITES the control record or does an EXFMT on the control record, the following occurs:

1. SFLDSP (Subfile Display) is on and the subfile will be displayed.
2. SFLDSPCTL (Subfile Display Control) is on and the header section of the control record will be displayed.
3. SFLCLR (Subfile Clear) is off and has no effect.

When indicator 50 is *OFF and the RPG program WRITES the control record, the following occurs:

1. SFLDSP is off and the subfile will not be displayed.
2. SFLDSPCTL is off and the header section of the control record will not be displayed.
3. SFLCLR is on and removes all records from the subfile.

Creating the Footer Record Description for Computers Are US

AS/400 standards that IBM developed and many organizations use require that we display the function key definitions at the bottom of the screen. To do so requires a third record definition for the footer record (see Figure 1.6). In the RPG program, this record is written to the screen first. It may seem a little odd to build the bottom of the screen first, but because this record does not require user input, it can be put on the screen (with a WRITE statement) before the other records are put on with a command that requires a response (EXFMT). Because DSP02 contains the OVERLAY keyword, the FOOTER record is displayed while the subfile is displayed. Remember: This approach requires that the rows used for the function key record (22 and 23) are not used by the record that is subsequently OVERLAYed. (Also remember that row 24 is reserved for error messages.)

Figure 1.6

Footer Record

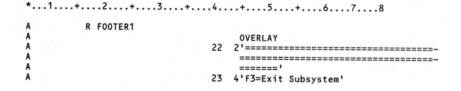

```
*...1....+....2....+....3....+....4....+....5....+....6....7....8
A
A          R FOOTER1
A                                        OVERLAY
A                                     22  2'=====================================-
A                                         =====================================-
A                                         ======='
A                                     23  4'F3=Exit Subsystem'
```

Some Notes on Using SEU

I usually begin my design with a rough layout that I create with the Source Entry Utility (SEU) editor. One of the reasons for this is that I typically copy an earlier example of a subfile's DDS (that's right, copy — many programming activities include copying earlier code). To copy in SEU, enter **SEU** with the name of your new DDS file and then press F15 (Shift F3). Notice the 1 that means view a member. Move down to the member definition and type in the Member name, Library, and File of the member that you want to copy from, and then press Enter.

Your SEU screen is now split horizontally. On top is your new work in Edit mode; below is the member that you copy from in Browse mode. You can quickly copy code by putting copy codes such as CC...CC or C9999 in the sequence number area of the Browse member and in the destination location for the lines — using A(fter) or B(efore) in the edit member.

This split-screen capability is also useful for editing your program because you can view the display member, the physical file member, or RPG code without exiting the editor.

F12 returns SEU to full-screen capabilities.

The Browse/Copy options (invoked by F15) are also extremely useful when you debug code. Option 2 displays the latest compile listing for the member that you are editing on the bottom of the screen. Move to the BROWSE session and page down to scan the listing.

When you use SEU in browse or edit mode, you can use the following controls on the command line:

- B — go to bottom
- T — go to top
- xxx F16 (shift F4) — search for xxx, or any other entry
- QRG F16 (shift F4) — search for RPG error messages
- *ERR F16 (shift F4) — search for next error in source listing

As you find each error, simply move to the top and use the search capability to find the code to be corrected and make the change. Return to the bottom and locate the next error. Once you are familiar with the diagnostic messages and how to use SEU, it is rarely necessary to print out the compile listing.

Exercise 1.1A Computers Are US Inventory Project

Purpose

To test your understanding of the information and examples provided. In the first section of this book — Chapters 1 through 7 — Exercise 1 (called Exercise 1.1 in Chapter 1, Exercise 2.1 in Chapter 2, Exercise 3.1 in Chapter 3, etc.) is based on the code samples provided and follows the development of the Computers Are US Inventory Project. You should do all of the segments of Exercise 1 as they occur throughout each chapter and this section of the book because each set of steps is used to build the concepts and code developed in subsequent sets.

General Program Specifications

Create the physical file, load sample data, and create the display file with all three records for the Computers Are US Inventory screen, as outlined below.

1. Create the physical file INVPF (Figure 1.3) and compile it.

2. Use Data File Utility (DFU) to enter the records shown in Table 1.1. An easy way to start DFU is with the Update command UPDDTA INVPF.

3. Create the DDS INVD011C with the three records DSP01, DSP02, and FOOTER1.

4. View and enhance the layout using Screen Design Aid (SDA).

Exercise 1.2A Purchase Order Line Project

Purpose

In the first section of this book, Exercise 2 (called Exercise 1.2 in Chapter 1, Exercise 2.2 in Chapter 2, Exercise 3.2 in Chapter 3, etc.) follows the development of the Purchase Order Line Project and requires that you draw from the concepts and applications presented to create a solution to a new problem. You should do all of the segments of Exercise 2 as they occur throughout each chapter and this section of the book because each set of steps builds upon the concepts and code developed in previous steps.

General Program Specifications

Computers Are US buys computers wholesale and resells them. The company needs to keep a record of the items that it has on order. Figure 1.7 contains a sample purchase order (PO) issued by Computers Are US.

The top section of the PO provides information specific to that order, such as

- the order number and date of order
- from whom the items are being ordered
- where and how to ship the items
- where to send the bill

This information is often referred to as the order header information and is stored in the Purchase Order Header File. Our current project is not concerned with the header information.

In the middle of the PO form is a table of items ordered. We can have multiple items ordered (sometimes referred to as lines) on the same PO. The data that relates to a single line from a PO is stored in a second file called the PO Line File. Our project is to create the physical file and display file to show the data in the PO Line File (ORDLNP).

1. Create the Physical File ORDLNP and compile it. This file will have a UNIQUE KEY and the following fields:

OLNUM	6A	-	Order Number	Key 1
OLSEQ	3S 0	-	Sequence or Line Number	Key 2
OLPN	11A	-	Part Number	
OLPRC	7S 2	-	Unit Price	
OLOQN	5S 0	-	Quantity Ordered	
OLEDT	8S 0	-	Expected Date	
OLADT	8S 0	-	Actual Delivery Date	
OLAQN	5S 0	-	Actual Delivery Quantity	

continued

Exercise 1.2A *Continued*

Figure 1.7
Purchase Order Form
for Computers Are US

Computers Are US

Purchase Order

PO #: 000015   **Date:** 09/21/99

TO: Fast Eddie's Computer Company
21 Fleet Street
Westmoreland, VA 53071

SHIP TO: Computers Are US   **BILL TO:**   Computers Are US
100 Broadway   PO Box 175100
St Louis, MO 63105   St Louis, MO 63100

SHIP VIA: Fastest Way

PART #	DESCRIPTION	QUANTITY	PRICE	EXTENDED PRICE
A123		250	1,250.00	$312,687.50
A124		150	2,050.00	$307,500.00

TOTAL   **$620,187.50**

continued

Exercise 1.2A *Continued*

2. Use DFU to enter the records shown in Table 1.2.

Table 1.2
Records to Create Table of Items Ordered

OLNUM	OLSEQ	OLPN	OLPRC	OLOQN	OLEDT	OLADT	OLAQN
000015	001	A123	1250.75	250	19980921	19980922	251
000015	002	A124	2050.00	150	19981030	19980922	150
000016	001	A123	1150.75	125	19981030	0	0
000017	001	A320	205.15	50	19981010	0	0
000017	002	A320	200.00	50	19981015	0	0
000017	003	A319	95.21	10	19981015	0	0
000018	001	A214	190.00	5	19980929	19980923	5
000018	002	A216	315.15	250	19981021	0	0
000018	003	A213	415.16	10	19981015	0	0

3. Create display file ORDD011C with the three records DSP01, DSP02, and FOOTER1. The subfile should display the fields OLNUM, OLSEQ, OLPN, OLPRC, OLOQN, and OLEDT in date format as well as a computed column, Extended Price (Extended Price = Price × Quantity) as shown in Figure 1.7. The subfile should be coded to display six records per page and have a maximum of six records in the subfile. The first record of the subfile should be displayed on line 7.

Figure 1.8 shows the screen design.

4. View and enhance the layout using SDA.

Figure 1.8
Computers Are US
Purchase Order
Line Data

```
    USERID                    COMPUTERS ARE US PURCHASING          12/18/99
                                 WORK WITH ORDER LINES

    ORDER  SEQ  PART       PRICE    QUANTITY     EXTENDED   EXPECTED
    NUMBER NUM  NUMBER                              PRICE       DATE
    ===================================================================
    000015 001  A123     1,250.75        250    312,687.50  09/22/98
    000015 002  A124     2,050.00        150    307,500.00  10/30/98
    000016 001  A123     1,150.75        125    143,843.80  10/30/98
    000017 001  A320       205.15         50     10,257.50  10/10/98
    000017 002  A320       200.00         50     10,000.00  10/15/98
    000017 003  A319        95.21         10        952.10  10/15/98

    ===================================================================
    F3=Exit Subsystem
```

Using a Subfile in RPG IV

Now that we have a well-designed display file — INVD011C — we are ready to develop the RPG program (INV011B) to load and display the subfile. The pseudocode for our design is provided in Figure 1.9.

Figure 1.9

Pseudocode for RPG Program INV011B

```
Start
    Execute Load Subfile (LOAD) subroutine
    Do while user has not pressed the F3 key
                            Note: This loop is entered the first time
                            before the display has been sent to the
                            screen because the indicator associated
                            with the function key F3 (*IN03) is initially
                            off and cannot be pressed until the
                            screen is displayed and read.
        Display and read the subfile and the subfile control
    End do
    Close files
End

LOAD subroutine
    Clear subfile
    Load the subfile
        Read a record from INVPF
        Do while not EOF(INVPF) and fewer than eight records have been
        written to the subfile
            Populate the fields of the subfile record
        Add 1 to the subfile Relative Record Number (RRN)
        Write a record to the subfile
        End do
    Write footer
End subroutine
```

The value of the variable RRN is most critical to the performance of this or any subfile. This variable positions the "pointer" for the subfile to the correct subfile record to be used. In the pseudocode shown in Figure 1.9, 1 is added to the Subfile RRN just before a record is written to the subfile. If the value of this variable were zero, the number of an existing record, or greater than the subfile size when the WRITE (Write a Record to a File) operation was attempted, an error would occur.

Figure 1.10 contains the RPG code for program INV011B, with extensive internal comments. Read the code over carefully. Consider how it resembles the pseudocode in Figure 1.9.

```
+....1....+....2....+....3....+....4....+....5....+....6....+....7....+....8

*Jefferson College   Professor Levinson   9/01/99
*APPLICATION NAME      - Inventory System
*PROGRAM NAME          - INV011B
*DESCRIPTION - 1. Clears Subfile    2. Loads Subfile  3.Displays Footer
*              4. Exercises the Screen Display with the Subfile
**********************************************************
*  L O G    O F    M O D I F I C A T I O N S
*
*  DATE    PGMR    DESCRIPTION
*  --------------------------------------------------------
*  / /
**********************************************************
*  F U N C T I O N    O F    I N D I C A T O R S
*IND                 FUNCTION
*--------------------------------------------------------
*  03                USED TO EXIT DISPLAY
*  50                USED TO DISPLAY/CLEAR SUBFILE
*  90                EOF FLAG FOR INVPF
*  LR                LAST RECORD
**********************************************************
*  S U B R O U T I N E    I N D E X
**********************************************************
*  LOAD        - CLEAR AND LOAD RECORDS IN TO SUBFILE DSP01
**********************************************************
*    FILES
**********************************************************
*  Inventory file
FINVPF    IF   E           K DISK

*  Display File with subfile DSP01
FINVD011C CF   E             WORKSTN
F                                 SFILE(DSP01:RRN)

* note: The function SFILE relates the subfile DSP01 to a variable
*       that operates as the relative record pointer. In this
*       example, the variable is named RRN.

**********************************************************
DRRN          S           4P 0
**********************************************************
*MAINLINE
**********************************************************
*                          Load the Subfile
C              EXSR   LOAD

C              DOW    *In03 = *OFF

*              Display the Control Record and the subfile
C              EXFMT  DSP02

C              ENDDO

C              MOVE   *ON      *INLR
C              RETURN
**********************************************************
*  LOAD - LOADS THE INVENTORY SUBFILE FROM THE DATA FILE INVPF
**********************************************************
C  LOAD        BEGSR

C              MOVE   *OFF     *IN50
C              WRITE  DSP02
*  Before you load the subfile, it is cleared of previous entries,
*  although in this case there are none.

C              Z-ADD  *ZERO    RRN
*  Because the subfile is empty, the Relative Record Pointer should be
*  reset to zero.

C              MOVE   *ON      *IN50
*  When Indicator 50 in *on, the control record and the subfile can
+....1....+....2....+....3....+....4....+....5....+....6....+....7....+....8
*  be displayed.
```

Figure 1.10
RPG Program INV011B

continued

Figure 1.10
continued

```
*   START LOADING
C                    READ       INVPF                                    90
*
* Load the first 8 records (or as many as exist) into the subfile.
C                    DOW        (*In90 = *OFF) and
C                               (RRN   <    8)

  *    Populate the subfile fields.
C                    MOVE       INPN            D1PN
C                    MOVE       INDESC          D1DESC
C                    MOVE       INQOH           D1QOH
C                    MOVE       INUCST          D1UCST
C       D1QOH        MULT       D1UCST          D1LTOT

  *    Update the Relative Record Pointer.
C                    ADD        1               RRN
C                    WRITE      DSP01
C                    READ       INVPF                                    90
C                    ENDDO
*    Write Footer Record.
C                    WRITE      FOOTER1

C                    ENDSR
```

Go back and read the RPG program code again. It seems rather long, but most of it is comments. When you write your programs, you should always include enough comments to make the logic and the details of the program clear to any programmer.

Figure 1.11 presents exactly the same code as Figure 1.10 but without comments. With comments, the program seems long, but without comments, the code comprises just 28 lines. The code without comments is harder to understand than the code with comments. Good comments are valuable. In fact, you will find that a large part of a programming job involves making changes to existing code — and it's much easier if the code includes good comments.

Figure 1.11
RPG Program INV011B
Without Comments

```
+....1....+....2....+....3....+....4....+....5....+....6....+....7....+....8

FINVPF     IF   E         K DISK
FINVD011C  CF   E           WORKSTN
F                                     SFILE(DSP01:RRN)
DRRN           S               4P 0
C                    EXSR       LOAD
C                    DOW        *IN03 = *OFF
C                    EXFMT      DSP02
C                    ENDDO
C                    MOVE       *ON             *INLR
C                    RETURN
C       LOAD         BEGSR
C                    MOVE       *OFF            *IN50
C                    WRITE      DSP02
C                    Z-ADD      *ZERO           RRN
C                    MOVE       *ON             *IN50
C                    READ       INVPF                                    90
C                    DOWEQ      (*IN90 = *OFF) and
C                               (RRN   < 8
C                    MOVE       INPN            D1PN
C                    MOVE       INDESC          D1DESC
C                    MOVE       INQOH           D1QOH
C                    MOVE       INUCST          D1UCST
C       D1QOH        MULT       D1UCST          D1LTOT
C                    ADD        1               RRN
C                    WRITE      DSP01
C                    READ       INVPF                                    90
C                    ENDDO
C                    WRITE      FOOTER1
C                    ENDSR
```

Exercise 1.1B Computers Are US Inventory Project

Purpose
To learn to enter, debug, and test RPG code that loads and displays a subfile.

General Program Specifications
In step 5, you develop the RPG program INV011B to load and display the inventory display. In step 6, you test this program under severe conditions.

> **Note:** If you have a problem compiling the program, remember that the library your *FILE objects are in must be included in your library list. You can use the DSPLIBL command to check your library list and the EDTLIBL command to add libraries to your library list. If you have further problems, remember that the compiler report in the spool file indicates the problems. You can view this when you edit in SEU by using F15 (Shift-F3) and then option 2.

5. Enter, compile, and test the RPG program INV011B as shown in Figure 1.10. To test your program call INV011B.

6. In this step, we will test the code to determine what happens if there are no records in the physical file. Testing is an important part of programming. It is the programmer's responsibility to develop virtually "bullet-proof" code.

   • Copy the file to INVPF2 (to save the records for later use) with the following command:

     CPYF YOURLIB/INVPF YOURLIB/INVPF2 CRTFILE(*YES)

   • Remove all records from the file: CLRPFM YOURLIB/INVPF.

   • Run the program. A runtime error occurs and the system displays an error screen — but don't despair. Solving this runtime error is the topic of the next section.

The No-Records Case

Our code works, but it won't pass quality control because it contains a ticking bomb: it will cause a runtime error under some special circumstances. If the inventory file is empty — which seems rather incredible for this particular file but is certainly possible in other subfile load situations — a runtime error occurs when the program attempts to display the subfile via the command EXFMT DSP02.

This error occurs when the subfile contains no record, and the system won't let you display a zero-record subfile.

The code shown in Figure 1.12 ensures that the subfile has at least one record, even if that record only displays the value NO RCDS. The code does so by testing the variable RRN, which is incremented every time a record is added. If the program flow reaches this code and RRN is zero, then this code writes the NO RCDS record to the subfile.

Figure 1.12

Code to Avoid the
No-Records Error

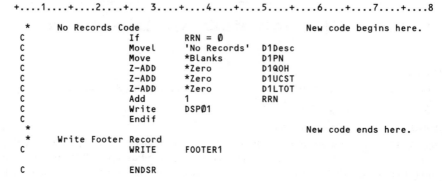

```
+....1....+....2....+... 3....+....4....+....5....+....6....+....7....+....8
  *      No Records Code                                   New code begins here.
  C                  If        RRN = 0
  C                  Movel     'No Records'  D1Desc
  C                  Move      *Blanks       D1PN
  C                  Z-ADD     *Zero         D1QOH
  C                  Z-ADD     *Zero         D1UCST
  C                  Z-ADD     *Zero         D1LTOT
  C                  Add       1             RRN
  C                  Write     DSP01
  C                  Endif
  *                                                        New code ends here.
  *      Write Footer Record
  C                  WRITE     FOOTER1

  C                  ENDSR
```

Exercise 1.1C Computers Are US Inventory Project

Purpose
To correct your code to remove a known error.

General Program Specifications
Finding and correcting errors is an important part of the programming process. Correct the inventory display program so that it does not fail when it encounters the no-records case.

7. Because you proved in step 6 that your code had a potential bug when it encountered the no-records case, you should correct it by adding the code presented in Figure 1.12.

   • Name your new program INV011C.
   • Test it with the empty file and print the screen.
   • Copy the data from INVPF2.
   • Once you've proven that your modified code works with no records, you must demonstrate that it still works with records. To do this, use the copy file command to copy your file with data back into your file:

   CPYF YOURLIB/INVPF2 YOURLIB/INVPF MBROPT(*REPLACE)

   • Test your program again to prove that it still works and print the screen.

Exercise 1.2B Purchase Order Line Project

Purpose

To reinforce your knowledge of the RPG needed to load and display subfiles and to get experience in restricting record selection when loading the subfile.

General Program Specifications

In steps 5 through 8 of the Purchase Order Project, you develop the code to display the purchase order line data. You use the physical file and display file that you created in Exercise 1.2, steps 1 through 4. Your code should include provisions for the no-records case. In steps 7 and 8, you create the code to restrict the selection of records further.

5. Write the RPG program to load the order-line data into subfile DSP01 and display it until F3 is pressed. Name the program ORDL21B. The expected date should be displayed in MM/DD/YY format. Print the compiler listing.

6. Call the program and print the screen.

7. For many of the uses that Computers Are US has for this data, the company is interested only in the PO lines that show orders that have not been delivered. As soon as the POs are marked as delivered, they are added to the inventory and show up on the inventory screens. If delivered lines continued to appear on the PO line screen, it might seem to indicate that more of these items still should be delivered.

In this step, you will create a second program to display only those lines for orders that have not yet been delivered. Although the Order Line Data file (ORDLNP) does not contain a field that specifically indicates the line status, it does have a field that contains the actual delivery date. When the actual delivery date is zero, the order for that line has not been delivered.

Copy program ORDL21B to ORDL21C. Modify ORDL21C so that it displays only records with OLADT = zero.

8. Call the program and print the screen.

Review

1. What is a subfile?
2. What is the role of the subfile record format?
3. How is the subfile record format specified?
4. What is the role of the subfile control record?
5. How is the subfile control record described?
6. Could you include the screen header and footer on the same format?
7. Define the following terms and their functions:

   SFLDSP

   SFLDSPCTL

   SFLCLR

   SFLSIZ

   SFLPAG

8. Could the SFLSIZ be smaller than the SFLPAG? Larger?
9. What is different about the RPG F-spec for a subfile record?
10. Before loading the subfile, we turned off indicator 50 and wrote the control record. Why?
11. RRN is a variable that we assigned to indicate the relative record number of the subfile record. If we wanted to call it RRN01, indicate the lines that would be changed.
12. Why did we move NO RECRD to D1DESC instead of to another field?

Chapter 2

The Option Column, Windows, and File Maintenance

Chapter Overview

Chapter 2 helps you understand and demonstrate how to use

- the READC (Read the Next Changed Record) operation
- popup windows
- display-file code and RPG code for interactive file maintenance
- Add, Delete, and Change options

Subfiles: User Interaction

Your first experiments in creating subfiles displayed the subfile but did not allow user interaction. In this chapter, you add another column to the subfile description, one that lets users make an entry beside any of the records displayed.

Your program then responds to the users' selection of codes for add, delete, change, or display, by locating the corresponding record and displaying a popup window. After users make the appropriate entries or changes in the window, the program updates both the physical file and the display.

Updating files interactively is referred to as interactive file maintenance. Interactive file maintenance is not the only process that uses subfiles, but it is frequently encountered in interactive systems. In this chapter, you learn more about subfiles as you develop a simple file-maintenance system.

The chapter steps you through the process of developing an interactive file-maintenance system in the following sequence. You learn to

1. Describe and demonstrate the changes to the subfile description that are required to provide a user-input-capable column.
2. Describe and demonstrate the development of window formats in the display file.
3. Develop the display file for the inventory maintenance system for Computers Are US.
4. Develop the display file for the purchase order line maintenance system for Computers Are US.
5. Describe and demonstrate the RPG code to detect and process a change request.
6. Develop the RPG code for the inventory maintenance system for Computers Are US to display the screen, support user selection, detect an entry, and process change requests.

7. Add the add, delete, and display capabilities to the inventory maintenance system for Computers Are US.

8. Develop the RPG code for the Computers Are US purchase order line maintenance system to display the screen; allow user selection; detect an entry; and process add, delete, change, and display requests.

Adding an Option Column

Figure 2.1 presents the inventory maintenance screen for Computers Are US.

Figure 2.1

Computers Are US
Inventory Maintenance
Display

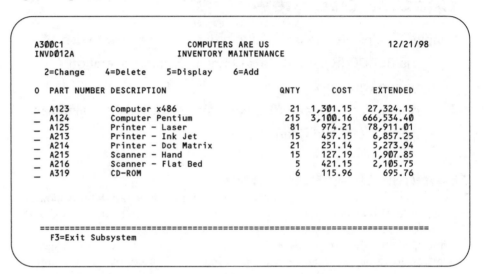

```
A300C1                    COMPUTERS ARE US                  12/21/98
INVD012A                  INVENTORY MAINTENANCE

   2=Change    4=Delete    5=Display    6=Add

O  PART NUMBER DESCRIPTION                   QNTY      COST     EXTENDED

_  A123        Computer x486                   21  1,301.15   27,324.15
_  A124        Computer Pentium               215  3,100.16  666,534.40
_  A125        Printer - Laser                 81    974.21   78,911.01
_  A213        Printer - Ink Jet               15    457.15    6,857.25
_  A214        Printer - Dot Matrix            21    251.14    5,273.94
_  A215        Scanner - Hand                  15    127.19    1,907.85
_  A216        Scanner - Flat Bed               5    421.15    2,105.75
_  A319        CD-ROM                           6    115.96      695.76



================================================================================
   F3=Exit Subsystem
```

The screen shown in Figure 2.1 is similar to the screen shown in Figure 1.2 (Chapter 1) except for the following:

- The display-file name (INVD012A) has been added on row 2. (Having an identification field on every screen is helpful both for user support in general and for tracking users' problems in particular.)
- The screen name on row 2 has been changed to Inventory Maintenance.
- A line has been added to the heading indicating how to select the Add, Change, and Delete options.
  - An option column has been added on the far left side of the subfile record. (This column is input capable.)
  - The column headings now have an O over the option column.
  - The column headings and subfile columns have been moved a few characters to the right to accommodate the new column.

The modified subfile code is shown in Figure 2.2. Only one line has been added — to accommodate the new field, D1PICK. Notice that D1PICK is input capable and that the other fields have been shifted to the right to accommodate it.

You also need to make cosmetic changes to the heading area of the control record. These changes include the column headings in the control record DSP02. I've used an O as the heading for the option column because it fits easily above the column. I've also added a line to the heading that presents the definitions of the available options, option 2=change, etc.

```
*...1....+....2....+....3....+....4....+....5....+....6
A* Subfile example DDS  - INVD012A
A* by Phil Levinson
A*********************************************
A                              PRINT
A                              CF03(03)
A*********************************************
A
A           R DSP01                    SFL
A             D1PICK       1A  I  8  2
A             D1PN        11A  O  8  4
A             D1DESC      30A  O  8 16
A             D1QOH        5Y 0O  8 47EDTCDE(1)
A             D1UCST       6Y 20  8 55EDTCDE(1)
A             D1LTOT       8Y 20  8 65EDTCDE(1)
A*********************************************
```

Figure 2.2
Subfile Definition
Including the Input-
Capable Option
Field D1PICK

Adding Windows

Your file-maintenance screen responds to the selection of an option by displaying a popup window. The window appears over part of the earlier display, and when an action is completed, disappears, revealing the entire earlier display. Figure 2.3 presents a sample display with the change window "open."

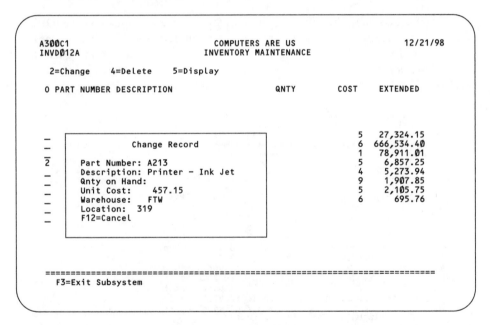

Figure 2.3
Work with Inventory Lists
That Have Popup Change
Windows

A window is defined as a separate record format within the same display file as the screen. Its definition is similar to the definition of a screen except that it begins with the window keyword. The parameters of this keyword define the location and size of the window.

A special keyword that can be used only with windows, WDWBORDER (Window Border), controls the color and appearance of the window's border.

The position of text and variables in the window is measured from the upper left corner of the window, not the upper left corner of the display.

For the inventory project, a single window could be used for all of the options, but it's a little simpler to design a separate window for each option. Table 2.1 contains a list of the formats needed in the INVD01xx display file. DSP02 must immediately follow DSP01, but the rest of the formats can be entered in any order.

Table 2.1
Window Names

Format Name	Format Function	Related to
DSP01	Subfile record	
DSP02	Subfile control record for DSP01	
FOOTER1	Displays the function key definitions	
WINDOW2	Change window	User option 2
WINDOW4	Delete window	User option 4
WINDOW5	Display window	User option 5
WINDOW6	Add window	User option 6

Figure 2.4 contains the window definition for the change window (WINDOW2). WINDOW2 contains a record-level keyword command function (CF) that enables function key F12 and turns on indicator 12 when that function key is pressed. As a record-level declaration, this function is only available in those records in which it is declared. The F12 key is used to exit the window and cancel the change.

Figure 2.4

Window2:
The Change Window

```
*...1....+....2....+....3....+....4....+....5....+....6

A*********************************************
A** Window2 - Change data *****************
A*********************************************
A          R WINDOW2
A                                      CF12(12 )
A                                      WINDOW(8 5 12 52)
A                                      WDWBORDER((*DSPATR HI RI) +
A                                      (*CHAR '       ') (*COLOR RED))
A                                    1 13'Change Record'
A                                    3  3'Part Number:'
A            W2PN          11A  B    3 17
A                                    4  3'Description:'
A            W2DESC        30A  B    4 17
A                                    5  3'Qnty on Hand:'
A            W2QOH          5Y 0B    5 17EDTCDE(1)
A                                    6  3'Unit Cost:'
A            W2UCST         6Y 2B    6 17EDTCDE(1)
A                                    7  3'Warehouse:'
A            W2WH           3A  B    7 17
A                                    8  3'Location:'
A            W2WHL          5A  B    8 17
A                                   10  3'F12=Cancel'
A                                      DSPATR(HI)
A*********************************************
```

The format for WINDOW2 — as shown in total in Figure 2.4 and in small segments in Figures 2.4A, 2.4B, and 2.4E — provides a good model for discussing the window keywords, including how to use them in designing windows.

The keyword WINDOW, shown in Figure 2.4A, is what declares to the system that this is a window (the record name WINDOW2 was fine, but had no special meaning to the system and gave the system no information). The complete command is

WINDOW(row column height width). Thus, the window pops up with the upper left corner at row 8 column 5; it will be 12 rows high and 52 columns wide. You must subtract three rows from the width and two columns from the height for the working width and height. The three "lost" rows are the top and bottom borders, as well as a line for error messages. The two "lost" columns are the right and left borders.

```
*...1....+....2....+....3....+....4....+....5....+....6

A*******************************************
A**  Window2 - Change data *****************
A*******************************************
A          R WINDOW2
A                                        CF12(12)
A                                        WINDOW(8 5 12 52)
```

Figure 2.4A
The Window Keyword
from Window2

The inner, usable portion of our window comprises 9 rows (12 − 3) — with row 10 reserved for messages — and 50 columns (52 − 2). We position our text and fields in this area as if the window were a little display. The words Change Record appear in row 1 of the window (not row 1 of the physical display) and in column 13 of the window (not column 13 of the display).

The Window Border keyword, WDWBORDER (Figure 2.4B), lets you define the frame around the window.

```
*...1....+....2....+....3....+....4....+....5....+....6

A                                        WDWBORDER((*DSPATR HI RI) +
A                                        (*CHAR '       ')( *COLOR RED))
```

Figure 2.4B
The Window Border
Keyword from
WINDOW2

The WDWBORDER keyword is not required (the default is shown in Figure 2.4C).

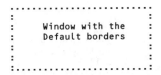

Figure 2.4C
Window with the
Default Borders

Also, the optional *CHAR part of the WDWBORDER can be used to redefine the characters used for the corners, top, bottom, and sides. The sequence for defining the eight positions is shown in Table 2.2.

Table 2.2
Window Position Default Characters

Window Position	Default	Position in definition *CHAR('12345678')
Top left corner	.	1
Top border	.	2
Top right corner	.	3
Left border	:	4
Right border	:	5
Bottom left corner	:	6
Bottom border	.	7
Bottom right corner	:	8

The optional *CHAR part of the WDWBORDER keyword can be used, as shown in Figure 2.4D, to create another border pattern.

Figure 2.4D
Window with *CHAR('/-\ I I\-/')

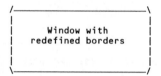

In the code for WINDOW2 (Figure 2.4) the *CHAR('   ') is filled with eight blanks, which means that there will be blank spaces around the border.

The color of the border can also be changed — with the optional *COLOR component of the WDWBORDER keyword. In Figure 2.4B, (*COLOR RED) makes the border red. The list of colors comprises BLU, GRN, WHT, RED, TRQ, YLW, and PNK. Actual colors vary based on the display unit.

The *DSPATR function of the WDWBORDER keyword offers three additional options for borders. These are high intensity (HI), reverse image (RI), and blinking (BL). Blinking makes the border characters blink and therefore has no effect if the border characters are blanks. Some displays may create different colors when HI is on. The latter function was shown in Figure 2.4B.

The rest of the code for WINDOW2 is shown in Figure 2.4E. This code is exactly the same as it would be if this were a simple screen instead of a window.

The row and column positions are all measured from the upper left corner of the window, not the screen, and all of the fields and text must fit within the border area of the window — or the compile of the display file will fail. Because this is the change window, the usage of all fields has been set to B, which allows both input and output.

When you use this window, the RPG program that is introduced in the next section of this chapter

- loads the selected record's data into the window field values
- issues the operation EXFMT WINDOW2 to display and read the window format
- transfers the values in the W2xxx fields to the file (unless F12 has been pressed)

```
*...1....+....2....+....3....+....4....+....5....+....6
A                                      1 13'Change Record'
A                                      3  3'Part Number:'
A          W2PN          11A  B  3 17
A                                      4  3'Description:'
A          W2DESC        30A  B  4 17
A                                      5  3'Qnty on Hand:'
A          W2QOH          5Y  ØB  5 17EDTCDE(1)
A                                      6  3'Unit Cost:'
A          W2UCST         6Y 2B  6 17EDTCDE(1)
A                                      7  3'Warehouse:'
A          W2WH           3A  B  7 17
A                                      8  3'Location:'
A          W2WHL          5A  B  8 17
A                                      9  3'F12=Cancel'
A                                          DSPATR(HI)
A*********************************************
```

Figure 2.4E
Window2
Remaining Code

Exercise 2.1A Computers Are US Inventory Exercise

Purpose
To create or modify an existing display file and test the modified display. The modifications add an option column in the subfile format and add windows for add, change, delete, and display of file data.

General Program Specifications
Create display file INVD012A for the Computers Are US inventory file-maintenance screen, as outlined in the steps that follow.

1. Copy member INVD011C to new member INVD012A, and make the changes to DSP01 and DPS02. Add the code for the WINDOW2 format. Compile the DDS.

   If you have problems, remember that the compiler makes a report. This spooled file will indicate the problems. You can view this report when you edit in SEU by using F15 (Shift-F3) and selecting option 2. Print the compiler listing.

2. Design and add the source code to define WINDOW4 (confirm delete); this should display the record to be deleted in output mode only. Also, add WINDOW5 (display record) at this point; both WINDOW4 and WINDOW5 are similar to WINDOW2, so some code can be copied and modified.

   Because WINDOW4 and WINDOW5 will be similar to WINDOW2, you can copy WINDOW2 code and modify it as needed. To copy multiple lines of code in SEU, mark the block by typing CC in the sequence number area of the first and the last lines to be copied. An A in the sequence number area of the destination indicates that you want the copy placed after that line; a B in place of the A indicates that you want the copy before that line.

   Compile and print the compiler listing.

3. Design and add the DDS definition for WINDOW6 (add record).

Exercise 2.2A Purchase Order Line Project

Purpose

To design screens and windows and create the code to support the designs. You will use the design functions to modify existing designs, adding an option column in the subfile format and adding windows for add, change, delete, and display of file data.

General Program Specifications

Create the display file ORDD022A for the Computers Are US Order Line File-Maintenance screen as outlined in the steps that follow.

1. Copy member ORDD021C to new member ORDD022A, make the following changes, and print:

   - Add a one-character input field to the left of the other subfile fields.
   - Add appropriate heading information to define the options.
   - Print the compiler listing.

2. Modify the DDS for this project to add WINDOW2 (change), WINDOW4 (delete), WINDOW5 (display), and WINDOW6 (add) to ORDD022A. The change window should have all fields designated as Both except the order number and the sequence-of-line number. The order number and sequence-of-line number should be display only.

Copying WINDOW2 Code

As we mentioned earlier, WINDOW2 is similar to the windows in the previous project, and it might save time to copy WINDOW2 from INVD012A into the ORDD022A member. To do so, edit ORDD022A, press F15 (Shift F3), choose option 1, and change the browse/copy member name to INVD012A. Edit now displays the file you were editing in the edit window at the top of the screen and the browse/copy member in the browse window at the bottom of the screen. You can find the format that you want to copy in the Browse window by typing WINDOW2 on the SEU==> line of the browse member. Press F16 to search that member. Mark the code that you want to copy with CC in the sequence-number area on the first and last lines. Move your cursor to the Edit window and type either an A or B (for after or before) to specify where you want to locate the copied code. Press F12 to close the Browse window. Of course, the field names and text must be changed for this project.

3. Users are not allowed to delete records that are not closed. Therefore, add a window (WBADDEL) for this type of bad delete request. The window should display the highlighted record data as well as highlight the following message:

   The requested record cannot be deleted because it is not closed.

Interactive File Maintenance

In the previous section of the chapter, you developed the display file INVD012A, the Computers Are US inventory file-maintenance display. It contained an option column in the subfile and windows for the change, display, delete, and add options. Now we explore the RPG code needed to manage the expanded system. During the exploration, you will learn how to read from the subfile, load, and display windows, as well as how to code the change option. In subsequent exercises, you will design and develop the additional coding for the display, delete, and add options.

The pseudocode expanded design is provided in Figures 2.6A, 2.6B, and 2.6C. Only minor changes are required to the program design from Chapter 1; these changes are bolded in Figure 2.6A. Two new subroutines are added to the design. The Respond (RESPD) subroutine processes user responses to the initial display (Figure 2.6B) and calls the appropriate subroutine to service the request. The Change (CHG) subroutine (Figure 2.6C) processes change requests.

```
Start
    Execute Load subroutine
    Display and read the subfile and the subfile control
    Do while user has not pressed the F3 key
            Execute the Respond (RESPD) subroutine
            Display and read the subfile and the subfile control
    End do
    Close files
End


LOAD subroutine
    Clear subfile
    Position to the top of INVPF
    Load the subfile
            Read a record from INVPF, but do not lock the record
            Do while not EOF(INVPF) and fewer than eight records have been
            written to the subfile
                    Populate the fields of the subfile record
                    Add 1 to the subfile relative record number (RRN)
                    Write a record to the subfile
            End do
    Write footer
End subroutine
```

Figure 2.6A
Pseudocode for RPG Program, Modified Code

Figure 2.6B

Pseudocode for the
RESPD Subroutine

RESPD subroutine

  Set the update flag to off (this flag will be set on if a change requires that the subfile be reloaded).

  Read the first changed record in the subfile (a changed record must have a new value in D1PICK field because that's the only field the user can change)

  Do while changed records exist

    Do selection

      Select when D1PICK is 2 (Change)

        Execute the Change (CHG) subroutine

      End selection

      Read the next changed record in the subfile

    End do

    If the update flag is on

        Execute the LOAD subroutine

    End if

End subroutine

Figure 2.6C

Pseudocode for the
CHG Subroutine

CHG subroutine

  Find and lock the correct record in the inventory physical file

  If inventory record found

    Move fields of the inventory record to the corresponding fields of WINDOW2

    Write and read the window (EXFMT WINDOW2)

    If neither F3 nor F12 was pressed

      Move the fields of WINDOW2 to the inventory physical file record fields

      Update the inventory physical file record

      Move the fields of WINDOW2 to the subfile record fields

      Update the subfile record

    Else

      Unlock the record

    End if

  End if

End subroutine

Now that you've looked over the changes to the pseudocode for the inventory-maintenance system, it's time to look at the actual RPG code. Throughout the next few pages, segments of the RPG code are presented, followed by discussion about each segment.

Figure 2.7A shows our first change — not surprisingly in the first active line of the program. To post changes to this file, we must open it in update mode. Later, when you add the add function, you will have to put an A code in the add-record column. However, because for the moment we are just tackling the change option, only the update status is necessary.

```
+....1....+....2....+....3....+....4....+....5....+....6....+....7....+....8

*Jefferson College    Professor Levinson     11/13/99
*APPLICATION NAME       - Inventory System
*PROGRAM NAME           - INV012A
*DESCRIPTION  - 1. Clears Subfile   2. Loads Subfile   3. Displays Footer
*                4. Exercises the Screen Display with the Subfile
*                5. Receives User Responses
*                6. Processes Change Requests
*                7. Repeats The Display
***********************************************************************
*     FILES
***********************************************************************
*  Inventory file    UPDATE ACCESS Requested
FINVPF    UF   E          K DISK
```

Figure 2.7A

Program Heading and F-Spec for Physical File Access

Notice that the display declaration (Figure 2.7B) is unchanged except for the use of the new display name. The display file used in Chapter 1 contains three record formats; this display contains seven. In your compiled listing, you will see information on all seven formats, including structural information on the fields in each. The listing of the display formats in the compiled listing can be a convenience. It lets programmers know what they have to work with in their program.

```
+....1....+....2....+....3....+....4....+....5....+....6....+....7....+....8

 *  Display File with subfile DSP01.
FINVD012A  CF   E          WORKSTN
F                              SFILE(DSP01:RRN)
```

Figure 2.7B

F-Spec for Display Station

The changes to the mainline code are shown in Figure 2.7C. The sequence — in which an initial execution of the display is followed by a loop to process the user response and redisplay the main screen — makes the DOW statement do double duty. The first time it is encountered — just after the initial screen is displayed and the user releases the screen by pressing Enter or F3 — the DOW acts as an IF statement, preventing entry to the looped code if F3 has been pressed. Once the loop is entered, it acts as a DOW, testing the status of indicator 03 after each return from the display screen.

```
+....1....+....2....+....3....+....4....+....5....+....6....+....7....+....8

 *                          Load the subfile.
C              EXSR    LOAD
 *                          Initial display.
C              EXFMT   DSP02
 *                          Loop until F3 is pressed.
C              DOW     *IN03 = *OFF
 *                          Process response.
C              EXSR    RESPD
 *                          Next display.
C              EXFMT   DSP02
 *                          Enddo
C              ENDDO

C              MOVE    *ON      *INLR
C              RETURN
```

Figure 2.7C

Changes to the Mainline Code

In the previous chapter, the LOAD subroutine left the record pointer in INVPF after the eighth record. Because we will now be reusing this subroutine to reload the subfile whenever we make an addition or deletion, we must reset this pointer. For now, we always want to load the subfile with the first eight records of INVPF. Therefore, we reset the file pointer to the top of the file (TOF) using *LOVAL SETLL INVPF (Figure 2.7D) to position the INVPF file at the top every time the LOAD subroutine is called. Regardless of the key, or even without a key, you can position to the TOF with *LOVAL SETLL file name.

Figure 2.7D

Beginning of the LOAD Subroutine

```
+....1....+....2....+....3....+....4....+....5....+....6....+....7....+....8

****************************************************************
*  LOAD - LOADS THE INVENTORY SUBFILE FROM THE DATA FILE INVPF
****************************************************************
C     LOAD          BEGSR
*                                          Clear the subfile.
C                   EVAL      *IN50 = *OFF
C                   WRITE     DSP02
C                   EVAL      RRN = *ZERO
C                   EVAL      *IN50 = *ON

*                   Position to the top of the physical file.
C     *LOVAL        SETLL     INVPF
```

When option 2 is selected and records are changed, we do not need to rebuild the subfile because we can use the UPDATE operation to update both the subfile record and the physical file.

The READ statement in Figure 2.7E includes a modifier to the read operation that we haven't used often. The operation READ (N) indicates that this read does not lock the record. This feature is required because we now open the file in the F-spec for update, which causes READ statements to lock the record until the next READ, CHAIN, UPDAT, or DELET. At the moment, our only objective is to read the records and transfer the data to the subfile. We have no intention of updating or deleting this record immediately; therefore, we use the N in the H/P/N column.

Figure 2.7E

LOAD Subroutine: Read of Physical File Without Locking the

```
+....1....+....2....+....3....+....4....+....5....+....6....+....7....+....8
*                                  Load first record.
C                   READ (N)  INVPF                                90
```

As Figure 2.7F shows, when we load the subfile, we clear the new field, D1PICK, by moving blanks to it.

Figure 2.7F

LOAD Subroutine (Continued)

```
+....1....+....2....+....3....+....4....+....5....+....6....+....7....+.....8
*
C                   DOW       (*IN90 = *OFF) and
C                             (RRN   <  8 )

C                   Eval      D1PICK = *BLANKS
```

The final section of the LOAD subroutine is shown in Figure 2.7G. This code requires only a single change from the code in Chapter 1. Like the initial or primary read shown in Figure 2.7E, the secondary read in Figure 2.7G must contain the N to unlock the record.

```
+....1....+....2....+....3....+....4....+....5....+....6....+....7....+....8
  *
.C                     Eval       D1PN    = INPN
.C                     Eval       D1DESC  = INDESC
.C                     Eval       D1QOH   = INQOH
.C                     Eval       D1UCST  = INUCST
.C                     Eval       D1LTOT  = D1QOH * D1UCST
.C                     Eval       RRN     = RRN   + 1
.C                     WRITE      DSP01
.C                     READ (N)   INVPF                               90
.C                     ENDDO
.C                     If         RRN = 0
.C                     Eval       D1DESC  = 'No Records'
.C                     Eval       D1PN    = *BLANKS
.C                     Eval       D1QOH   = *ZERO
.C                     Eval       D1UCST  = *ZERO
.C                     Eval       D1LTOT  = *ZERO
.C                     Eval       RRN = 1
.C                     Write      DSP01
.C                     Endif
. *    Write Footer Record.
.C                     WRITE      FOOTER1                              .
C                      ENDSR
```

Figure 2.7G
LOAD Subroutine
(Continued)

Mod-Marks

Notice the XXX that I put to the left of the specification type on one of the lines in Figure 2.7D. The compiler does not use positions 1 through 5 of every RPG and DDS specification, so those positions can be used to indicate which lines were changed as part of a specific modification. This tool can be valuable in maintenance programming; it is very helpful to know when and why specific lines of code were modified.

The standard for indicating modifications varies widely from one organization to the next, but a good standard includes the following elements:

1. The modification is described at the beginning of the program, along with the date, the programmer's name, and the reason for the change. These comments use the same Mod-Marks that are used in the subsequent code.

2. The Mod-Mark can be an IS work-request number. It should be some combination of letters and digits that differentiates this change from others in the program. In many standards, the length of the Mod-Mark is restricted to four characters or digits.

3. The Mod-Mark is preceded by a letter designating the action taken, such as A for add or D for delete.

> **Note:** According to some shop standards, lines cannot be changed. This ensures that the original code and the nature of the changes are not hidden from future programmers. Changes are made by using the Delete Mod-Mark and an asterisk (*) in column 7 to declare the line a comment. A new line is then added with the corrected code. Using Delete Mod-Mark and retaining the old code as comments lets programmers see what changes occurred, but it can cause confusion if a programmer fails to realize that the line is no longer active.

The RESPD subroutine (Figure 2.7H) processes all user requests that were entered on the main screen when Enter was pressed. It initially sets the update flag (UPDFLG) off, then loops through all the requests. If the Add or the Delete subroutine turned the flag on, then at the end of the RESPD subroutine, the subfile is reloaded.

READC and CHAIN (Random Retrieval from a File, based on a record number) are the only input operations that let you access the subfile record. The READC operation in Figure 2.7H reads the first record that was changed and drops the flag for that record. The READC shown later in Figure 2.7J reads subsequent changed records.

Figure 2.7H
Beginning of
RESPD Subroutine

```
+....1....+....2....+....3....+....4....+....5....+....6....+....7....+....8
 *
C                   Eval      D1PN    = INPN
C                   Eval      D1DESC  = INDESC
C                   Eval      D1QOH   = INQOH
C                   Eval      D1UCST  = INUCST
C                   Eval      D1LTOT  = D1QOH * D1UCST
C                   Eval      RRN     = RRN   + 1
C                   WRITE     DSP01
C                   READ (N)  INVPF                                      90
C                   ENDDO
C                   If        RRN = 0
C                   Eval      D1DESC  = 'No Records'
C                   Eval      D1PN    = *BLANKS
C                   Eval      D1QOH   = *ZERO
C                   Eval      D1UCST  = *ZERO
C                   Eval      D1LTOT  = *ZERO
C                   Eval      RRN = 1
C                   Write     DSP01
C                   Endif
 *        Write Footer Record
C                   WRITE     FOOTER1
C                   ENDSR
```

The indicator comes on at the EOF (when no more changed records exist). If the user changes any field in the record, the flag is set. In our case, only the D1PICK field can be changed, so we will check that field to see what option was requested.

A selection structure is used in the RESPD subroutine (Figure 2.7I-1) to branch to the various options selected by the user.

Figure 2.7I-1
RESPD Subroutine
(Continued)

```
+....1....+....2....+....3....+....4....+....5....+....6....+....7....+....8
 ***********************************************************************
 *   PROCESS RESPONSE TO SUBFILE
 *        Field UPDFLG defined in D-Spec as 1 Alpha
 ***********************************************************************
C     RESPD         BEGSR
C                   Eval      UPDFLG = *OFF
C                   READC     DSP01                                      90
```

If the changed record that was just acquired with the READC operation has a 2 in D1PICK, we run the CHG subroutine. You can imagine how to modify this code for options 4, 5, and 6, but remember that options 4 and 6 must turn on UPFLG if they actually write or delete a record.

Walk through the code and see whether you can determine how it will respond when someone types an option value of 6 or any other value that isn't coded.

Your users may prefer to use a C for change, but to be consistent with standard AS/400 screens, you also want to respond to a 2 for change. This can be easily accommodated in the selection structure in either of two ways, as shown in Figures

2.7I-2 and 2.7I-3. The code shown in Figure 2.7I-2 uses two When clauses, each calling the same subroutine. If either is true, the CHG subroutine is executed.

```
+....1....+....2....+....3....+....4....+....5....+....6....+....7....+....8
    C                   DoW         *IN94 = *OFF
    C                   Select
    C                   When        D1PICK = '2'
    C                   ExSR        CHG
    C                   When        D1PICK = 'C'
    C                   ExSR        CHG
    C                   EndSL
```

Figure 2.7I-2
Selection Structure
with Two Values Using
Two WHEN Clauses for
the CHG Subroutine

The code in Figure 2.7I-3 uses a complex When/Or to accomplish the same task. A selection structure with complex When/And or When/Or clauses can create clear and simple code, which is especially useful when the alternative is nested Ifs or nested Selects.

```
+....1....+....2....+....3....+....4....+....5....+....6....+....7....+....8
    C                   DoW         *IN94 = *OFF
    C                   Select
    C                   When        D1PICK = '2'
    C                   ExSR        CHG
    C                   EndSL
```

Figure 2.7I-3
Selection Structure
with Two Values Using
Complex WHEN Clause
for the CHG Subroutine

You will recall that the READC operation shown in Figure 2.7J reads subsequent changed records and sets the indicator on at the EOF (when no more changed records exist). If the user changes any field in the record, the update flag (UPFLG) is set on.

```
+....1....+....2....+....3....+....4....+....5....+....6....+....7....+....8
    *
    C                   READC       DSP01                           94
    C                   ENDDO
    C                   IF          UPDFLG = *on
    C                   EXSR        LOAD
    C                   ENDIF
    C                   ENDSR
```

Figure 2.7J
End of the RESPD
Subroutine

Because the code shown in Figures 2.7I through 2.7J loops until the READC finds no more changed records, the RESPD subroutine processes all requested changes before it reloads the subfile (if necessary) and returns to the mainline code. The mainline code then redisplays the main screen.

The CHG subroutine is shown in Figure 2.7K. This subroutine is called from the Respond subroutine when the user requests a change.

The READC operation in the RESPD subroutine locks the record, allowing an UPDAT of the record in the subfile. The value of D1PN, the part number of the record acquired by the READC operation, is used at the beginning of the CHG subroutine to CHAIN into the inventory file (which was conveniently keyed on — you guessed it — part number). This chain acquires the physical-file record and locks it for subsequent update.

The CHG subroutine loads the window's fields from the physical-file record and executes the window. When control returns to the program from the window and the user has not pressed F12 or F3, the design assumes that the values of one or more fields were changed. The code would be somewhat more efficient if the fields were compared and updates done only if a change actually occurred, but the performance improvement would be minor. If no changes were made, the code updates the file and subfile, and — if no damage has been done to the files since — the record looks exactly the same before and after the operation.

The processing continues by moving the returned window fields to the physical-file fields and updating the physical file. Then the returned window fields are moved to the subfile fields and that record is updated. Because the subfile is updated in this subroutine, the update flag that would update the subfile by reloading it is unnecessary. That flag, however, is necessary with adds or deletes.

If the user presses F12 or F3 to cancel or exit the process, the inventory physical-file record that was locked is unlocked.

Figure 2.7K
CHG Subroutine

```
+....1....+....2....+....3....+....4....+....5....+....6....+....7....+....8
******************************************************************
*   PROCESS CHANGE REQUEST
******************************************************************
C     CHG           BEGSR

C     D1PN          CHAIN     INVPF                               93
C                   IF        *IN93 = *OFF
* Copy the record to be changed to WINDOW2 fields.
C                   Eval      W2PN   = INPN
C                   Eval      W2DESC = INDESC
C                   Eval      W2QOH  = INQOH
C                   Eval      W2UCST = INUCST
C                   Eval      W2WH   = INWH
C                   Eval      W2WHL  = INWHL
*     Display change window.
C                   EXFMT     WINDOW2
* Unless EXIT or Cancel move window values to PF Fields and Update PF
C                   IF        *IN03 = *OFF and *IN12 = *OFF
C                   Eval      INPN   = W2PN
C                   Eval      INDESC = W2DESC
C                   Eval      INQOH  = W2QOH
C                   Eval      INUCST = W2UCST
C                   Eval      INWH   = W2WH
C                   Eval      INWHL  = W2WHL
* and update the physical file record.
C                   UpDate    INVPFR
*   Prepare the subfile record data for update
C                   Eval      D1PN   = W2PN
C                   Eval      D1DESC = W2DESC
C                   Eval      D1QOH  = W2QOH
C                   Eval      D1UCST = W2UCST
C                   Eval      D1LTOT = D1QOH * D1UCST
* and update the subfile record.
C                   UpDate    DSP01
C                   Else
C                   UnLock    INVPF
C                   EndIf
C                   EndIf
C                   ENDSR
```

Exercise 2.1B Computers Are US Inventory Project

Purpose

To create or modify and test RPG program code that

- loads and displays a subfile
- receives user input from the subfile
- branches to the appropriate subroutine based on the value of the user selection
- performs changes to the data
- performs display, delete, and add functions on the data

General Program Specifications

Create the maintenance program INV012A, which provides interactive file maintenance on the Computers Are US inventory file. The program uses the screen INVD012A. The steps of the process follow.

4. Copy source member INV011C to new member INV012A and make the changes as outlined in Figures 2.7A through 2.7K.

   - Test and debug.
   - Print the compiler listing.
   - Print the screens as well as a "before" and an "after" example of a change.

5. Design and develop the display components of the RPG code.

   - Test and debug.
   - Print the compiler listing.
   - Print the display screen.

6. Design and develop the delete components of the RPG code.

   - Test and debug.
   - Print the compiler listing.
   - Print the screens and a "before" and "after" example of a change.

7. Design and develop the add components of the RPG code.

   - Test and debug.
   - Print the compiler listing.
   - Print the screens and a "before" and "after" example of a change.

Exercise 2.2B Purchase Order Line Project

Purpose

To design and code an interactive file-maintenance system with subfiles, basing it upon a similar solution.

General Program Specifications

Create RPG program ORDL22A, which displays *all* purchase order lines. It lets the user

- select records to add, delete, change, or display
- change all of the fields except the order number and line sequence
- delete records that have been delivered with OLADT not equal to zero
- if the user requests a delete of a record with OLADT equal to zero, display a window that presents the record and informs the user that the line cannot be deleted because the record is not closed

4. Copy source member ORDL21C to new member ORDL22A. Make the modifications equivalent to the modifications in Figures 2.7A through 2.7K. The CHG subroutine should not change the values of the order number or sequence number fields, but they should be displayed on the change window.

- Test and debug.
- Print the compiler listing.
- Print the screens and a "before" and "after" example of a change.

5. Add the display capability to the program.

- Test and debug.
- Print the compiler listing.
- Print the screen.

6. Add the delete capability to the program.

- Only delete records with a OLADT not equal to zero.
- If OLADT is equal to zero load and display the Bad Delete Window.
- Test and debug.
- Print the compiler listing.
- Print demonstrations of a good delete and a bad delete.

7. Add the add capability to the program.

- Test and debug.
- Print the compiler listing.
- Print demonstrations of an add.

Review

1. What does the READC do? What does it mean when the READC indicator is on?
2. Write the code change necessary to allow entry of 2 or C, 4 or D, and 5 or A.
3. Write the DDS code for the following window:

```
                     DELETE ORDER REQUESTED

      OK to Delete ORDER NO:_____

      and all ORDER LINES?

      Enter=Accept    F12=Cancel
```

4. F3 was opened as a file-level function key: CF03. What would happen if F3 were pressed on the Delete window?

    a. How would you code the Delete subroutine so that this key cancels the request but does not exit the program?
    b. How would you code the Delete subroutine so that the application ends if F3 is pressed on the delete Window?

5. F12 was used to cancel an option; however, if pressed, F12 remains on.

    a. What happens to subsequent options?
    b. How can that be avoided?

6. You should be familiar with the option column.

    a. What happens when someone puts a 7 in the option column?
    b. Write the window definition and the changes to the RPG code to send the following message: You have chosen an invalid code _____! (The window should display the actual code that the user typed.)

7. Step by step, identify what the program does if no options are selected and the Enter key is pressed.
8. Describe why the Change option doesn't require that the subfile be rewritten.
9. If the N were left off the READ statement in the LOAD subroutine, what would happen if a second user attempted to load the same screen from the same physical file?
10. Why must you reload the subfile after an add or delete?

Chapter 3

Managing Multipage Subfiles

Chapter Overview

Chapter 3 helps you understand the implications of the following three subfile load options and be able to demonstrate their use:

- Subfile load option 1 — for loading all records
- Subfile load option 2 — for a growing subfile
- Subfile load option 3 — for a single-page subfile

When you complete the chapter, you will also be able to demonstrate how to use the following keywords

- SFLEND (Subfile End)
- ROLLUP (Roll Up) and ROLLDOWN (Roll Down)
- SFLRCDNBR (Subfile Record Number)

Managing Multipage Subfiles

As you studied the first two chapters, you also created some useful code. Your programs load and display subfiles and provide fully operational file-maintenance systems with pop-up windows for the options. The code you have developed has, however, one serious limitation: It displays and processes only the number of records that fit on a single screen. In this chapter, you learn how to develop code that manages a multipage subfile and lets the user move through the file.

We explore the following three options for managing a multipage subfile. Table 3.1 presents code-related and user-related issues for all options.

- Subfile load option 1, which loads the entire file into a large subfile before displaying the first screen.
- Subfile load option 2, which loads the records to fill a single page and displays the subfile. It adds a page of records to the subfile when the last page of loaded records is displayed and the user requests more data by pressing the Page down key.
- Subfile load option 3, which loads a single page of records and displays the subfile. It replaces the current page with the next page whenever the user presses the Page down key and replaces the current page with the previous page whenever the user presses the Page up key.

Table 3.1
Subfile Load Options

Subfile Load Option	Code Issues	User Issues
1. Load entire file.	Simplest code. Limit of 9999 records.	• User has to wait until entire file is loaded. • Data is only updated when a user makes a change that requires reloading the subfile. • Changes made to the data by other users or other programs after the subfile is loaded will not be apparent.
2. Add a page at a time.	Code is more complex. Limit of 9999 records.	• Brief delay whenever a page is loaded. • Pages added when the Page down key is pressed are up-dated at the time they are added to the subfile. However, subsequent changes to the data made by other users or programs are not displayed until a user makes a change that requires reloading the subfile.
3. Replace the page with the next or previous page of data.	Most complicated code. Uses least memory. No size limit.	• Brief delay whenever the Page up key or the Page down key is pressed. • Data is always updated at the time of processing a Page up/ Page down request.

Subfile Size and Subfile Page

Before we examine the details of the three load options, we will explore how each subfile load option controls the subfile's size. You recall that in Chapters 1 and 2, we worked with a single page only and declared the subfile size and the subfile page size as equal (Figure 3.1A). Subfile load option 3, covered later in the chapter, also works with single pages, and, as in the previous chapters, it, too, uses the same value for subfile size and subfile page.

Figure 3.1A
Subfile Size=Subfile Page

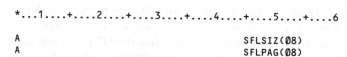

```
*...1....+....2....+....3....+....4....+....5....+....6
A                                      SFLSIZ(08)
A                                      SFLPAG(08)
```

Subfile load options 1 and 2 require a subfile that is larger than a single page. The subfile page value remains the number of records that are to be displayed on a single page, but the subfile size has a larger value than the page size.

A fixed-size subfile can be declared by putting the maximum size of the subfile in the subfile size field. Figure 3.1B shows this declaration with a maximum subfile size of 250 records. When the file is opened, a block of memory large enough to accommodate 250 records is claimed. This method of defining a subfile size works well when the maximum number of records is known and does not change.

```
*...1....+....2....+....3....+....4....+....5....+....6

A                                    SFLSIZ(250)
A                                    SFLPAG(08)
```

Figure 3.1B
Subfile Size=Maximum
Number of Records
in Subfile

A growing subfile is declared by setting the subfile size as one greater than the subfile page value (Figure 3.1C). A growing subfile can increase up to 9999 records.

```
*...1....+....2....+....3....+....4....+....5....+....6

A                                    SFLSIZ(09)
A                                    SFLPAG(08)
```

Figure 3.1C
Subfile Size Is One
Greater Than Subfile Page

As the subfile grows, the system gives the program new blocks of memeory. This method of defining subfile size works well whenever you code load options 1 or 2.

More Than 9999 Records

Only subfile load option 3 accommodates more than 9999 records. The code that we introduce for subfile load option 1 loads the entire file if it is fewer than 9999 records or the first 9999 records of the file. Subfile load option 2 loads a page each time the user request a new page until either the entire file is loaded or 9999 records are loaded.

If the program displays eight records (like our sample program), then the user would have to press the Page down key 1,250 times to run into the limitation of options 1 and 2. And that number brings up another point. Obviously, when users work with large files, they need a quick way to move to a specific area of the file. Chapter 5 introduces a way to design the capability to quickly locate a record, and using it makes either load option 1 or load option 2 an effective solution for virtually all subfiles.

I recommend using subfile load option 1 for any file smaller than a few hundred records and subfile load option 2 for any larger files. If possible, avoid subfile load option 3, with its complex code. However, because you must be ready to do maintenance on existing code and to develop new code to the specifications of your organization, we will explore all three options.

Subfile Load Option 1: Loading All the Records (Up to 9999) at One Time

The coding of subfile load option 1 requires only minor changes to the code developed in the previous chapters. You change the SFLSIZ value to one more than the subfile page value. Because the SFLSIZ value is greater than the SFLPAG value, the system adds a page of records whenever needed — up to 9999 records. In the Load subroutine, you change the RPG loop control code to limit the value of RRN LT 9999, which keeps the program from attempting to load more than 9999 records. The loop control also ends at the end of file (EOF) of the physical file.

Exercise 3.1A Computers Are US Inventory Project

Purpose
To modify existing code to develop and test a simple multiple-page subfile display.

General Program Specifications
Create maintenance program INV013A and display file INVD013A. The program loads all of the records in the inventory file INVPF into the subfile (up to 9999 records) using subfile load option 1.

1. Copy display file INVD012A into the new member INVD013A and increase the subfile size by one.

2. Copy program INV012A into the new member INV013A and change the limit in the Load subroutine from 8 records to 9999 records.

3. Add the 10 records shown in Table 3.2 to the file, using either the Add option that you created in the last chapter or Display File Utility (DFU).

Table 3.2
Ten Records to Be Added to the File

A325	14" MULTI-SYNC MONITOR	00025	021500	STL	SL1
A326	15" MULTI-SYNC MONITOR	00006	027500	STL	SL2
A327	17" MULTI-SYNC MONITOR	00005	037500	FTW	F21
D2115	3 1⁄2" DISK DRIVE	00127	002141	STL	S27
D2116	DISK DRIVE - 5 1⁄4 "	00007	002141	STL	211
CP07	CABLE PRINTER 7'	00015	000575	STL	S1L
CP10	CABLE PRINTER 10'	00019	000325	STL	S42
CS10MM	CABLE SERIAL 10' MALE–MALE	00015	000412	DAL	D21
D511	511 MBYTE HARD DISK	00023	015715	STL	S15
D1022	1.022 GIG-BYTE HARD DISK	00047	025319	DAL	D25

Compile and test. Note that you must compile the DSPF first and get a "clean" compile before you compile the RPG.

Test the effects of the Page up and Page down keys.

Using + or MORE ...

The program that you just created works, but users might find it hard to know when they can press the Page down key. Therefore, as long as pressing the Page down key will show more records, the standard display on the AS/400 displays the term More... in the lower right corner of the display. When the display shows the last available records, it says Bottom.

The Subfile End keyword (SFLEND) can be added to the control record in the display file as in Figures 3.2A and 3.2B. The SFLEND keyword — when entered without the *MORE parameter (Figure 3.2A) — displays a plus sign (+) in the right-most column of the subfile display whenever there are more records.

```
*...1....+....2....+....3....+....4....+....5....+....6

A  90                              SFLEND
```

Figure 3.2A
Subfile End Keyword
with No Parameter

When the *MORE parameter is added to the SFLEND keyword (Figure 3.2B), the keyword displays the term More... on the rightmost end of the line immediately below the end of the subfile display. When no more records are available for display, either the + is removed or More... becomes Bottom.

```
*...1....+....2....+....3....+....4....+....5....+....6

A  90                          SFLEND(*MORE)
```

Figure 3.2B
Subfile End Keyword
with *MORE

The display file determines whether there are more records based on two rules.

1. If the conditioning indicator (in this example, the conditioning indicator is 90) is off, there are more records — because more records can be loaded from the source file. This indicator is usually the same indicator used to sense the end of the physical or logical file that is the source of records to be loaded into the subfile. In our inventory example, that file is INVPF and the indicator used in the READ statements is 90.

2. If the conditioning indicator is on, the display shows + or More... when the subfile is positioned above the last page of records.

Exercise 3.1B Computers Are US Inventory Project

Purpose
To modify existing code to add the subfile end keyword to a simple multiple-page subfile display.

General Program Specifications
Create maintenance program INV013A and display file INVD013A. The program loads all of the records in the inventory file INVPF into the subfile (up to 9999 records) using subfile load option 1. The program indicates to users whether more records are available to view.

4. Modify INVD013A. Add the subfile end keyword without parameters to the control record. Compile the display and the RPG program and test. Print out the display with the + and without it.

5. Modify INVD013A. Add the subfile end keyword with the *MORE parameters to the control record. Compile the display and the RPG program and test. Print out the display with More... and with Bottom. Using the MORE* parameter will be our standard throughout the remainder of this text.

Exercise 3.2A Purchase Order Line Project

Purpose
To design and code a subfile that loads using subfile load option 1.

General Program Specifications
Create the RPG program ORDL23A, which displays all purchase order lines. It lets the user press the Page down key to perform maintenance on the data and loads and displays the word More... when there are more records to be displayed.

1. Copy the display file source member ORDD022A to a new member, ORDD023A. Make the necessary modifications to prepare this display file for subfile load option 1. Your modification should include More.../Bottom on the subfile display. Compile and test the display.

2. Copy the source member ORDL22A to new member ORDL23A. Make the necessary modifications to load all of the records in the file using subfile load option 1.

   - Test and debug.
   - Print the compiler listing.
   - Print the screens and a "before" and "after" example of a change.

3. Add the records shown in Table 3.3 to the order line file.

continued

Exercise 3.2A *Continued*

Table 3.3
Order Line File

OLNUM	OLSEQ	OLPN	OLPRC	OLOQN	OLEDT	OLADT	OLAQN
000019	001	A123	1175.00	50	19981114		0
000019	002	A124	2000.00	50	19981114		0
000020	001	A320	150.00	75	19981115	0	0
000021	001	A124	1900.10	50	19981201	0	0
000021	002	A320	200.00	50	19981201	0	0
000021	003	A319	95.21	10	19981201	0	0
000022	001	A214	200.00	15	19981229	19980923	5
000022	002	A216	305.15	200	19981229	19980923	200
000022	003	A213	415.16	10	19981229	0	0
000023	001	A214	200.00	25	19981222	0	0
000023	002	A216	305.15	150	19981222	0	0
000023	003	A213	415.16	12	19981222	0	0
000023	004	A319	100.00	14	19981222	0	0
000023	005	A320	150.15	225	19981222	0	0
000023	006	A321	400.16	1	19981222	0	0

Subfile Load Option 2: Adding a Page at a Time

Although subfile load option 1 is accomplished with the simplest code, the option could cause a significant waste of processing time in loading records beyond those needed. It could also mean that users would have to wait an unacceptably long time for the display to appear on their screen.

Subfile load option 2 minimizes the wait for the first screen because only the first page of records is loaded. However, there is a slight wait for each new page to be added to the subfile. (This wait is not repeated when the user is paging through any data already loaded.)

Only two changes to the display file are required. Both changes require that new keywords be added to the control record DSP02. The first keyword activates the Page down key and turns on an indicator when the key is pressed.

The keyword ROLLUP, shown in Figure 3.3A, is equivalent to the keyword PAGEDOWN. (IBM display terminals use the term roll up to mean the same thing that page down means on PCs; either keyword can be used with either type of display.) When the last page of the subfile has been displayed and either the Rollup or Page down key has been pressed, the display-file code will turn on the indicator enclosed in parentheses (in Figure 3.3A, indicator 25) and return control to the RPG program.

We will not want this keyword active once all the records in the physical file have been loaded into the subfile. The PAGEDOWN and ROLLUP keywords can be controlled by a conditioning indicator that the RPG program can set to a false condition when the physical file has been completely loaded. In Figure 3.3A, this control value is N90. When indicator 90 is off, the keyword is active, and when indicator 90 is on, the keyword is inactive. When the subfile is loaded from physical file INVPF, the RPG program uses indicator 90 as the EOF. As long as the RPG program has not encountered the end of the physical file, indicator 90 is off and the keyword is active (when the program comes to the end of physical file INVPF, indicator 90 is turned on and the keyword is inactive).

Figure 3.3A

Rollup Keyword Returns Indicator 25 On When Indicator 90 Is Off

```
*...1....+....2....+....3....+....4....+....5....+....6
A N90                           ROLLUP(25)
```

The second keyword that must be added to the control record is used to control which page of the subfile is displayed and which record the cursor is located on when the subfile is displayed. The SFLRCDNBR keyword receives a value from the program through a variable defined on the same line with the keyword. This variable, which in the example shown in Figure 3.3B is named SFLRCD, must be signed (4 0), and its usage must be (H) hidden.

Figure 3.3B

Subfile Record Number Locates the Cursor

```
*...1....+....2....+....3....+....4....+....5....+....6
A           SFLRCD     4S 0H     SFLRCDNBR(CURSOR)
```

A hidden variable is one whose value is available to the display file and the RPG program, but it is not displayed on the screen. The RPG program must include code that determines which record should be displayed at the top of the screen whenever a new page is added. The RPG program loads this value into the variable associated with the SFLRCDNBR keyword before it displays the subfile. That value is the relative record number (RRN) of the first record of the page displayed. Keywords with variables must appear after the general subfile keywords, as shown in Figure 3.3C.

Figure 3.3C

Subfile Control Record for Subfile Load Option 2

```
*...1....+....2....+....3....+....4....+....5....+....6....+....7....+....8
A*****************************************************************
A           R DSP02              SFLCTL(DSP01)
A 90                             SFLEND(*MORE)
A                                SFLSIZ(0009)
A                                SFLPAG(0008)
** The rollup function will turn on the desired indicator when the
** rollup (Display station words for PageDown) key is pressed
** IN25 is turned when PgDn is pressed, but this command is only
** in effect until indicator 90 is on.
** If IN90 is off and PgDn is pressed, the screen returns IN25 on.
** If 90 is on, the PgDn key will be processed by the screen code,
** either displaying the next page or a message warning about bottom
** of data.  We will use IN25 to detect when another page should be
** loaded.
*
```

continued

```
*...1....+....2....+....3....+....4....+....5....+....6....+....7....+....8
A N90                                    ROLLUP(25 'ROLLUP OR PGDN')
A                                        OVERLAY
A  50                                    SFLDSP
A  50                                    SFLDSPCTL
A N50                                    SFLCLR
  **
  ** We've taken more control of the system and must now take control of
  ** the cursor. Otherwise, the PgDn key will load another page but we
  ** will still display the first page. As we load the subfile, the RPG
  ** code will compute new values for the CURSOR location. The value
  ** will be loaded into the variable SFLRCD as a hidden value. The
  ** compiler gets "upset" if it encounters the SFLRCDNBR keyword
  ** before the SFLDSP and SFLCLR keywords.
  *
A           SFLRCD       4S 0H           SFLRCDNBR(CURSOR)
A                                      1 31'COMPUTERS ARE US'
A                                      2 31'WORK WITH INVENTORY LISTS'
A                                      1  2USER
A                                      1 71DATE
A                                        EDTCDE(Y)
A                                      6  4'PART NUMBER'
A                                      6 16'DESCRIPTION'
A                                      6 47'QNTY'
A                                      6 55'COST'
A                                      6 65'EXTENDED'
A                                      6  2'0'
A                                      4  3'2=Change'
A                                      4 15'4=Delete'
A                                      4 27'5=Display'
```

Figure 3.3C
Continued

The pseudocode for the RPG program for subfile load option 2 is shown in Figures 3.4A through 3.4C. The Respond (RESPD) subroutine (Figure 3.4A) has been modified to call the subroutine to locate the position of the physical file just beyond the last record previously loaded, read the next record from the physical file, and load a page whenever indicator 25 is on. If indicator 25 is off, the subroutine works just as it did in Chapter 2.

Figure 3.4A

Pseudocode for the
Respond (RESPD)
Subroutine with
the Subfile Load
Option Added

RESPD subroutine
    If indicator 25 is on (the Page down key was pressed at the current bottom of the subfile)
        Position in the physical file immediately after the last record loaded
        Read the record
        Execute the Load Page (LOADPG) subroutine
    ELSE
        Set the update flag to off (this flag will be set on if a change requires that the subfile be reloaded)
        Read the first changed record in the subfile (a changed record must have a new value in D1PICK field because that's the only field the user can change)
        Do while changed records exist
            Do selection
                Select when D1PICK is 2 (Change)
                    Execute the Change (CHG) subroutine
            End selection
            Read the next changed record in the subfile
        End do
        If the update flag is on
            Compute the number of pages up to the last changed record
            Execute the Clear Subfile (CLRSF) subroutine
            Repeat for the number of pages up to the last changed record
                Execute the LOADPG subroutine
            If SFL>RRN then SFLRCD=RRN (occurs only if the last records were deleted)
        End if
    End if
End subroutine

Figure 3.4B shows the pseudocode for the LOADPG subroutine, which includes most of the LOAD subroutine from the previous examples. The code to clear the subfile is moved to another subroutine, CLRSF, because that code will only be used when you initially create or rebuild the subfile.

The LOAD subroutine needs a few additional variables: (load count) is used to count the number of records loaded during this execution of the subroutine. RRNHLD contains the number of records in the subfile. This value, obtained from the value of RRN at the end of each execution of the LOADPG subroutine, lets RRN be set to the number of records that are in the subfile prior to adding the next page. RRN must point at the EOF of the subfile whenever records are added. Between executions of this subroutine, the value of RRNs will change to point at the record accessed with a READC (Read Next Changed Record) operation in the Respond subroutine. RRN must be reset every time this subroutine runs to make certain that it is pointing to the EOF; this is accomplished at the beginning of the routine by moving the value of RRNHLD to RRN.

```
LOADPG subroutine
    Initialize load count to zero
    Move the value of the relative record number hold area (RRNHLD) to the
    relative record number (RRN)
    Set subfile record to one greater than the previous RRN
    Do while not EOF and load count < 8 and RRN < 9999
        Load source file fields into SFL record fields
        Add 1 to load count
        Add 1 to RRN
        Write subfile record
        Save the value of the last part number loaded
        Read the next record from the source file
    End do
    IF RRN = 0
        Create a 'no records' record
        Add 1 to RRN
        Write subfile record
    End if
    Set RRNHLD = RRN
End subroutine
```

Figure 3.4B

Pseudocode for the
LOADPG Subroutine

The value of the key (part number) of the last record loaded into the subfile is stored in the variable LASTPN. This variable is used when the Page down key is pressed to position the physical file to the first record for the next page.

The LOAD subroutine also sets the value into SFLRCD, the variable used in the display file by the SFLRCDNBR keyword. Loading the RRN of the first record of the new screen into SFLRCD causes the display file to position the cursor on the first record of the new screen.

Figure 3.4C shows the pseudocode for the CLRSF subroutine. It contains the code to clear the subfile, reset the value of RRN, and position and read the first record from the physical file.

```
CLRSF subroutine
    Turn indicator 50 *off
    Write to Dsp02 (clear the subfile)
    Turn indicator 50 *on
    Set RRN and  RRNHLD to zero
    Position INVPF at the top of file (TOF)
    Read the first record from INVPF
End subroutine
```

Figure 3.4C

Pseudocode for the
CLRSF Subroutine

Because the LOAD subroutine has been replaced with the LOADPG and CLRSF subroutines, the mainline of our code is changed to call both subroutines, as shown in Figure 3.5A.

Figure 3.5A

Mainline Code for
Subfile Load
Option 2

```
....+....1....+....2....+....3....+....4....+....5....+....6....+....7.

      ***********************************************************
      *  MAINLINE
      ***********************************************************
      *                                       Clear the subfile.
A3B  C                   EXSR      ClrSF
      *                                       Load page.
A3B  C                   EXSR      LoadPG

     C                   EXFMT     DSP02
     C                   DOW       *IN03 = *OFF
     C                   EXSR      RESPD
     C                   EXFMT     DSP02
     C                   ENDDO

     C                   MOVE      *ON            *INLR
     C                   RETURN
```

Figure 3.5B contains the code for the RESPD subroutine for subfile load option 2. When the update flag has been set by the Delete or Add subroutines, the subfile will be reloaded from record 1 to the page containing the last change. To do that, the number of pages (LOOPC) is computed by dividing the RRN (which contains the location of the last READC performed by the RESPD subroutine) by the number of lines per page. The result is the number of complete pages. If the division has a remainder, one additional page must be loaded.

Figure 3.5B

Code for RESPD
Subroutine for Subfile
Load Option 2

```
....+....1....+....2....+....3....+....4....+....5....+....6....+....7....+....8

      *************************************************************
      *  PROCESS RESPONSE TO SUBFILE
      *************************************************************
     C     RESPD         BEGSR
A3B  *                                          Process page down req.
A3B  C                   If        *IN25 = *ON
A3B  C     LastPN        SetGT     INVPF
A3B  C                   Read (N)  INVPF                          90
A3B  C                   Exsr      LoadPG
A3B  C                   Else
A3B  *
     C                   Eval      UPDFLG = *OFF
     C                   READC     DSP01                          94
      *
     C                   DoW       *IN94 = *OFF
A3B  C                   Eval      SFLRCD = RRN
     C                   Select
     C                   When      D1PICK = '2' or D1PICK = 'C'
     C                   ExSR      CHG
     C                   EndSL
      *
     C                   READC     DSP01                          94
     C                   ENDDO
     C                   IF        UPDFLG = *on
A3B  * Compute the number of pages to load.
A3B  C     RRN           DIV       8              LoopC          4 0
A3B  C                   MVR                      LoopM          1 0
A3B  C                   If        LoopM > 0
```

continued

```
....+....1....+....2....+....3....+....4....+....5....+....6....+....7....+....8
A3B C                    Eval      LoopC = LoopC + 1
A3B C                    EndIf
A3B C                    ExSR      ClrSF
A3B  * Load the computed number of pages.
A3B C                    Do        LoopC
A3B C                    ExSR      LoadPG
A3B C                    EndDo
A3B C                    If        SFLRCD > RRN
A3B C                    Eval      SFLRCD = RRN
A3B C                    EndIF
A3B C                    ENDIF
    C                    ENDIF
    C                    ENDSR
```

Figure 3.5B
Continued

Figure 3.5C contains the CLRSF subroutine, which resembles the first portion of the Load subroutine used in previous programs.

```
....+....1....+....2....+....3....+....4....+....5....+....6....+....7....+....8
A3B  ****************************************************************
A3B  * Clear the Subfile.
A3B  ****************************************************************
A3B C    ClrSF       BEGSR
A3B
A3B C                    Eval      *IN50 = *Off
A3B C                    Write     DSP02
A3B C                    Eval      *IN50 = *On
A3B C                    Eval      RRN = 0
A3B C                    Eval      RRNHLD = RRN
A3B C    *LOVAL        SETLL     INVPF
A3B C                    READ (N)  INVPF                                90
A3B
A3B C                    Write     FOOTER1
A3B
A3B C                    ENDSR
```

Figure 3.5C
The CLRSF Subroutine
for Subfile Load
Option 2

```
....+....1....+....2....+....3....+....4....+....5....+....6....+....7....+....8
     ****************************************************************
     * LoadPG - Loads the next 8 records into the Subfile
     ****************************************************************
     C    LoadPG      BEGSR

A3B C                    z-add     *zero        LoadCt        1 0
A3B C                    Eval      RRN = RRNHLD
A3B C                    Eval      SFLRCD = RRN + 1

     C                    DOW       (*IN90 = *OFF) and
A3B C                              (LoadCt < 8 ) and
A3B C                              (RRN     < 9999)
     C                    Eval      D1PICK = *BLANKS

     *        Populate the subfile fields.
     *
     C                    Eval      D1PN   = INPN
     C                    Eval      D1DESC = INDESC
     C                    Eval      D1QOH  = INQOH
     C                    Eval      D1UCST = INUCST
     C                    Eval      D1LTOT = D1QOH * D1UCST
A3B C                    Eval      LoadCt = LoadCt + 1
     C                    Eval      RRN    = RRN    + 1
A3B  * Save the Last Part Number Loaded.
A3B C                    Move (P)  INPN         LastPN        11
```

Figure 3.5D
The LOADPG
Subroutine for Subfile
Load Option 2

continued

Figure 3.5D
Continued

```
....+....1....+....2....+....3....+....4....+....5....+....6....+....7....+....8
       C                        WRITE     DSP01
       C                        READ (N)  INVPF                                90
       C                        ENDDO
       C                        If        RRN = 0
       C                        Eval      D1DESC = 'No Records'
       C                        Eval      D1PN    = *BLANKS
       C                        Eval      D1QOH   = *ZERO
       C                        Eval      D1UCST  = *ZERO
       C                        Eval      D1LTOT  = *ZERO
       C                        Eval      RRN = 1
       C                        Write     DSP01
       C                        Endif
  A3B  C                        Z-Add     RRN        RRNHLD        4 0
       C                        ENDSR
```

Except for the changes to the LOAD subroutine — which was replaced by the CLRSF and LOADPG subroutines, as well as the RESPD subroutine and mainline — the other subroutines developed in Chapters 1 and 2 need not be altered to work with subfile load option 2.

Exercise 3.1C Computers Are US Inventory Project

Purpose

To modify existing code to add the subfile end keyword to a growing multiple-page subfile display.

General Program Specifications

Create maintenance program INV013B and display file INVD013B. The program loads one page at a time into the Subfile DSP01 using subfile load option 2. The program lets users know whether there are more records available to view.

6. Copy display file INVD013A to new member INVD013B and modify it. Add the subfile keywords ROLLUP and SFLRCDNBR. Compile the display and test it.

7. Copy program INV013A to new member INV013B, modify the mainline code and the RESPD subroutine, and replace the LOAD subroutine with the CLRSF and LOADPG subroutines shown in Figures 3.5A through D. Compile the RPG program and test it.

Exercise 3.2B Purchase Order Line Project

Purpose

To design and code a subfile using subfile load option 2.

General Program Specifications

Create the RPG program ORDL23B, which displays all purchase order lines. It lets users press the Page down key to perform maintenance on the data, and it displays the word More... when there are more records available to be displayed.

4. Copy the display file source member ORDD023A to a new member ORDD023B. Make the necessary modifications to prepare this display file for Subfile Load Option 2. Compile and test the display.

5. Copy the source member ORDL23A to a new member, ORDL23B. Make the necessary modifications to load all of the records in the file using subfile load option 2.

   • Test and debug.
   • Print the compiler listing.

Subfile Load Option 3: Loading a Single Page

In subfile load option 3, the subfile is never more than a single page long. Whenever the user presses the Page up or the Page down key, the program clears the subfile and loads the next or previous page.

With this option, we programmatically manage the file as blocks of eight records (remember that eight was an arbitrary number based on how many records would look good on the screen layout). When the user presses the Page down key, the program clears the subfile and loads the next page. When the user presses the Page up key, the program clears the subfile and repositions a sufficient number of records above the current page in the physical file to cause the previous page to be loaded. This load option allows fast access to each page of data but requires a good deal of coding to determine and locate the records to load when a Page up or Page down key is pressed.

This option is preferred for working with dynamic data. All the subfile load options show the data as it existed at the time that the page displayed was actually loaded, regardless of the subsequent changes made by other users or other programs. Because every PageUp/PageDown request causes this option to reload that page from the physical data, the display always shows data that was up-to-date the last time that the Page up or Page down keys were pressed. To make certain that a page loaded by this option is up-to-date, a user could simply press the Page down key and then press the Page up key.

The description and code samples for subfile load option 3 specify only differences from subfile load option 2.

In addition to the ROLLUP keyword used in the display file in option 2, a ROLL-DOWN keyword is used to activate the Page up key. This keyword is conditioned by an indicator that indicates when the top of the file has been reached (Figure 3.6).

Figure 3.6

Page Up and
Page Down Keys

```
*...1....+....2....+....3....+....4....+....5....+....6....+....7....+....8
A N90                                       ROLLUP(25 'ROLLUP OR PGDN')
A N91                                       ROLLDOWN(26 'ROLLDN OR PGUP')
```

In subfile load option 3, the subfile is never longer than one page. Therefore, the subfile page size and subfile file size both equal the number of records displayed on a single screen. Finally, the SFLRCDNBR keyword is unnecessary. (This keyword was used in subfile load option 2 to control which page is displayed.) It is unnecessary because only a single page of subfile records exists in subfile load option 3.

The pseudocode for subfile load option 3 is shown in Figures 3.7A through 3.7C. The LOAD subroutine resembles the LOAD subroutine from Chapters 1 and 2 in that it clears the subfile and loads a single page. The LOAD subroutine stores the part numbers of the first and last records in the current page of the subfile. This makes it easy to locate the physical file properly when the next page is loaded or the current page updated.

To load the previous page, the program selects a point before the first record of the current page, reads back the number of records in a screen plus one additional record, and then reads that record. (Initially, the first record will be read in the mainline code, which you will see in Figure 3.8A, page 61.)

The RESPD subroutine has been modified as shown in Figure 3.7A. When the BACKUP subroutine is called, it reads backwards in the physical file until it reaches the point where the previous screen begins.

If the Page down key is pressed, *IN91 is turned off. Indicator 91 is used to signal the TOF, and if we've gone down one or more pages, we are no longer at the top of the physical file. Also, the physical file is positioned after the last record in the current subfile page and that record is read.

Both Page up and Page down cause the LOAD subroutine to be called, which loads the next page from the current record in the physical file.

Near the end of the RESPD subroutine, the update flag is tested to determine whether the subfile page has changed and needs to be reloaded. To reload the current page, the physical file is positioned just above the first record of the current page and that record is read and the LOAD subroutine is called.

Figure 3.7B shows the pseudocode for the LOAD subroutine. This subroutine includes most of the LOAD subroutine that appears in Chapters 1 and 2, including the code to clear the subfile.

RESPD subroutine
    If either indicator 25 or 26 is on (page down or page up)
        If indicator 26 is on (page up)
            Execute the Backup subroutine
        Else (page down)
            Move *off to indicator 91 (top-of-file (TOF) indicator)
            Position the physical file just beyond the last record loaded into the subfile page
            Read the next record from the physical file
        End if
            Execute the LOAD subroutine

    Else
        Set the update flag to off (this flag is on if a change requires that the subfile be reloaded)
        Read the first changed record in the subfile (a changed record must have a new value in D1PICK field because that's the only field the user can change)
        Do while changed records exist
            Do selection
                Select when D1PICK is 2 (Change)
                    Execute the CHG subroutine
            End selection
            Read the next changed record in the subfile
        End do
        If the update flag is on
            Position the physical file just above the first record loaded into the subfile page
            Read the next record from the physical file
            Execute the LOAD subroutine
        End if
    End if
End subroutine

Figure 3.7A

Pseudocode for the RESPD Subroutine with Subfile Load Option 3 Added

Figure 3.7B

Pseudocode for the
LOAD Subroutine

```
LOAD Subroutine
   Clear the Subfile
   Read the next record from the physical file
   Write the Footer
   Store the (Key)Part Number of the first record in FirstPN
   Do while not EOF and RRN less than Subfile Size
      Load physical file fields into subfile fields
      Add 1 to RRN
      Store the (Key)Part Number of the first record in LastPN
      Read the next record from the physical file
   Enddo
   If RRN = 0
      Create 'No Record' entry and write it to the subfile
      Add 1 to RRN
   EndIF
End subroutine
```

FirstPN is the part number of the first record loaded into the current page. LastPN is the part number of the last record loaded into the current page.

Figure 3.7C shows the pseudocode for the BACKUP subroutine. It uses the READP operation code to read backwards through the file until either the TOF is reached or the file has been positioned at the correct location. It then does the initial read from the data file preparing the data for the LOAD subroutine.

Figure 3.7C

Pseudocode for the
BACKUP Subroutine

```
BACKUP Subroutine
         Position physical file above first record loaded into the current subfile
         page
         Set indicator 90 off
   Do while indicator 91 is off (TOF) and the count is less than the page size+1
         Read the previous record from the data file
         Add 1 to count
   End do
   If indicator 91 is on (TOF)
         Position at TOF
   End if
   Read from the data file
End subroutine
```

If either the top of the data file (during backup) or the bottom of the data file (during load) is encountered, the record pointer must be repositioned to the TOF or EOF for subsequent read or read previous operations to be successful. These tests and the SETLL (Set Lower Limit) or SETGT (Set Greater Than) operations are also included in the Backup subroutine.

The RPG code for the mainline code, and the RESPD, LOAD, and BACKUP subroutines are shown in Figures 3.8A through 3.8D.

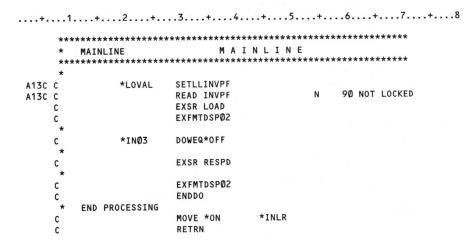

```
....+....1....+....2....+....3....+....4....+....5....+....6....+....7....+....8
        ****************************************************************
        *   MAINLINE                      M A I N L I N E
        ****************************************************************
        *
A13C C            *LOVAL     SETLLINVPF
A13C C                       READ INVPF                      N     90 NOT LOCKED
     C                       EXSR LOAD
     C                       EXFMTDSP02
        *
     C            *IN03      DOWEQ*OFF
        *
     C                       EXSR RESPD
        *
     C                       EXFMTDSP02
     C                       ENDDO
        *  END PROCESSING
     C                       MOVE *ON       *INLR
     C                       RETRN
```

Figure 3.8A
Mainline Code for Subfile Load Option 3

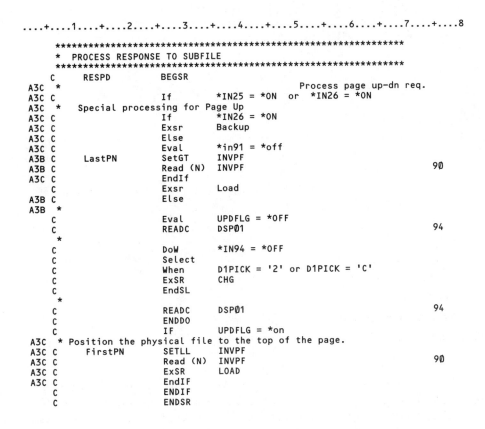

```
....+....1....+....2....+....3....+....4....+....5....+....6....+....7....+....8
        ****************************************************************
        *   PROCESS RESPONSE TO SUBFILE
        ****************************************************************
     C      RESPD      BEGSR
A3C  *                                       Process page up-dn req.
A3C  C                 If        *IN25 = *ON  or  *IN26 = *ON
A3C  *   Special processing for Page Up
A3C  C                 If        *IN26 = *ON
A3C  C                 Exsr      Backup
A3C  C                 Else
A3C  C                 Eval      *in91 = *off
A3B  C      LastPN     SetGT     INVPF
A3B  C                 Read (N)  INVPF                          90
A3C  C                 EndIf
     C                 Exsr      Load
A3B  C                 Else
A3B  *
     C                 Eval      UPDFLG = *OFF
     C                 READC     DSP01                          94
        *
     C                 DoW       *IN94 = *OFF
     C                 Select
     C                 When      D1PICK = '2' or D1PICK = 'C'
     C                 ExSR      CHG
     C                 EndSL
        *
     C                 READC     DSP01                          94
     C                 ENDDO
     C                 IF        UPDFLG = *on
A3C  *  Position the physical file to the top of the page.
A3C  C      FirstPN    SETLL     INVPF
A3C  C                 Read (N)  INVPF                          90
A3C  C                 ExSR      LOAD
A3C  C                 EndIF
     C                 ENDIF
     C                 ENDSR
```

Figure 3.8B
RESPD Subroutine Code for Subfile Load Option 3

Figure 3.8C
LOAD Subroutine
Code for Subfile Load
Option 3

```
....+....1....+....2....+....3....+....4....+....5....+....6....+....7....+....8
*******************************************************************
     *  Load    - Load 8 records into the Subfile.
     *******************************************************************
     C        Load          BEGSR

     C                      Eval      *IN50 = *Off
     C                      Write     DSP02
     C                      Eval      *IN50 = *On
     C                      Eval      RRN = 0
     C                      READ (N)  INVPF                                    90
     C                      Write     FOOTER1

A3C  * Save the First Part Number Loaded.
A3C  C                      Move      INPN          FirstPN          11

     C                      DOW       (*IN90 = *OFF) and
     C                                (RRN    < 8 )
     C                      Eval      D1PICK = *BLANKS

        *        Populate the subfile fields.
        *
     C                      Eval      D1PN   = INPN
     C                      Eval      D1DESC = INDESC
     C                      Eval      D1QOH  = INQOH
     C                      Eval      D1UCST = INUCST
     C                      Eval      D1LTOT = D1QOH * D1UCST
     C                      Eval      RRN    = RRN    + 1
A3B  * Save the Last Part Number Loaded.
A3B  C                      Move (P)  INPN          LastPN           11
     C                      WRITE     DSP01
     C                      READ (N)  INVPF                                    90

     C                      ENDDO
     C                      If        RRN = 0
     C                      Eval      D1DESC = 'No Records'
     C                      Eval      D1PN   = *BLANKS
     C                      Eval      D1QOH  = *ZERO
     C                      Eval      D1UCST = *ZERO
     C                      Eval      D1LTOT = *ZERO
     C                      Eval      RRN = 1
     C                      Write     DSP01
     C                      Endif
     C                      ENDSR
        *
```

```
....+....1....+....2....+....3....+....4....+....5....+....6....+....7....+....8
A3C   ****************************************************************
A3C   *  Backup - Locate before first record of current page.
A3C   *          Read back the number of records plus 1.
A3C   ****************************************************************
A3C C     Backup        BEGSR
A3C   * Position the file before the first record of the current pg.
A3C C     FirstPn       SetLL    INVPF
A3C C                   Eval     *IN90 = *OFF
A3C C                   Z-ADD    *ZERO    RcdCt          1 0
A3C   * Read back through the file to the top of the previous page.
A3C C                   DoW      *in91 = *OFF and RcdCt < 9
A3C C                   ReadP (N) INVPF                               91
A3C C                   Eval     RcdCt = RcdCt + 1
A3C C                   EndDo
A3C   * If the top of file has been reached the file must be repositioned
A3C   *   with the setLL command and the TOF indicator turned off.
A3C C                   If       *IN91 = *ON
A3C C     *loval        SETLL    INVPF
A3C C                   Eval     *IN91 = *OFF
A3C C                   Endif
A3C   * Perform priming read.
A3C C                   Read (N)  INVPF                               90
A3C
A3C C                   ENDSR
```

Figure 3.8D
BACKUP Subroutine
Code for Subfile Load
Option 3

Exercise 3.1D Computers Are US Inventory Project

Purpose
To modify existing code to add the subfile end keyword to a growing multiple-page subfile display.

General Program Specifications
Create the maintenance program INV013C and the display file INVD013C. The program loads one page at a time into the subfile DSP01, using subfile load option 3. The program indicates to users whether there are more records to be displayed.

8. Copy display file INVD013A to new member INVD013C and modify it. Add the subfile keywords ROLLUP and ROLLDOWN. Compile and test the display.

9. Copy program INV013A to new member INV013C. Modify the mainline code as well as the RESPD and LOAD subroutines and add the BACKUP subroutine shown in Figures 3.8A through 3.8D. Compile and test the RPG program.

Exercise 3.2C Purchase Order Line Project

Purpose

To design and code a subfile that loads using subfile load option 3.

General Program Specifications

Create RPG program ORDL23C, which displays all purchase order lines. It lets the user press the Page down key to perform maintenance on the data and displays the word More... when there are more records to be displayed.

6. Copy the display-file source member ORDD023A to a new member, ORDD023C. Make the necessary modifications to prepare this display file for subfile load option 3. Compile and test the display.

7. Copy the source member ORDL23A to a new member ORDL23C. Make the necessary modifications to load all of the records in the file using subfile load option 3.

   • Test and debug.
   • Print the compiler listing.

Review

1. For each of the subfile load options, state what is displayed if — after the initial load and while a user is viewing the first screen — another program deleted all of the records. What would happen with each load option if the Page down key were pressed? What would happen if the Page up key were pressed?

2. If we have a small number of records to display, which option would be most appropriate? Why?

3. Explain how the BACKUP subroutine works. Why is it necessary to use a SETLL on the physical file if the TOF is encountered during backup?

4. The bottom of the physical file is displayed and the Page up key is pressed. What happens in the RPG code for each of the following load options?

    a. Option 1
    b. Option 2
    c. Option 3

5. The first page is displayed, there are more physical records available to load, and the Page down key is pressed. What happens in the RPG code for each of the following load options?

    a. Option 1
    b. Option 2
    c. Option 3

6. The first page is displayed, the user has already pressed the Page down key once followed by the Page up key, there are more physical records available to load, and the Page down key is pressed. What happens in the RPG code for each of the following load options?

    a. Option 1
    b. Option 2
    c. Option 3

Chapter 4

Adding Drop and Fold Capabilities and Using the Header and Footer

Chapter Overview

When you finish Chapter 4, you will be able to describe and use

- the SFLDROP (Subfile Drop) and SFLFOLD (Subfile Fold) keywords
- the SFLPAG (Subfile Page) keyword with the SFLDROP and SFLFOLD keywords
- the SFLCSRRRN (Subfile Cursor Relative Record Number) keyword
- the layout of the SFL record to accommodate drop and fold
- the layout of the SFL record to place a blank row between records
- the Input, Output, or Both fields on the header record
- the Output fields on the footer record

Introduction to Drop and Fold

The data to be displayed on a screen frequently exceeds the space available to display it. This is especially true when you design displays with subfiles that are usually limited to a single row of 80 characters. The first part of this chapter introduces a new display-file keyword that lets the user press a function key and expand the display of each record from a single-row layout to a multiple-row layout. Adding this feature to a subfile display lets the screen designer lay out the first row with the frequently viewed data and subsequent rows with data that users would view less often.

Figure 4.1 shows the inventory file maintenance screen. The display is well laid out, easy to read, and presents the most frequently needed data. However, the inventory file (INVPF) contains fields for warehouse and warehouse location that are not shown. Although these fields are included in the display window (option 5), this isn't convenient for users who need to scan the data for items in a particular warehouse or location.

Figure 4.2 shows the display after the user presses F6 to display the additional fields. F6 works like a toggle for the user; pressing it again switches the display shown in Figure 4.2 back to the display shown in Figure 4.1.

Figure 4.1
Initial Display with
SFLDRP Keyword

```
 A300C1                           COMPUTERS ARE US                 12/21/98
 INVD012A                      INVENTORY MAINTENANCE

   2=Change     4=Delete    5=Display    6=Add

 O  PART NUMBER     DESCRIPTION              QNTY        COST      EXTENDED

 _   A123           Computer x486              21    1,301.15    27,324.15
 _   A124           Computer Pentium          215    3,100.16   666,534.40
 _   A125           Printer - Laser            81      974.21    78,911.01
 _   A213           Printer - Ink Jet          15      457.15     6,857.25
 _   A214           Printer - Dot Matrix       21      251.14     5,273.94
 _   A215           Scanner - Hand             15      127.19     1,907.85
 _   A216           Scanner - Flat Bed          5      421.15     2,105.75
 _   A319           CD-ROM                      6      115.96       695.76
                                                                More ...

 ==========================================================================
    F3=Exit Subsystem         F6=Display Details
```

Figure 4.2
Display After
F6 Is Pressed

```
 A300C1                           COMPUTERS ARE US                 12/21/98
 INVD012A                      INVENTORY MAINTENANCE

   2=Change     4=Delete    5=Display    6=Add

 O  PART NUMBER       DESCRIPTION              QNTY       COST     EXTENDED

 _  A123            Computer x486                21    1,301.15   27,324.15
                       WAREHOUSE: DLS  LOCATION: 15A
 _  A124            Computer Pentium            215    3,100.16  666,534.40
                       WAREHOUSE: FTW  LOCATION: 21901
 _  A125            Printer - Laser              81      974.21   78,911.01
                       WAREHOUSE: DLS  LOCATION: X19
 _  A213            Printer - Ink Jet            15      457.15    6,857.25
                       WAREHOUSE: FTW  LOCATION: 319
                                                                  More ...
 ==========================================================================
    F3=Exit Subsystem         F6=Display Details
```

The subfile keyword that initially displays only the first line of the subfile records (as in Figure 4.1) and reacts to a function key by switching into a multiline format (as in Figure 4.2) is **SFLDROP**. Conversely, the keyword **SFLFOLD** initially displays the subfile in a multiline format (as in Figure 4.2) and reacts to a function key by switching to a single-line format (as in Figure 4.1). These keywords are mutually exclusive; only one of them should be used in a subfile control record.

Creating the Subfile Record for Subfile Drop and Fold

To add drop and fold, the additional fields are added to the subfile record as shown in Figure 4.3. Fields to be displayed on the first line are entered with the first line number of the subfile (8 in this example). Fields to be displayed on the second line are coded with the next line number (9). If a third or fourth line were needed, the line numbers would be 10 and 11. If you look back at Figure 4.2, you can see that 'WAREHOUSE:' and 'LOCATION:' precede the fields on the second line of each record. The coding for these constants is shown shaded in Figure 4.3. Because these constants are to be displayed on the second line of each subfile record, they are entered with the line position of the second line of the first record (9).

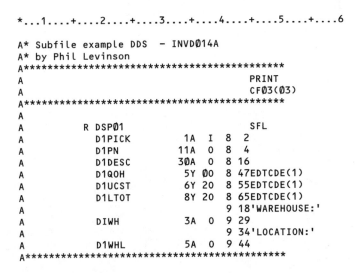

```
*...1....+....2....+....3....+....4....+....5....+....6

A* Subfile example DDS  - INVD014A
A* by Phil Levinson
A*********************************************
A                                    PRINT
A                                    CF03(03)
A*********************************************
A
A           R DSP01                  SFL
A             D1PICK      1A   I  8  2
A             D1PN       11A   O  8  4
A             D1DESC     30A   O  8 16
A             D1QOH       5Y 00  8 47EDTCDE(1)
A             D1UCST      6Y 20  8 55EDTCDE(1)
A             D1LTOT      8Y 20  8 65EDTCDE(1)
A                                    9 18'WAREHOUSE:'
A             D1WH        3A   O  9 29
A                                    9 34'LOCATION:'
A             D1WHL       5A   O  9 44
A*********************************************
```

Figure 4.3
Subfile Record Definition Including Drop/Fold Fields

Creating the Subfile Control Record for Subfile Drop and Fold

A sample subfile control record is shown in Figure 4.4. Although this is the control record for subfile load option 2, the same two changes would be required in any subfile control record. The SFLDROP keyword has been added, followed by CF06. CF06 is the function key that causes the display file to switch from the drop (single-line format) to the fold (multiline format).

The subfile page size (SFLPAG) has been changed to the number of folded records that can be displayed. The value of SFLPAG has been changed to 4 (four two-line records occupy eight lines). In drop mode, eight records are displayed per page; in folded mode, only four records are displayed per page.

Modifying the Footer Record for Drop and Fold

The footer record is used to display function key definitions to the user. Because the drop or fold is going to be activated by pressing F6, the footer record should inform the user about that.

Modifying the RPG Program for Drop and Fold

Because the display file manages the fold-and-drop process without returning to the RPG program, the only modifications to the RPG program are in the subroutines that write or update the subfile records. The subfile records contain some new fields (D1WH and D1WHL). Therefore, the subroutines that write or update the subfile records must be modified to move the appropriate data into these fields along with the rest of the subfile fields prior to the write or update process.

Figure 4.4
Subfile Control Record
for Subfile Load Option
2 with Subfile Drop

```
*...1....+....2....+....3....+....4....+....5....+....6....+....7....+....8
A*******************************************************************
A           R DSP02                      SFLCTL(DSP01)
A   90                                    SFLEND(*MORE)
A                                         SFLDROP(CF06)
A                                         SFLSIZ(0009)
A                                         SFLPAG(0004)
A  N90                                    ROLLUP(25 'ROLLUP OR PGDN')
A                                         OVERLAY
A   50                                    SFLDSP
A   50                                    SFLDSPCTL
A  N50                                    SFLCLR
A           SFLRCD          4S 0H         SFLRCDNBR(CURSOR)
A                                       1 31'COMPUTERS ARE US'
A                                       2 31'WORK WITH INVENTORY LISTS'
A                                       1  2USER
A                                       1 71DATE
A                                         EDTCDE(Y)
A                                       6  4'PART NUMBER'
A                                       6 16'DESCRIPTION'
A                                       6 47'QNTY'
A                                       6 55'COST'
A                                       6 65'EXTENDED'
A                                       6  2'0'
A                                       4  3'2=Change'
A                                       4 15'4=Delete'
A                                       4 27'5=Display' n
```

Adding a Blank Line Between Records

The folded screen can sometimes be difficult to read. A blank line between folded records makes the screen easier to read, as is apparent in Figure 4.5.

Creating the folded record layout with a blank line between the records (Figure 4.5) requires two changes to the display file. The first change is to the subfile record. One additional field is added, as shown in shaded type in Figure 4.6.

Figure 4.5
Folded Display
with a Blank Line
Between Records

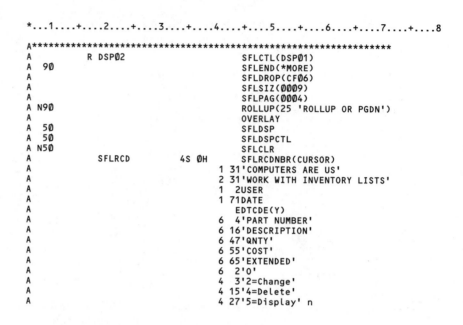

```
A300C1                    COMPUTERS ARE US                    12/21/98
INVD012A                  INVENTORY MAINTENANCE

  2=Change      4=Delete      5=Display      6=Add

O  PART NUMBER  DESCRIPTION                   QNTY     COST      EXTENDED

_  A123         Computer x486                  21   1,301.15    27,324.15
                  WAREHOUSE: DLS  LOCATION: 15A

_  A124         Computer PentIUM              215   3,100.16   666,534.40
                  WAREHOUSE: FTW  LOCATION: 219

_  A125         Printer - Laser                81     974.21    78,911.01
                  WAREHOUSE: DLS  LOCATION: X19

                                                             More ...
================================================================================
  F3=Exit Subsystem       F6=Display
```

```
*...1....+....2....+....3....+....4....+....5....+....6

A* Subfile example DDS  - INVD014A
A* by Phil Levinson
A*******************************************
A                                     PRINT
A                                     CF03(03)
A*******************************************
A
A         R DSP01                     SFL
A           D1PICK      1A  I  8  2
A           D1PN       11A  O  8  4
A           D1DESC     30A  O  8 16
A           D1QOH       5Y 00  8 47EDTCDE(1)
A           D1UCST      6Y 20  8 55EDTCDE(1)
A           D1LTOT      8Y 20  8 65EDTCDE(1)
A                              9 18'WAREHOUSE:'
A           DIWH        3A  O  9 29
A                              9 34'LOCATION:'
A           D1WHL       5A  O  9 44
A                             10  1' '
A*******************************************
```

Figure 4.6

Subfile Record
Definition Including
Drop and Fold Fields

The other change that might be required is in the definition of page size in the subfile control record. Because the folded record now takes more rows, you may have to reduce the page size. The display shown in Figure 4.5 was created with a subfile page size of 3. If, however, your program uses subfile load options 2 or 3 and loads eight records at a time, then in folded mode, you will see two pages of three followed by one page of two. This accounts for the eight records loaded into the subfile.

The next use of the Page down key causes the program to load eight more records — and, in folded mode, you will again see two pages of three records each followed by one page of two records. The pattern of 3-3-2-3-3-2 is not a technical problem, but users might find it distracting. If we modify the LOAD subroutine to load nine records at a time instead of eight, then the display will show nine dropped records or three pages of three folded records.

Exercise 4.1A Computers Are US Inventory Project

Purpose

To modify existing code to develop and test a subfile with subfile fold capability.

General Program Specifications

Create the maintenance program INV014A and the display file INVD014A. The program and display are modified to display the folded record when the user presses F6.

1. Copy display file INVD013B into the new member INVD014A. Modify INVD014B by adding the additional fields from the inventory file to a second line of the subfile record. Add SFLDROP(CF06) to the control record and modify the footer record to indicate that Function key 6 will display details. Modify the SFLPAG value to 4.

2. Copy program source member INV013B into new member INV014B. Modify your program to load additional fields into the subfile in the LOAD subroutine.

3. Compile and test your program. Select folded mode (multiline record). Select option 5 to display a record. Did the screen remain folded after you exited the display window?

4. Modify your code to provide a blank line between records, as shown in Figure 4.5.

Exercise 4.2A Purchase Order Line Project

Purpose

To demonstrate that you can add drop and fold capabilities to subfiles.

General Program Specifications

Create the RPG program ORDL24A, which will display all purchase order lines. This file will have drop and fold capabilities.

1. Copy the display file source member ORDD023B to new member ORDD024A. Add the fields in the file ORDLPF that were not previously included in the subfile display. Make the necessary modifications to prepare this display file for subfile display fold. Include a blank line between records when they are folded.

2. Copy the source member ORDL23B to a new member ORDL24A. Make the necessary modifications to load the additional fields.

Review

1. Describe two differences between SFLDROP and SFLFOLD.
2. Describe how to compute the SFLPAG value when you use drop or fold.
3. What is the impact of leaving out the SFLDROP and the SFLFOLD keywords with a multiline subfile?

Maintaining the Subfile Mode

With drop and fold, you've added a nice feature to your code. However, you may have noticed in testing it that every time the program loops and executes the format DSP02, the drop and fold reverts to its default setting. For some applications, that might be fine, but it is possible to keep the drop and fold mode the way that the user sets it. This requires a few changes and one new keyword.

Changes to the Subfile Control Record to Maintain the Subfile Mode

To take control of the subfile drop and fold, the RPG program needs to know what mode the display was in when it turned over control to the program. The keyword that passes the drop and fold mode to the program is SFLMODE (Subfile Mode). This keyword, shown in Figure 4.7, is followed by an ampersand (&) and the name of a one-character hidden variable: SFLMODE(&SFLMD). When you code display-file keywords, the name of a field that transfers data from the display file to the program is preceded by an &. The field SFLMD is defined on the next specification after the SFLMODE keyword. This variable must be one character long and hidden.

Table 4.1 shows the meaning of the values of the variable associated with SFLMODE.

Table 4.1
SLFMODE Values

Value	Subfile mode
'0' or *OFF	Folded (multiline)
'1' or *ON	Dropped (single line)

The subfile control record also contains both the SFLDROP and SFLFOLD keywords. They are conditioned by opposite modes of the same indicator. In Figure 4.7, this indicator is 55. If indicator 55 is on, the screen appears in drop (single-line) format because the SFLDROP keyword is conditioned with 55. If indicator 55 is off, the screen appears in fold (multiline) format because the SFLFOLD keyword is conditioned with N55.

Figure 4.7

Subfile Control Record
with Subfile Drop
Default and
SLFMODE Keyword

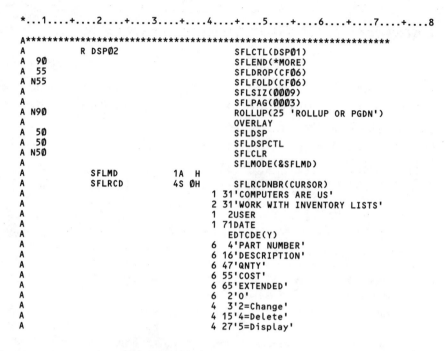

```
*...1....+....2....+....3....+....4....+....5....+....6....+....7....+....8
A******************************************************************
A            R DSP02                          SFLCTL(DSP01)
A 90                                           SFLEND(*MORE)
A 55                                           SFLDROP(CF06)
A N55                                          SFLFOLD(CF06)
A                                              SFLSIZ(0009)
A                                              SFLPAG(0003)
A N90                                          ROLLUP(25 'ROLLUP OR PGDN')
A                                              OVERLAY
A 50                                           SFLDSP
A 50                                           SFLDSPCTL
A N50                                          SFLCLR
A                                              SFLMODE(&SFLMD)
A              SFLMD         1A  H
A              SFLRCD        4S  0H             SFLRCDNBR(CURSOR)
A                                          1 31'COMPUTERS ARE US'
A                                          2 31'WORK WITH INVENTORY LISTS'
A                                          1  2USER
A                                          1 71DATE
A                                              EDTCDE(Y)
A                                          6  4'PART NUMBER'
A                                          6 16'DESCRIPTION'
A                                          6 47'QNTY'
A                                          6 55'COST'
A                                          6 65'EXTENDED'
A                                          6  2'0'
A                                          4  3'2=Change'
A                                          4 15'4=Delete'
A                                          4 27'5=Display'
```

Changes to the RPG Program to Maintain the Subfile Mode

Figure 4.8 shows the mainline code for subfile load option 2. Before the initial display of the screen, indicator 55 should be set on if the screen should be shown initially in SFLDROP mode. Later in the same subroutine, the mode value returned at the completion of the previous execution of the display is used to set the value of indicator 55 appropriately, so the display will be activated in the same mode in which it ended.

Figure 4.8

Mainline Code for Subfile
Load Option 2 with
Subfile Mode Control

```
....+....1....+....2....+....3....+....4....+....5....+....6....+....7....+....8

          ********************************************************
          *  MAINLINE
          ********************************************************
A3B  C                     EXSR      ClrSF
A3B  C                     EXSR      LoadPG
     *  Set ind 55 to initially display the file in SFLDROP mode.
A4B  C                     Eval      *in55 = *on

     C                     EXFMT     DSP02
     C                     DOW       *IN03 = *OFF
     C                     EXSR      RESPD
A4B  *  Set ind 55 based on the SFLDrop mode.
A4B  C                     Eval      *In55 = SFLMD
     C                     EXFMT     DSP02

     C                     ENDDO
     C                     MOVE      *ON            *INLR
     C                     RETURN
```

Exercise 4.1B Computers Are US Inventory Project

Purpose

To modify existing code to develop and test a subfile that maintains the subfile display mode.

General Program Specifications

Create the maintenance program INV014B and the display file INVD014B. The program and display will be modified to display the folded record when the user presses F6 and to maintain the latest selection of mode.

5. Copy display file INVD014A into new member INVD014B. Modify INVD014B by adding the SFLMODE keyword and its variable. Also include both SFLDROP and SFLFOLD conditioned with the opposite values of the same indicator.

6. Copy RPG source member INV014A into new member INV014B. Modify your program to bring the subfile up initially in SFLDROP mode and to maintain the user's preferred mode.

7. Test your program carefully. Switch into folded mode and press the Enter key. While still in folded mode, press the Page down key to move to the next set of records. Press the Enter key. What records are displayed each time you press the Enter key?

Exercise 4.2B Purchase Order Line Project

Purpose

To demonstrate that you can add drop and fold capabilities to subfiles and maintain the user-selected subfile display mode.

General Program Specifications

Create the RPG program ORDL24B, which will display all purchase order lines. This file will have drop and fold capabilities. Initial display mode should be folded.

3. Copy the display file source member ORDD024A to the new member ORDD024B. Make the necessary modifications to prepare this display file for subfile display fold. Include a blank line between records when they are folded.

4. Copy the source member ORDL24A into new member ORDL24B. Make the necessary modifications to initially show the display file in fold mode and then maintain the user's selected mode.

Using the Subfile Cursor Keyword to Improve Screen Control

In Exercise 4.1, step 7, you saw that pressing the Enter key

- returned the cursor to the top of a page
- caused a different page to be displayed occasionally

In subfile load option 2, the RPG program controls the cursor position by setting the value of the variable associated with the SFLRCDNBR (Subfile Record Number) keyword in the subfile control record. The current page can be kept on the display and the cursor can be returned to its correct location. To do so, set the value of this variable to the record number of the record the cursor was pointing to when a user action caused the screen to turn over control to the RPG program.

The subfile control keyword SFLCSRRRN returns to the RPG program the number of the subfile record that the cursor is pointing to when control returns to the program. If the cursor is not pointing to a subfile record, then SFLCSRRRN returns a zero. This keyword identifies a field that transfers data to the program. In Figure 4.9, the field to transfer the subfile record cursor location is CSRLOC, and the variable name is preceded with an ampersand (&) in the keyword to indicate that it transfers data to the program. As shown in Figure 4.9, this variable must be defined in the display file (as 5 0 signed and hidden).

Figure 4.9
Subfile Control Record with Subfile Cursor Relative Record Number Keyword

```
*...1....+....2....+....3....+....4....+....5....+....6....+....7....+....8
A******************************************************************
A           R DSP02                    SFLCTL(DSP01)
A   90                                  SFLEND(*MORE)
A   55                                  SFLDROP(CF06)
A  N55                                  SFLFOLD(CF06)
A                                       SFLSIZ(0009)
A                                       SFLPAG(0003)
A  N90                                  ROLLUP(25 'ROLLUP OR PGDN')
A                                       OVERLAY
A   50                                  SFLDSP
A   50                                  SFLDSPCTL
A  N50                                  SFLCLR
A                                       SFLMODE(&SFLMD)
A                                       SFLCSRRRN(&CSRLOC)
A             SFLMD          1A  H
A             CSRLOC         5S  0H
A             SFLRCD         4S  0H     SFLRCDNBR(CURSOR)
A                                      1 31'COMPUTERS ARE US'
    * code continues as in previous examples
```

The RPG program (shown in Figure 4.10) uses the value the SFLCSRRRN keyword creates (if it is not zero) to set the subfile record variable. The subfile record variable is used by the SFLRCDNBR keyword to locate the cursor on the subsequent EXFMT (Execute Format) operation. If this is done immediately after the execution of the display, as shown in Figure 4.10, no other changes to the RPG program are needed.

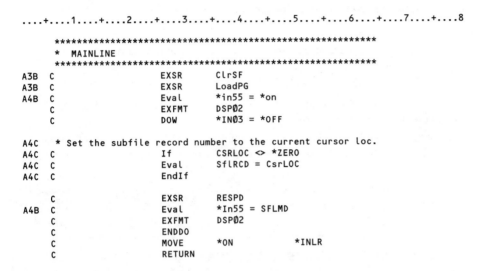

```
....+....1....+....2....+....3....+....4....+....5....+....6....+....7....+....8

             ********************************************************
         *   MAINLINE
             ********************************************************
A3B  C                     EXSR      ClrSF
A3B  C                     EXSR      LoadPG
A4B  C                     Eval      *in55 = *on
     C                     EXFMT     DSP02
     C                     DOW       *IN03 = *OFF

A4C     * Set the subfile record number to the current cursor loc.
A4C  C                     If        CSRLOC <> *ZERO
A4C  C                     Eval      SflRCD = CsrLOC
A4C  C                     EndIf

     C                     EXSR      RESPD
A4B  C                     Eval      *In55 = SFLMD
     C                     EXFMT     DSP02
     C                     ENDDO
     C                     MOVE      *ON            *INLR
     C                     RETURN
```

Figure 4.10

Mainline Code for Subfile Load Option 2 Loading Current Subfile Position into SFLRCD

After the subfile record number is set, the remainder of the processing cycle takes place. Based on the subsequent processing, a better location might be computed for the cursor (i.e., when a new page is added to the subfile). The last value of the variable SFLRCD when the subfile is displayed again will control the position of the cursor. Therefore, setting the value at this point ensures that a good value will be in the SFLRCD variable, but it will leave the opportunity for it to be changed by later processing.

Exercise 4.1C Computers Are US Inventory Project

Purpose
To modify existing code to develop and test a subfile that maintains the cursor position.

General Program Specifications
Modify the inventory maintenance program INV014B and the display file INVD014B. The program and display are modified to maintain the correct records on the display and keep the cursor in the correct position.

8. Modify display file INVD014B to return the subfile cursor position as shown in Figure 4.9.

9. Modify the program INV014B to return the cursor to the correct position when redisplaying the screen. Refer to the code sample in Figure 4.10.

10. Test your program carefully. Switch into folded mode and press the Enter key. While still in folded mode, press the Page down key to move to the next set of records. Press the Enter key. Move the cursor to the top of the page and press Enter.

Exercise 4.2C Purchase Order Line Project

Purpose
To demonstrate that you can apply the SFLCSRRRN keyword to control the cursor location.

General Program Specifications
Modify the RPG program ORDL24B, which will display all purchase order lines. Add the SFLCSRRRN keyword and the necessary program modifications to control the cursor location.

5. Make the necessary modifications to display file ORDD024B to include the SFLCSRRRN keyword.

6. Make the necessary modifications to ORDL24B to control the cursor location.

Review

6. Describe the SFLCSRRRN keyword and its use in subfile processing.

The Screen Header

In the past few chapters, we've concentrated on the subfile. However, the screen also has a header area, which we've defined in the subfile control record, and a footer area defined in the footer record. These screen areas can play a role in communicating a more complete set of information to users or in making the programs easier to use.

Frequently, an input field is added to the header that lets users indicate a value to which they want to position the subfile. I will explore this tool in Chapter 5.

Output fields can also be added to the header area of the display to provide information that applies to the whole set of records displayed. The example in Figure 4.11 displays the general information about an order in the header, and the subfile contains the "lines" of the order.

```
A300C1                    Jefferson College                    10/24/98
                          Bookstore Order

 ORDER NUMBER:  2113              Order Status: 0
 TO:        Duke Press                          SHIP TO:   BOOKSTORE
            221 E. 29th Street                             JEFFERSON COLLEGE
            Loveland, CO 80538                             1000 VIKING ROAD
                                                           HILLSBORO, MO 63050
 SHIPPING INSTRUCTIONS: FASTEST WAY           ORDER DATE:  10/25/98

 1=Add 2=Change 4=Delete 5=Display
                                                                 *
 O    PART#       Description        Quantity    Cost      Extended

 _    ISBN1245A   RPG/400 by Judy Yaeger      30   60.00      1,800.00
 _    ISBN2144B   Advanced RPG by P.Levinson  20   45.00        900.00
 _
 _
 _

                                       Total              2,700.00
 ------------------------------------------------------------
 F3= Exit      F6=Display Detail    F12= Cancel
```

Figure 4.11

Display File with Subfile, Data Fields in the Header Area, and a Grand Total in the Footer Area

If the header is included in the subfile control record, then the fields in the header can be output capable, input capable, or both. When the RPG program issues an Execute Format (EXFMT) operation on the control record, all input and both fields in the header are returned — along with values for which we have already coded. This provides the user with a large number of options and the programmer with more processing options to accommodate in the code.

The user can

- change any input-capable field on the header
- select options by entering values into the options field
- press the Page up or Page down keys
- press any activated function key

The Footer

The footer can contain output fields, such as the Total field in Figure 4.11. This value was accumulated as the subfile was loaded. For the total to be correct, the entire subfile must be loaded (load option 1).

To keep the total up-to-date when changes, deletes, or adds occur, its value must be recomputed or corrected. The simplest way to do this is to reload the subfile whenever any type of change occurs. The subfile routine would begin by setting the value of the Total field to zero and subsequently add the extended price of each line as it is computed to the total.

Whenever the Total field is recomputed, the footer record must be rewritten to the screen, or it continues to show the old value. We do this by including the WRITE FOOTER statement at the end of the Load Subfile (LOAD) subroutine. We've been including this write in the LOAD subroutine from the beginning, but now you know why.

The header can have input or both fields included in the control record. The fields work because we do an EXFMT operation on the control record. EXFMT causes the control record to return its input and both fields, function keys, and subfile changes.

You cannot use input or both fields in the footer record because it will be written to but never read from (with a READ or an EXFMT operation).

Exercise 4.1D Computers Are US Inventory Project

Create INV014C and INVD014C, which will be similar to INV013A.

1. Load entire subfile (load option 1).
2. Display the extended total in the footer properly labeled and formatted and in reverse image and color.
3. Total should be updated whenever changes, deletes, or adds occur.

Purpose

To modify existing code to develop and test a program that loads and displays all records in a subfile and that displays a grand total field in the footer.

General Program Specifications

Create maintenance program INV014C and display file INVD014C. These programs should function like INV013A, but they display the extended price total in the footer. The total should be updated when records are added, deleted, or changed.

11. Copy display file INVD013A to member INVD014C and add the Grand Total field to the footer record.
12. Copy RPG source member INV013A to new member INV014C. Modify the code to compute and display the total. Test the program to make certain that the total is correct when records are added, deleted, and changed.

Review

7. Consider the program developed in Exercise 4.1D, steps 11 and 12. It displays a grand total on the footer record. If the user changes a record, it is possible to execute that change without reloading the subfile. Use a flowchart or pseudocode of the Change (CHG) subroutine to demonstrate how that subroutine can keep the total up-to-date without reloading the subfile.

Chapter 5

Positioning the Subfile and Selecting Records

Chapter Overview

Chapter 5 teaches you the programming techniques you need to load records from the correct position in a physical file by

- using a selection screen
- using a selection field in the header record

You will also learn techniques for

- locating records based on various fields and loading the subfile from different logical files
- creating a display file and writing a program with more than one subfile

Loading Records from the Physical File

Although you have learned a lot about programming subfiles in the first four chapters, there are many additional techniques to learn. In this chapter, we explore various ways of determining which records in the physical file are to be loaded and displayed.

In the real world, physical files contain thousands — sometimes millions — of records. With large files, your users' Page down keys could wear out long before they reach the records they need. Clearly, there has to be a better way.

Instead of displaying the first page of records to the user, the program begins by displaying a selection screen (Figure 5.1). Once the user enters a part number, the RPG program will position the file to that part. The program will then load the subfile from that position in the file and display the first page. For example, if the user typed the part number A214 on the selection screen, the RPG program would locate the file at A214, and the first record loaded and displayed would be A214. If the user types the partial value A3, the first record that would be loaded and displayed would be the first record with a part number equal to or greater than A3.

The file will be positioned using the SETLL (Set Lower Limits) operation. This operation positions the file at the record that is equal to or greater than the specified value. If the user leaves the selection field blank, then the SETLL operation positions the file at the first part number.

Once the file is positioned, we can use any of the load options. Remember, however, that load option 1 shouldn't be used for large loads and a subfile cannot contain more than 9999 records.

By pressing F12, the user can exit the subfile display screen and return to the selection screen. F3 exits the program from either screen.

Figure 5.1

Selection Screen

```
A300C1                    COMPUTERS ARE US                      09/21/98
                INVENTORY PART NUMBER SELECTION SCREEN




    Locate Part Number:_____




    ====================================================================
    * F3=Exit Subsystem
```

Using the Selection Screen

Selection screens are used frequently because they are both easy to program and
simple to use. Users can enter the first part of or the entire entry of interest, and the
subfile is loaded and displayed beginning at that value.

The screen definition is a simple record with one field designated as both (input
and output), which will be in the same display file as the subfile record, the subfile
control record, and the footer record. The field should be the same size and type as
the key to the physical file. The subfile control record must be changed to activate
function key F12.

The RPG program must be altered to

- display the selection screen
- use the value from the input screen instead of *LOVAL to position the
  physical file before reading records and loading the subfile
- if F12 is pressed, display the selection screen
- if F3 is pressed, exit the program

All of the changes to the RPG program will be located in the mainline code.
These changes appear in boldface in the pseudocode shown in Figure 5.2.

```
Mainline
    Do while indicator 03 is off
        Execute the select screen format
        Position the file with the setLL operation using the value from the
            select screen
        Read the next record
        Execute the Load (LOAD) subroutine
        Use the EXFMT (Execute Format) operation to display the control record
            and the subfile (DSP02)
        Do while indicator 03 and 12 are off
            Execute the Respond (RESPD) subroutine
            Execute the format display the control record and subfile (DSP02)
        End do
    End do
End program
```

Figure 5.2
Mainline Pseudocode
for Subfile Load Option
3 with Selection Screen

Exercise 5.1A Computers Are US Inventory Project

Purpose

To modify existing code to add a selection screen.

General Program Specifications

Create maintenance program INV015A and display file INVD015A. The program will display a selection screen (Figure 5.1) and use subfile load option 3.

1. Copy display file INVD013C into new member INVD015A. Modify INVD015A by

   • adding a new record for the selection screen
   • adding CA12(12) to the subfile control record so function key F12 can be used

2. Copy program source INV013C into new member INV015A. Modify your program's mainline code as shown in the pseudocode in Figure 5.2. Compile and test your program.

Exercise 5.2A Purchase Order Line Project

Purpose

To design and add a selection screen to a subfile program.

General Program Specifications

Create RPG program ORDL25A, which displays all purchase order lines. This program uses a selection screen to locate the correct records to load and display. Records are loaded using subfile load option 2.

Figure 5.3

Selection
Screen

```
USERID                    COMPUTERS ARE US PURCHASING              09/21/98
                               Order Lines Selection


             Locate Order Number:   _____



  ==============================================================================
      F3=Exit Subsystem
```

1. Copy the display file source member ORDD024B to new member ORDD025A. Design and add a record for the selection screen (Figure 5.3).

2. Write the pseudocode for the necessary changes to incorporate the selection screen into the RPG program ORDL25A (from ORDL24B).

3. Copy the source member ORDL24B to new member ORDL25A. Modify ORDL25A to provide the selection-screen capabilities.

Review

1. How would you design the selection screen for the following file keyed on CSTZIP, CSTLN, and CSTFN?

Customer File

CSTZIP	10A	CUSTOMER'S ZIP CODE
CSTLN	25A	CUSTOMER'S LAST NAME
CSTFN	25A	CUSTOMER'S FIRST NAME
CSTA1	25A	CUSTOMER'S ADDRESS LINE 1
CSTA2	25A	CUSTOMER'S ADDRESS LINE 2
CSTCT	10A	CUSTOMER'S CITY
CSTST	02A	CUSTOMER'S STATE

Keyed on: CSTZIP, CSTLN, CSTFN

Adding a Selection Field
to the Screen Header

With the selection screen, we've provided a quick way for users to locate the first record that they need. However, whenever users need to move to another location in this file, our current design requires that they press F12, then key the new value on the selection screen. We can provide users with a simpler way to locate records by adding a selection field to the header section of the display (Figure 5.4).

```
    USERID                    COMPUTERS ARE US                    09/21/98
                        WORK WITH INVENTORY LISTS

      2=Change      4=Delete     5=Display     6=Add

      Locate Part Number: A
  O   PART NUMBER DESCRIPTION            QNTY        COST     EXTENDED

  _   A123        Computer x486            21    1,301.15    27,324.15
  _   A124        Computer PentIUM        215    3,100.16   666,534.40
  _   A125        Printer - Laser          81      974.21    78,911.01
  _   A213        Printer - Ink Jet        15      457.15     6,857.25
  _   A214        Printer - Dot Matrix     21      251.14     5,273.94
  _   A215        Scanner - Hand           15      127.19     1,907.85
  _   A216        Scanner - Flat Bed        5      421.15     2,105.75
  _   A319        CD-ROM                    6      115.96       695.76



  ======================================================================
      F3=Exit Subsystem
```

Figure 5.4
Inventory List with Selection Field

The selection field that is added to the header record in Figure 5.4 is the same type and size as the key field of the physical file. This field is coded as both input and output capable.

The code in the RPG program must be able to determine whether the user has changed the value in the selection field. One way to determine whether the value has been changed is to maintain a selection hold field. In the Respond (RESPD) subroutine, the current value of the selection field and the hold field are compared. If the values are different, the program will

- reposition the file to the new location and read the first record
- load a page
- update the hold value with the new value

These steps can be included in the RESPD subroutine. The pseudocode for this subroutine using subfile load option 3 is shown in Figure 5.5. Because there are now three positioning options (Page up, Page down, and Locate), the new pseudocode uses a select structure rather than the if-then-else structure the previous code used.

Figure 5.5

Pseudocode for the
RESPD Subroutine
with Subfile Load
Option 3 and a
Select Value Field

RESPD Subroutine
   If indicator 25 or 26 is on (page down or page up) **or SELPN is not equal to SELPNH**
      Do selection
         Select when indicator 26 is on (page up)   Note: if/then/else
                                                                structure replaced with
                                                                selection structure
            Execute the Backup (BACKUP) subroutine
            Execute the LOAD subroutine
         Select when indicator 25 is on (page down)
            Move *off to indicator 91 (top of file indicator)
            Position the physical file just beyond the last record loaded into the subfile page
            Read the next record from the physical file
            Execute the LOAD subroutine
         Select when SELPN is not equal to SELPNH
            Position the physical file just before SELPN
            Read the next record from the physical file
            Execute the LOAD subroutine
            Update SELPNH to value of SELPN
         End select
      Else
         Set the update flag to off
         Read the first changed record in the subfile
         Do while changed records exist
         Do selection
            Select when D1PICK is 2 (change)
               Execute the Change (CHG) subroutine
            Logic continues with other options
         End selection
         Read the next changed record in the subfile
        End do
        If the update flag is on
         Position the physical file just above the first record loaded into the subfile page
         Read the next record from the physical file
         Execute the LOAD subroutine
        End if
      End if
End subroutine

Exercise 5.1B Computers Are US Inventory Project

Purpose

To modify existing code to add a selection field.

General Program Specifications

Create maintenance program INV015B and display file INVD015B. The program will display a selection screen (Figure 5.1) and use subfile load option 3. It will also have a selection field (Figure 5.4).

3. Copy display file INVD015A into new member INVD015B. Modify INVD015B by adding text and the selection field to the subfile control record (Figure 5.4).

4. Copy program source INV015A into new member INV015B. Modify your program by adding the RESPD subroutine as shown in the pseudocode shown in Figure 5.5. Compile and test your program.

Exercise 5.2B Purchase Order Line Project

Purpose

To design and add a selection field to a subfile program (the program will not have a selection screen).

General Program Specifications

Create RPG program ORDL25B, which will display all purchase order lines. This program will use a selection field to locate the correct records to load and display. Records will be loaded using subfile load option 2.

4. Copy the display-file source member ORDD024B to new member ORDD025B. Design and add the text and selection field.

5. Write the pseudocode for the necessary changes to incorporate the selection field into the RPG program ORDL25B (from ORDL24B).

6. Copy source member ORDL24B to new member ORDL25B. Modify ORDL25B to provide the selection field capabilities.

Review

2. What differences are there in handling the user input from a selection screen and a selection field?

Locating Data on Other Fields

In the Computers Are US example, we've provided a quick way to locate a record if the user knows the part number. However, users find the program hard to use when they don't know the part number. To make this program more useful, users have requested that it be able to locate and load records based on either the part number or the part description.

Users often need more than one way to access records. In an employee file, Human Resources users might need access by social security number or name, and in a customer file, users might need access by customer number or customer name.

In the Computers Are US example, the RPG program could search the physical file INVPF and load only those records that matched the desired description into the subfile. However, if the file is large, this could take quite awhile. Online programs must be quick and easy to use. To get good performance, we need a logical file that provides an alternative sequence keyed on the other field or fields.

About Logical Files

Logical files are real winners from the perspective of online performance, but they have their own performance costs. Whenever a physical file record is updated, added, or deleted, the logical files over that physical file must also be posted. (The only exception to this rule is logical files with maintenance values of REBUILD or DELAY.) However, to meet our quick response needs, our logical files must have a maintenance value of IMMEDIATE, which means that they are kept up-to-date at all times.

In the real world, we don't create a logical file until we check to see whether one that can serve our needs might already exist. You can check on existing logical files with the CL command DSPDBR (Display Database Relations), which lists logical files for the physical file with which you are working. The DSPDBR command (Figure 5.6) can be run from any command line.

Figure 5.6

CL Command Display
Database Relations

```
Parameters or command
===> DSPDBR FILE(INVPF)
```

The results of the DSPDBR command are shown in Figure 5.7. This report shows that the file INVPF has a dependent file INVLF1.

Figure 5.7

List of Dependent
(Logical) Files Created
with the DSPDBR
Command

```
Number of dependent files . . . . . . . . :              1
   Files Dependent On Specified File

   Dependent File         Library                   Dependency    JREF
Constraint
     INVLF1               A300C1_BOK        Data
```

The next step is to check each logical file to determine whether any will meet our basic needs. If the source code for the logical files is available, it can be used, but the data we need on each logical file exists as a component of that file. The CL command DSPFD (Display File Description), shown in Figure 5.8, provides the information that we need to determine whether the logical file will meet our needs.

```
Parameters or command
===> DSPFD INVLF1
```

Figure 5.8
CL Command DSPFD
(Display File Description)

A lot of information is available from via the DSPFD command. Figure 5.9 shows data extracted from the display file description command for the file INVLF1. Each of the pieces of information about INVLF1 will be useful in determining whether this file suits our needs.

```
Access path maintenance . . . . . . . . . . : MAINT      *IMMED
   Record format . . . . . . . . . . . . . . .:            INVPFR
      Key field . . . . . . . . . . . . . . .:             INDESC
         Sequence . . . . . . . . . . . . . .:             Ascending
      Key field . . . . . . . . . . . . . . .:             INPN
         Sequence . . . . . . . . . . . . . .:             Ascending
   Select/omit specified . . . . . . . . . .:             No

                         Record    Format Level
   Format      Fields    Length    Identifier
   INVPFR        6         60       2A224C68C1F19
```

Figure 5.9
Partial Listing of Output of DSPFD (Display File Description) for a Logical File

The logical file record format should have the same name, length, and format-level identifier as the record format in the physical file. If any of these things is different, the logical file may not access all of the fields of the physical file. This would limit our ability to use this logical file.

As shown in Figure 5.9, the logical file INVLF1 uses a composite key of the fields INDESC INPN. This composite key lets us find items by description, and items with the same description will be ordered by part number.

Finally, check the select/omit specifications, which indicate what rules are used to include or exclude records from the logical file. Excluded or omitted records that exist in the physical file are not available through the logical file. If there is a selection rule, only those records selected are available through the logical file. If these rules exclude some of the records that your application will need, then the logical file will not be useful in solving your problem.

If no logical file that meets the key and selection requirements exists, then one must be created. In the inventory project, we know that there are no logical files over the physical file INVPF. To provide quick access based on the description field, a new logical file must be created.

Exercise 5.1C Computers Are US Inventory Project

Purpose

To create a logical file that provides an alternate key to a physical file.

General Program Specifications

Users have requested that the inventory program locate records by descriptions as well as part number. Create logical file INVLF1, which provides an alternate key structure to the physical file INVPF. INVLF1 will be keyed on the description and the part number.

    5. Enter the member INVLF1 logical file using the specifications shown in Figure 5.10. Compile the member.

Figure 5.10

Specifications for INVLF1

```
                              *...1....+....2....+....3....+....4....+....5....+....6
                              *************** Beginning of data ********************************
                   0001.00        *  JEFFERSON COLLEGE      10/19/99   PHIL LEVINSON     INVLF1
                   0002.00        *  LOGICAL FILE INVLF1 OVER INVPF ON DESCRIPTION FIELD AND PART N
                   0003.00     A        R INVPFR                      PFILE(INVPF)
                   0004.00     A        K INDESC
                   0005.00     A        K INPN
                              ***************** End of data **********************************
```

    6. Test how the logical file delivers records to our application by using DFU to view the data. A quick way to do this is with the UPDDTA command. Once the key fields are displayed on DFU, press the Page down (Roll up) keys on your keyboard to step through the file. This is the sequence in which these records will be presented to programs using read statements. You can also do the equivalent of a CHAIN by pressing F12 — so that just the fields for the key are shown — and typing in a value.

    7. Enter the CL command DSPDBR and press F4 to prompt the command entry. Enter the file name INVPF and change the output to *PRINT. *PRINT directs the command to spool the DSPDBR report. Issue the command and print out the spool file with the DSPDBR report.

    8. Enter the CL command DSPFD and press F4 to prompt the command entry. Enter the file name INVPF and change the output to *PRINT. *PRINT directs the command to spool the DSPFD report. Issue the command and print out the spool file with the DSPFD report.

Exercise 5.2C Purchase Order Line Project

Purpose

To design and create a logical file that provides an alternate key structure to a physical file.

General Program Specifications

Modify the purchase order line display program to locate and display records based on order number or part number. When you use part number to locate and display records, display only the records of orders that have not been received.

Create logical file ORDLNLF1. This file should provide an alternate key structure to the physical file ORDLNP. The key should be based on part number, order number, and sequence. It should include only records of items that haven't yet been delivered (i.e., the actual delivery date equals zero).

7. Enter member ORDLNLF1 as a logical file over physical file ORDLNP. This logical file should use the same record name and structure as the physical file. It should be keyed on the part number, order number, and sequence number fields. The logical file definition should contain a selection rule to limit the available records to those records for which the received date is equal to zero, as shown in Figure 5.11. Compile the member.

```
*...1....+....2....+....3....+....4....+....5....+....6

A          S OLADT                  COMP(EQ 0)
```

Figure 5.11

Specifications to Select Records with OLADT Equal to Zero

Review

3. Why are logical files used in conjunction with online processing?
4. What are the "costs" of logical files?

Loading the Subfile from One of Two Sources

In the inventory project, you've created a logical file because users needed to be able to find parts in the inventory by the description. Now that we have the logical file with the required keys, we need to modify the program INV015B to provide the necessary access. An easy way to do this would be to clone the program. The clone could be modified by substituting the logical file for the physical file and making a few other minor changes. That would be simple and effective, but there would be little learning involved.

Instead, we will modify our program to load the subfile from either the keyed physical file or a logical file based on the field on the selection screen (Figure 5.12) into which users enter data. Later, users can request repositioning of the subfile by entering the request in one of the two selection fields in the header (Figure 5.13).

Each time that our program returns from the screen, we will check the fields. If either field has been changed, then our program will reload the subfile from the physical or logical file, depending on which field the user updated.

We need to modify our display program to provide the selection screen shown in Figure 5.12.

Figure 5.12

Selection Screen with
Alternate Selection Fields

```
  A300C1                    COMPUTERS ARE US                   11/02/99
                       INVENTORY LIST SELECTION SCREEN




              Locate Part Number: _____

                 or

              Locate Part Description: _____




  ======================================================================
    F3=Exit Subsystem
```

The subfile control record must also be changed to allow entry into a selection field by either a part number or a part description (Figure 5.13). On both the selection screen and the control record, these fields are SELPN and SELDES.

Figure 5.13

Work with Inventory Lists
with Selection Fields on
Both Part Number and
Part Description

```
  A300C1                      JEFFERSON COLLEGE                 11/02/99
                           Work with Inventory Lists

      1=Add      2=Change      4=Delete      5=Display

      Locate Part Number: B_____  or Part Descp: _____
  O PART NUMBER DESCRIPTION              QNTY     COST      EXTENDED

    _ CP07       CABLE PRINTER 7'          15     5.75        86.25
    _ CP10       CABLE PRINT 10'           19     3.25        61.75
    _ CS10MM     CABLE SERIAL 10' MALE-MALE 15    4.12        61.80
    _ D2115      3 1/2" DISK DRIVE        127 2,141.00    271,907.00
    _ D2116      DISK DRIVE - 5 1/4         7    21.41       149.87
    _ D511       512 MBYTE HARD DISK       23   157.15      3,614.45


                                                             Bottom


  ----------------------------------------------------
    F3=Exit Subsystem       F6=Display Details
```

The RPG program positions and reads from INVPF unless the user has changed the value in the Locate by Description field (SELDES). When the user changes the SELDES value, the display in part number order flag (DPNFLG) is turned off, and both positioning and reading are done from the logical file INVLF1. To control the source of data, the RPG code needs the following changes:

- Add an F-spec for the logical file INVLF1 (Figure 5.14).
- Add a call to a subroutine to position the file in the mainline code (Figure 5.15).
- Add a subroutine to position the file based on the value in either the selection part number or the selection description and set the flag DPNFLG on if part number is used (Figure 5.16).
- Modify the RESPD subroutine (Figure 5.17).
- Test the Description field.
- If there is a change in the Part Number field or the Description field, call the subroutine to position the file.
- If the update flag is on, reposition and read from file INVPF or INVLF1 based on the value of DPNFLG.
- Modify the LOAD subroutine (Figure 5.18).
- Read from either INVPF or INVLF1 based on the value of DPNFLG.
- Modify the BACKUP subroutine (subfile load option 3) to perform both the READ and READP operations from file INVPF when DPNFLG is on and from file INVLF1 when DPNFLG is off.

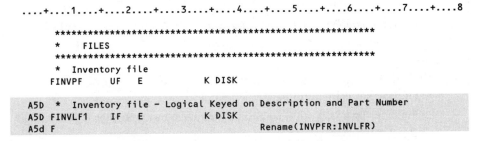

```
....+....1....+....2....+....3....+....4....+....5....+....6....+....7....+....8

          **********************************************************
          *    FILES
          **********************************************************
          *  Inventory file
          FINVPF    UF   E           K DISK

A5D  *  Inventory file - Logical Keyed on Description and Part Number
A5D  FINVLF1   IF   E           K DISK
A5d  F                                Rename(INVPFR:INVLFR)
```

Figure 5.14
F-Specs for Program INV015C with Logical File INVLF1 Added

Figure 5.14 shows the first minor change required. Using the logical file INVLF1 requires an additional F-spec (shaded). This file can be input only. The CHANGE, DELETE, and ADD subroutines can continue to locate and update records in the physical file.

The third line in the RPG program is new. It contains the keyword Rename and assigns a different record name to be used within this program for the file INVLF1. RPG demands unique record names for each file open because commands such as UPDATE or DELETE require the record name and must designate a single target file.

The task of positioning the file after the selection screen has been removed from the mainline code, as the crossed-out lines in Figure 5.15 illustrate. This task will be placed in a new subroutine.

Figure 5.15

Mainline Pseudocode
for Subfile Load
Option 3 and a
Selection Screen with
Two Fields

```
Mainline
    Do while indicator 03 is off
        Execute the select screen format
        Execute the subroutine to position the file
        Execute the Load (LOAD) subroutine
        Use the EXFMT (Execute Format) operation to display the control record
            and the subfile (DSP02)
        Do while indicator 03 and 12 are off
            Execute the Respond (RESPD) subroutine
            Execute the format display the control record and subfile (DSP02)
        End do
    End do
End program
```

The new subroutine for positioning the file (Figure 5.16) is called by the main routine — as is the RESPD subroutine.

Figure 5.16

Pseudocode for the
Position the File
(POSFIL) Subroutine

```
POSFIL subroutine
    If the Description Selection field (SELDES) is not equal to the Description
    Selection Hold field (SELDEH)
        Turn off the display on part number flag (DPNFLG)
        Update SELDEH with SELDES
        Position file INVLF1 with the set lower limits operation using SELDES
        Read INVLF1
    Else
        Turn on the display on part number flag (DPNFLG)
        Update SELPNH with SELPN
        Position file INVPF with the SETLL operation using SELPN
        Read INVPF
    End if
End subroutine
```

If the user has changed the Locate by Description field on the selection screen or on the main screen, the POSFIL subroutine will detect it because the SELDES field will not equal the value of SELDEH. The subroutine then sets the display on part number flag (DPNFLG) off, updates the hold area SELDEH, positions the logical file on the entered value, and reads the next record from the logical file.

If the POSFIL is called but the description has not changed, then the SELPN field is used to locate the physical file INVPF and the first record is read. The flag DPNFLG is set on and the hold area SELPNH is updated.

The RESPD subroutine (Figure 5.17) is changed to call the FILE subroutine if either the Locate on Part Number (SELPN) or the Locate on Description (SELDES) field has been changed.

RESPD Subroutine

  IF indicator 25 or 26 is on (Page down or Page up) or SELPN is not equal to SELPNH or SELDES is not equal to SELDEH

    Do Selection

      Select when indicator 26 is on (Page up)   note: if/then/else structure

        Execute the BACKUP subroutine   replaced with Selection

        Execute the LOAD subroutine

      Select when indicator 25 is on (Page down)

        Move *off to Indicator 91 (Top of File (TOF) indicator)

        Position the physical file just beyond the last record loaded into the subfile page

        Read the next record from the physical file

        Execute the LOAD subroutine

      Select when SELPN is not equal to SELPNH **or SELDES is not equal to SELDEH**

        Execute the POSFIL subroutine

        ~~Position the physical file just before SELPN~~

        ~~Read the next record from the physical file~~

        Execute the LOAD subroutine

        ~~Update SELPNH to value of SELPN~~

    END Select

  ELSE

    Set the update flag to off

    Read the first changed record in the subfile

    Do while changed records exist

      Do selection

        Select when D1PICK is 2 (Change)

          Execute the CHG subroutine

        Logic continues with other options

      End selection

      Read the next changed record in the subfile

    End do

    If the Update flag is on

      If DPNFLG is on

        Position the file INVPF just above the first record loaded into the subfile page

        Read the next record from the file INVPF

        Execute the LOAD subroutine

      Else

        Position the file INVLF1 just above the first record loaded into the

Figure 5.17

Pseudocode for the Respond (RESPD) Subroutine with Subfile Load Option 3 and Two Selection Fields

continued

Figure 5.17
Continued

> **subfile page**
> **Read the next record from the file INVLF1**
> **Execute the LOAD subroutine**
> **End if**
>   End if
> END IF
> End subroutine

The update task in the RESPD subroutine is changed to position and read from the file INVPF if the flag DPNFLG is on and from the file INVLF1 if the flag is off.

The LOAD subroutine must be changed to read from either INVPF or INVLF1 based on the value of the flag DPNFLG (Figure 5.18; note shaded lines). The READ from file INVPF must contain the N for not locked, but the READ from file INVLF1 does not require the N because, as an input-only file, the READ does not lock the record when accessing it. The value of the DPNFLG field should be used to determine whether the physical file INVPF or the logical file INVLF1 is used in READ, READP, and CHAIN operations whenever records are accessed.

Figure 5.18
The Part of the LOAD
Subroutine that Uses
the Value of DPNFLG
to Determine Which
File to Read

```
....+....1....+....2....+....3....+....4....+....5....+....6....+....7....+....8
      *
      C                   WRITE     DSP01
A5C   C                   If        DPNFlg = *off
A5C   C                   READ      INVLF1                              90
A5C   C                   Else
      C                   READ (N)  INVPF                               90
A5C   C                   EndIf
      C                   ENDDO
      *
```

Exercise 5.1D Computers Are US Inventory Project

Purpose

To modify a subfile program to load data from either of two access paths.

General Program Specifications

Users have requested that the inventory program locate records by description as well as part number. Modify display file INVD015C and program INV015C to locate and access data from file INVPF or file INVLF1.

9. Copy member INVD015B to INVD015C. Modify the selection screen to appear with the fields SELPN and SELDES, as shown in Figure 5.12. Also, modify the subfile control record to provide both fields, as shown in Figure 5.13.

10. Copy program source member INV015B to INV015C and modify it per the code in Figures 5.14 and 5.18 and the pseudocode in Figures 5.15 through 5.17. Modify the BACKUP subroutine to locate the correct record — in the file INVPF if the flag DPNFLG is on and in the file INVLF1 if the flag DPNFLG is off.

Exercise 5.2D Purchase Order Line Project

Purpose

To design and modify a subfile program to provide records via two access paths to the file.

General Program Specifications

The purchasing department needs to be able to enter a part number and see the display of order lines in part-number order, starting with the part number entered. They are interested in viewing only those parts that have not been received (Received date=0). Modify the pseudocode and the program to load the records from ORDLNPF or ORDLNLF1 based on a user's most recent entry in the Locate field.

8. Copy display-file source member ORDD025B to new member ORDD025C. Modify the subfile control record to add the text and selection fields for locating records by order number or by part number.

9. Write the pseudocode for the necessary changes to incorporate the two selection fields into the RPG program ORDL25C (from ORDL25B). Data is to be loaded from ORDLNPF or ORDLNLF1 based on the user's most recent entry in the Locate fields.

10. Copy the source member ORDL25B to new member ORDL25C. Modify ORDL25C to provide the selection field capabilities.

Eliminating the Initial Selection Screen

We have duplicated the function of the initial selection screen with the selection fields on the subfile control screens. To support this redundancy, we have had to add some redundant RPG code. Both the initial selection screen and the redundant code can be eliminated, in which case you depend exclusively on the selection fields on the control record to determine what should be displayed. This change can be accomplished by either of two alternative methods.

You've actually coded one of these alternatives — in ORDL25B and ORDL25C. In this case, the program initially loads and displays the first page of the physical file or loads the entire file from record 1 depending on the design of the load process. The user can then use the header fields to relocate the file to the desired position.

Eliminating the Initial Selection Screen with Finesse

The only criticism of the simple solution just described is its inefficiency: It requires the program to load a page of the subfile that is not likely to be of interest. An alternative is to begin the process by displaying the subfile control record without the actual subfile. This lets the user make an entry in one of the select fields.

Separating the display of the header from the display of the subfile requires a change to the DDS and a couple of lines of code.

First, the SFLDSP keyword in the control record is changed to use an additional control indicator, indicator 52 (Figure 5.19; note shaded number).

Figure 5.19
Portion of Subfile Control
Record with SFLDSP
Controlled by Two
Conditioning Indicators

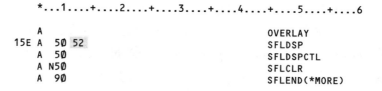

```
*...1....+....2....+....3....+....4....+....5....+....6
     A                                        OVERLAY
15E  A  5Ø 52                                 SFLDSP
     A  5Ø                                    SFLDSPCTL
     A N5Ø                                    SFLCLR
     A  9Ø                                    SFLEND(*MORE)
```

Here's how the additional control indicator — indicator 52 — works:

IN50	IN52	RESULT
*OFF	*ON	SFLCLR clears subfile
*OFF	*OFF	SFLCLR clears subfile
*ON	*OFF	Control record is displayed
*ON	*ON	Control record and subfile are displayed

The mainline pseudocode shown in Figure 5.20 would initially display the main screen without the subfile. It displays the footer and the header (IN50 on) but not the subfile (IN52 off). But after the initial screen, the subfile is displayed (IN52 on).

```
Mainline
    Do while indicator 03 is off
        Set Part Number Hold Field (SELPNH) to *LOVAL
        Turn off indicator 52  (do not display the subfile)
        Turn on indicator 50  (display the control record)
        Write the Footer
        Execute the format to display the screen without the subfile
        Do while indicator 03 is off
                Execute the Respond (RESPD) subroutine
                Execute the format display the control record and subfile (DSP02)
            End do
End program
```

Figure 5.20
Mainline Pseudocode
for Subfile Load Option
3 Displayed Initially
Without the Subfile

Exercise 5.1E Computers Are US Inventory Project

Purpose
To modify a subfile program to initially display the control record without the subfile.

General Program Specifications
Modify display file INVD015D and program INV015D to initially display the main screen without the subfile.

11. Copy member INVD015C to INVD015D. Remove the record for the selection screen. Also, modify the subfile control record to provide two conditioning indicators for the SFLDSP field (Figure 5.19).

12. Copy program source member INV015C to INV015D and modify the mainline code per the pseudocode in Figure 5.20.

Multiple Subfiles

We know we've got a good basic program, but users still want more. When they select to position based upon a description value, the screen is confusing if that description value is not in the leftmost column. Figure 5.21 shows a screen sequenced by description but with description in the second column.

Figure 5.21

Description Displayed in Sequence in the Second Column

```
 A300C1                      COMPUTERS ARE US                    11/02/99
                          Work with Inventory Lists

        1=Add    2=Change    4=Delete    5=Display

       Locate Part Number: _____ or Part Des: C_____
     O Part Number Description                       Qnty       Cost        Extended

       _ A124        Computer PENTIUM                 300    2,100.16      630,048.00
       _ A123        Computer X486                     22    1,301.15       28,625.30
       _ CP10        CABLE PRINT 10'                   19        3.25           61.75
       _ CP07        CABLE PRINTER 7'                  15        5.75           86.25
       _ CS10MM      CABLE SERIAL 10' MALE-MALE        15        4.12           61.80
       _ A319        CD-ROM                             7      115.96          811.72
       _ A155        COMPUTER STAND                     4       21.00           84.00
       _ D2116       DISK DRIVE - 51/4                  7       21.41          149.87
                                                                             More...


        F3=Exit Subsystem       F6=Display Details
```

The screen would be easier to understand if the leftmost column were the description column. When the data is displayed in description sequence, users like the clarity of having the description in the leftmost column, as shown in Figure 5.22.

Figure 5.22

Description Displayed in Sequence in the First Column

```
 A300C1                      COMPUTERS ARE US                    11/02/99
                          Work with Inventory Lists

         1=Add       2=Change    4=Delete      5=Display

        Locate Part Des: C_____ or Part Number: _____
     O Description                 Part Number Qnty       Cost        Extended

       _ Computer PENTIUM            A124       300    2,100.16      630,048.00
       _ Computer X486               A123        22    1,301.15       28,625.30
       _ CABLE PRINT 10'             CP10        19        3.25           61.75
       _ CABLE PRINTER 7'            CP07        15        5.75           86.25
       _ CABLE SERIAL 10' MALE-MALE  CS10MM      15        4.12           61.80
       _ CD-ROM                      A319         7      115.96          811.72
       _ COMPUTER STAND              A155         4       21.00           84.00
       _ DISK DRIVE - 51/4           D2116        7       21.41          149.87
                                                                         More...


        --------------------------------------------
        F3=Exit Subsystem       F6=Display Details
```

Only a few minor changes are necessary to meet the users' request. We create two new records in the display file. DSP03 is a subfile record with the description in the leftmost column, and DSP04 is the subfile control record for DSP03. The RPG program writes the subfile records either to DSP01 or DSP03 and executes the format of DSP02 or DSP04 when it clears or displays the subfile.

The following changes are required:

1. Edit the display file by making copies of the subfile record format DSP01 and subfile control record format DSP02. Name the new formats DSP03 and DSP04. Change the field locations in DSP03. Change the column headings in DSP04. Change the SFLCTL reference from DSP01 to DSP03 in record DSP04.

2. In the RPG code, add the F-spec to key for the subfile DSP03 (Figure 5.23; note shaded line). Each subfile in a display file requires a continuation specification that identifies the field that will be used as the RRN. In this case, the same field can be used for both subfiles because only one or the other will be loaded and displayed.

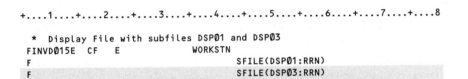

```
+....1....+....2....+....3....+....4....+....5....+....6....+....7....+....8

 *  Display File with subfiles DSP01 and DSP03
FINVD015E  CF   E              WORKSTN
F                                       SFILE(DSP01:RRN)
F                                       SFILE(DSP03:RRN)
```

Figure 5.23
Adding the F-Spec to Subfile DSP03

3. In the RPG code, make every reference to DSP01 conditional on the value of DPNFLG. When DPNFLG is on, use DSP01; when it is off, use DSP03.

4. In the RPG code, make every reference to DSP02 conditional on the value of DPNFLG. When DPNFLG is on, use DSP02; when it is off, use DSP04.

Exercise 5.1F Computers Are US Inventory Project

Purpose
To modify a subfile program to load and display one of two subfiles.

General Program Specifications
Modify display file INVD015E and program INV015E to display one of two subfiles.

13. Copy member INVD015D to INVD015E. Copy records DSP01 and DSP02 to DSP03 and DSP04. Modify records DSP03 and DSP04 to display the part-description column to the left of the part-number column, with the appropriate headings above the columns, as shown in Figure 5.22.

14. Copy program source member INV015D to INV015E and modify the program to use DSP01 and DSP02 when DPNFLG is on and DSP03 and DSP04 when DPNFLG is off.

Exercise 5.2E Purchase Order Line Project

Purpose
To design and modify a subfile program to load and display records in two different formats.

General Program Specifications
Users request that the order-line screen show the display with the column on which the data is sequenced to the left of all other data columns. For example, when an order number is entered, the order-number column should be shown to the left, and when a part number is entered, the part-number column should appear to the left. Modify ORDD025D and ORDL25D to add these screens.

11. Copy the display-file source member ORDD025C to new member ORDD025D. Add records DSP03 and DSP04 and modify these records to display the part number in the leftmost column.

12. Copy the source member ORDL25C to new member ORDL25D. Modify ORDL25D to use DSP01 and DSP02 when the user requests an order number and DSP03 and DSP04 when the user requests a part number.

Review

5. How can the headers and footers be displayed without the subfile? What would be the advantage of doing so?
6. What is the purpose of the Rename keyword in th F-spec?
7. Why is a logical file needed?
8. What are hidden fields used for?

Subfile Bookstore Order Project 1

Project Overview

To demonstrate that you can design, code, debug, and test a system with two subfiles.

The Bookstore Order System

It's time for a new project that will serve as a good review. The bookstore system will require a number of programs, but our task of the moment is a single program that creates the two displays shown in Figures SF1.1 and SF1.2.

When the system is started, SCREEN1 (Figure SF1.1) is displayed. This screen lists and supports user interaction with bookstore orders.

```
A300C1                    Jefferson College              10/24/99
SCREEN1                   Bookstore Orders


1=Add 2=Change  5=Lines

O   ORDER STS  DATE      INSTR         TO

_   2112   O   11/23/98  UPS           BEST PUBLISHERS
_   2113   O   11/24/98  FASTEST WAY   29TH STREET PRESS
_   2114   C   11/25/98  FED X         BEST PUBLISHERS
_   2115   O   11/25/98  FED X         UNIVERSITY OF MISSOURI PRESS
_



F3=Exit     F6=Display Details    F12=Cancel
```

Figure SF1.1
Subfile Project
Screen 1 —
List of Orders

When option 5 is selected on an order, the system loads and displays SCREEN2 (Figure SF1.2).

```
A300C1                    Jefferson College              10/24/99
                          Bookstore Order

ORDER NUMBER: 2113            ORDER STATUS: O
TO:      29TH STREET PRESS              SHIP TO:  BOOKSTORE
         221 E. 29TH STREET                       JEFFERSON COLLEGE
         LOVELAND, CO 80538                       1000 VIKING ROAD
                                                  HILLSBORO, MO 63050
SHIPPING INSTRUCTIONS: FASTEST WAY     ORDER DATE:  10/25/98

1=Add 2=Change 4=Delete 5=Display
                                                              *
O   PART#    DESCRIPTION                   QUANTITY   COST  EXTENDED

_   ISBN1245A  RPG/400 by Judy Yaeger            30   60.00  1,800.00
_   ISBN2144B  Subfile Programming Essentials by P.Levinson 20  45.00  900.00
_
_
_                                  Total            2,700.00
------------------------------------------------------------
F3= Exit     F6=Display Details    F12= Cancel
```

Figure SF1.2
Subfile Project
Screen 2 —
Order Details

continued

Subfile Project 1 *Continued*

SCREEN2 displays and lets users interact with and maintain the details of an order. The order selected on SCREEN1 is the one displayed on SCREEN2. The subfile on SCREEN2 is loaded with the lines of the order selected on SCREEN1.

Instructions

1. Create a file to hold the header information. This information occurs once per order whereas the line information is unique to each "line." Figure SF1.3 shows the header information for order 2113.

Figure SF1.3
Subfile Project —
Order Header

```
ORDER NUMBER: 2113                    ORDER STATUS: O
TO:        29TH STREET PRESS       SHIP TO: BOOKSTORE
           221 E. 29TH STREET               JEFFERSON COLLEGE
           LOVELAND, CO 80538               1000 VIKING ROAD
                                            HILLSBORO, MO
63050
SHIPPING INSTRUCTIONS: FASTEST WAY    ORDER DATE:  10/25/99
```

This file, often referred to as the Order Header file, will be named **BSORH01** for Bookstore Order Header 01. It will be keyed on order number, which is unique.

Fields are

BSHON	4	A		TEXT('ORDER NUMBER')
BSHSTS	1	A		TEXT('STATUS O / C')
BSHODT	6	S	0	TEXT('ORDER DATE')
BSHSI	25	A		TEXT('SHIP INSTR')
BSHTO1	30	A		TEXT('TO: LINE #1')
BSHTO2	25	A		TEXT('TO: LINE #2')
BSHTO3	25	A		TEXT('TO: LINE #3')
BSHTO4	25	A		TEXT('TO: LINE #4')
BSHFM1	25	A		TEXT('FROM: LINE #1')
BSHFM2	25	A		TEXT('FROM: LINE #2')
BSHFM3	25	A		TEXT('FROM: LINE #3')
BSHFM4	25	A		TEXT('FROM: LINE #4')

2. Enter the following records into your file.

BSHON	2112	2113	2114	2115
BSHSTS	O	O	C	O
BSHODT	961123	961124	961125	961125
BSHSI	UPS	FASTEST WAY	FED X	FED X
BSHTO1	BEST PUBLISHERS	DUKE PRESS	BEST PUBLISHERS	UNIVERSITY OF MISSOURI PRESS
BSHTO2	21 BROADWAY	221 E. 29TH STREET	21 BROADWAY	PO BOX 1241
BSHTO3	NEW YORK, NY 29101	LOVELAND, CO 80538	NEW YORK, NY 29101	COLUMBIA, MO 63901
BSHTO4				
BSHFM1	BOOKSTORE	BOOKSTORE	BOOKSTORE	BOOKSTORE

continued

Subfile Project 1 *Continued*

BSHFM2	JEFFERSON COLLEGE	JEFFERSON COLLEGE	JEFFERSON COLLEGE	JEFFERSON COLLEGE
BSHFM3	1000 VIKING DRIVE	1000 VIKING DRIVE	1000 VIKING DRIVE	1000 VIKING DRIVE
BSHFM4	HILLSBORO, MO 63050	HILLSBORO, MO 63050	HILLSBORO, MO 63050	HILLSBORO, MO 63050

3. Create a file to hold the line information. This information occurs multiple times, once for each line of the order. Below is the type of information that it should hold.

ISBN1245A RPG/400 by Judy Yaeger	30	60.00
ISBN2144B Subfile Programming Essentials by Philip J. Levinson	20	45.00

The extended price is not included in the file because, as we know, it can be computed whenever needed.

The line file, which we'll name BSORL01, will contain the data on all orders. Therefore, it is necessary to include a way to tie the line to the parent order. We will accomplish this by including the order number in the line file. But F6=Display Details shows more about these lines, as you see below.

ISBN1245A RPG/400 by Judy Yaeger   30   60.00
LINE STATUS: O Date Received / / Actual
ISBN2144B Subfile Programming Essentials by Philip J. Levinson 20   45.00
LINE STATUS: C Date Received 11/15/98   Actual 19 44.50

The file **BSORL01** should be keyed on both the order number and the line number, and the key should be unique. The fields in this file are

BSLON	4	A		TEXT('ORDER NUMBER')
BSLLN	4	S	0	TEXT('LINE NUMBER')
BSLPN	12	A		TEXT('PART NUMBER')
BSLDS	50	A		TEXT('PART DESCRIPTION')
BSLQO	4	S	0	TEXT('QUANT ORDERED')
BSLOP	7	S	2	TEXT('ORDER PRICE')
BSLSTS	1	A		TEXT('LINE STATUS')
BSLRDT	6	S	2	TEXT('REC DATE')
BSLQA	4	S	0	TEXT('QUANT ACTUAL')
BSLAP	7	S	2	TEXT('ACTUAL PRICE')

continued

Subfile Project 1 *Continued*

4. Enter the data below into the file BSORL01.

BSLON	BSLLN	BSLPN	BSLDS	BSLQO	BSLOP	BSLSTS	BSLRDT	BSLQA	BSLAP
2112	1	ISBN414	ENGLISH I	250	4712	O			
2112	2	ISBN312	ENGLISH II	75	5300	O			
2113	1	ISBN1245A	RPG/400 by Judy Yaeger	30	6000	O	0	0	0
2113	2	ISBN2144B	SUBFILE PROGRAMMING ESSENTIALS by Philip J. Levinson	20	4500	C	961115	19	44.50
2114	1	ISBN912	HISTORY 1	300	6500	C	961201	300	65.00
2115	1	ISBN311	HISTORY 2	150	7200	O			

5. Create the display DDS for SCREEN1 with windows for Add Order, Delete Order, and Change Order. Make the SFL Size 1500. Name the DDS BSORDD01.

6. Develop the code to manage SCREEN1 using LOAD OPTION 1 (load all orders at one time). This code should provide all services to the header file (add, delete, and change). The only option that will not be activated is option 5 (detail), which will bring up SCREEN2 and will be coded as indicated in steps 7 and 8. The ADD option should assign the order number, which will be 1 higher than the highest order number previously assigned. The user will not be allowed to change the order number. Name this program BSORDR01.

7. Modify the DDS for BSORDD01, adding the displays for SCREEN2 with windows for Add Line, Delete Line, and Change Line. Make the SFL Size 500. Name the DDS as BSORDD01.

8. Modify the code BSORDR01 to service option 5 from SCREEN1. When it is selected, load the subfile for SCREEN2 with the lines for the selected order and provide code to handle the Add Line, Delete Line, and Change Line. When F12 is pressed on SCREEN2 the program should return to SCREEN1.

9. Add the field SELORD to SCREEN1 Header Control Record, as is shown in the screen at the top of page 107. If the user types in a new value to which the subfile is to be positioned, reload the subfile starting with that value. To test this function, add 15 or 20 header records to the file.

continued

Subfile Project 1 *Continued*

```
A300C1                      Jefferson College              10/24/99
SCREEN1                     Bookstore Orders
ORDER 2112
1=Add 2=Change   5=Lines
O   ORDER STS  DATE      INSTR        TO
_   2112   O   11/23/98  UPS          BEST PUBLISHERS
_   2113   O   11/24/98  FASTEST WAY  29TH STREET PRESS
_   2114   C   11/25/98  FED X        BEST PUBLISHERS
_   2115   O   11/25/98  FED X        UNIVERSITY OF MISSOURI PRESS
_


F3= Exit     F6=Display Details    F12= Cancel
```

10. Add the following three function keys to SCREEN1:

       F9 - Show All Orders
       F10 - Show Open Orders
       F11 - Show Closed Orders

   Only two of these definitions should be displayed at any time — the two that aren't currently used to select header records. When F10, F11, or F12 is selected, reload the header subfile with only the appropriate records from the header physical file.

11. Add a function key to SCREEN1 that works as a "switch" when the screen first appears:

       F7 - TO: Sequence

   The orders are now shown in sequence based on the values in the field BSHT01, which requires a logical file over the header file.

   Because record names must be unique within a program, if the logical file has the same record name as the physical file, you must use an FK format to rename the records for the logical file.

   When the data is redisplayed, the function key displays the message

       F7 - Order Num Sequence

   Selecting F7 again will bring the display back to the original status, order number sequence, and the footer message F7 - TO: Sequence.

Chapter 6

Developing User-Friendly Subfiles

Chapter Overview

Chapter 6 helps you understand and develop subfiles that let users change the data on the screen. When you complete the chapter, you will be able to

- understand and use hidden fields
- create prompts for fields
- add Help at field and screen levels

Updating Data Directly on the Screen

In the previous chapters, you've developed a fully functional system to support users who maintain data files. The system you've developed is typical of many in existence today. This chapter introduces some techniques that help you make the system more user friendly.

The subfiles that you have created have looked a lot like spreadsheets, but most users would find them harder to work with. End users experienced with spreadsheet software, such as Excel or Lotus 1-2-3, would complain that the subfile we've created makes it too difficult to make changes. Using our subfile, a user would have to move to the correct record, type a 2 for change, wait for the change screen, move to the field targeted for change, and finally make the change.

In the first part of this chapter, you will learn to modify your subfiles so they have much more of the look and feel of spreadsheets. This change lets users make changes directly on the subfile instead of on a change screen.

First, you will learn to modify the subfile record in the display file as follows:

1. Change all of the fields except the Key field from a designation of output to both. If you allow changes to the Key field, you won't be able to find the record in the physical file to update it!

2. The fields that are changed to Both should also have the CHANGE (Change) keyword added to them to determine whether a change has occurred. The CHANGE keyword is followed by an indicator number. This indicator is turned on when READC (Read the Next Changed Record) accesses a record that includes a field with the CHANGE keyword and that has, in fact, been changed. If we need to know which field has been changed, we can use a different indicator for each field.

Figure 6.1 shows the display file with the fields changed to use Both and the CHANGE keyword. Notice that to make the second line easier to read, the text 'WAREHOUSE' and 'LOCATION' is displayed.

Figure 6.1

Record DSP01 with
Fields Changed to Both
and the CHANGE
Keyword Added

```
....+....1....+....2....+....3....+....4....+....5....+....6....+....7....+....8
        *subfile record - DSP01
A          R DSP01                        SFL
A            D1PICK      1A  I  8  2
A            D1PN       11A  0  8  4
A            D1DESC     30A  B  8 16
A                                       CHANGE(27)
A            D1QOH       5Y 0B  8 47EDTCDE(1)
A                                       CHANGE(27)
A            D1UCST      6Y 2B  8 55EDTCDE(1)
A                                       CHANGE(27)
A            D1LTOT      8Y 20  8 65EDTCDE(1)
A                                    9 10'WAREHOUSE'
A            D1WH        3A  B  9 25
A                                       CHANGE(27)
A                                    9 35'LOCATION'
A            D1WHL       5A  B  9 45
A                                       CHANGE(27)
```

Changes to the RPG program are primarily in the Respond (RESPD) subroutine
and a new subroutine, the On-Screen Change (ONSCHG) subroutine. Indicator 27
will be the first test in the select structure (Figure 6.2); if indicator 27 is on, the
ONSCHG subroutine (Figure 6.3) will be executed.

Figure 6.2

Part of the
Respond (RESPD)
Subroutine Showing
SELECT

```
....+....1....+....2....+....3....+....4....+....5....+....6....+....7....+....8
        *
        C                    DoW        *IN94 = *OFF
        C                    Select
A16A    C                    When       *in27 = *ON
A16A    C                    ExSR       ONSCHG

        C                    When       D1PICK = '2' or D1PICK = 'C'
        C                    ExSR       CHG
        *     The other options have been omitted to save space.
        *
        C                    EndSL
```

Figure 6.3

On-Screen Change
(ONSCHG) Subroutine

```
+....1....+....2....+....3....+....4....+....5....+....6....+....7....+....8

    ****************************************************************
    *  ONSCHG - Process on screen changes
    ****************************************************************
C     ONSCHG        BEGSR

C     D1PN          Chain      INVPF                           99
C                   If         *IN99 = *off
C                   Eval       InDESC = D1Desc
C                   Eval       InQOH  = D1QOH
C                   Eval       InUCST = D1UCST
C                   Eval       InDESC = D1Desc
C                   Eval       InWH   = D1WH
C                   Eval       InWHL  = D1WHL
C                   UpDATE     INVPFR
C                   Eval       D1LTOT = D1QOH * D1UCST
C                   If         DPNFlg = *on
C                   UpDATE     DSP03
C                   Else
C                   UpDATE     DSP01
C                   EndIF
C                   EndIF
C                   ENDSR
```

The ONSCHG subroutine chains into the physical file on the part number and updates the fields in the physical file from the subfile update. Also, because the subfile contains a computed field, we need to recompute that field and update the subfile record to reflect changes in quantity or price.

On-Screen Changes : A Simpler Solution?

What might seem an even simpler solution to making on-screen changes involves the following elements:

1. Except for the key field, all of the fields in the subfile record DSP01 are defined with a usage of both.

2. The CHANGE keyword is not used.

3. Modify the RESPD subroutine by adding an OTHER clause at the end of the Selection structure. The OTHER clause, which is executed if none of the previously defined clauses are true statements, will be coded to call the ONSCHG subroutine shown in Figure 6.3.

There is, however, a potential problem with this solution: It gives preference to the value in D1PICK.

If any previous user interaction leaves a value in the field D1PICK (e.g., if a canceled delete leaves a 4 in D1PICK), and the user attempts to make an on-screen change to that record, the code would branch to the Delete subroutine instead of to the ONSCHG subroutine.

Because this is not a robust solution, I don't recommend it. It is included for your information.

Exercise 6.1A Computers Are US Inventory Project

Purpose
To modify existing code to provide on-screen edit capabilities.

General Program Specifications
Create the maintenance program INV016A and the display file INVD016A.

1. Copy display-file member INVD015E to new member INVD016A. Modify the code to designate the subfile fields (except for the Key field) as both. Add the Change keyword for these fields. Refer to Figure 6.1.

2. Copy RPG program source member INV015E to new member INV016A. Add the necessary code as shown in Figures 6.2 and 6.3.

Exercise 6.2A Purchase Order Line Project

Purpose

To design and code subfiles with on-screen change capability.

General Program Specifications

Create the RPG program ORDL26A, which lets users make on-screen changes.

1. Copy the display-file source member ORDD025D to new member ORDD026A. Make the necessary modifications to prepare this display for on-screen changes.

2. Copy the RPG source member ORDL25D to new member ORDL26A. Make the necessary modifications to add on-screen change capabilities to this program.

Use of Hidden Fields

With what you've done so far, life will be good for about 15 minutes — until users discover that they cannot modify the Key field (in our example, the part number field). We prevented a change to that field because it was the Key field to the physical file. We needed its value to chain into the physical file to find the record to update. If we let the user change the Key field, we would no longer be able to find the record.

In this section, we introduce a way to make even the Key field update capable. As you may suspect from the title of this section, that's where hidden fields come into play.

A hidden field is stored in the display file but not displayed to the user. Although hidden fields are not displayed on the screen, programs can treat them exactly the same way they treat fields designated as both. Hidden fields are defined with a width, type, number of decimals, and a designation as hidden. On a hidden field, the Location Line and Position fields are left blank. If the field is defined in the subfile record, there will be one value of the hidden field for each subfile record.

To satisfy the users' additional need, we will have to change the field D1PN, designating it both. We will also need a second copy of the original part number, which is used to chain into the physical file. Figure 6.4 shows the modified specifications for D1PN and D1PNH, the hidden copy of the part number in the subfile.

Figure 6.4

Adding the Hidden
Field DIPNH to the
Subfile Record

```
*...1....+....2....+....3....+....4....+....5....+....6
A            D1PN         11A  B  8  4
A                                        CHANGE(27)
A  88                                    DSPATR(RI)
A            D1PNH        11A  H
```

Two other changes are shown in Figure 6.4. First, the D1PN field has the field-level keyword CHANGE with the same indicator value as is used on the other fields defined in the subfile record. Second, indicator 88 causes the value in the Part Number field to be displayed in reverse video. The program turns this indicator on to warn users who attempt to change the part number listed in the Part Number field to a number that already exists. The file INVPF identifies a unique key of part number and will not allow an add or update operation that would create a second record with an existing part number. (Part number was established as a unique key because that fits the company's business rules.)

> **Note:** To establish what fields should be defined with unique keys, you must understand how the company operates. For example, when we establish that the key field INPN is unique in the file INVPF, we are interpreting a company business rule. The file INVPF defines the part, cost, quantity on hand, and warehouse location of stored parts. For this key field to work correctly, the business rule must be that any product (number) will be stored in only one of the organization's warehouses and in only one location within that warehouse.

Whenever our RPG program loads a value into D1PN, it loads the same value into the field D1PNH. Later, when the program reads changed records from the subfile, we can be certain that D1PNH will still contain the key value of the corresponding record in the physical file.

Keep in mind two additional issues:

1. Because INPN is a unique key, we must test the changed value against the file to prevent a change of the key value to that of an existing key.

2. If this field's value is used to relate this file to other files, you may want to prevent or at least test any change of the value to see that the necessary relationships are not destroyed. The code may need to change the value in both the

```
....+....1....+....2....+....3....+....4....+....5....+....6....+....7....+....8
         *
       C                   Eval      D1PN  = INPN
A16B   C                   Eval      D1PNH = INPN
```

Figure 6.5
Loading Fields
D1PN and D1PNH

current file and the related files. In the RPG code, as is shown in Figure 6.5, whenever the value of D1PN is updated, the value of the hidden field D1PNH is also updated.

The pseudocode for the ONSCHG subroutine shown in Figure 6.6 compares D1PN to D1PNH. If the values are different, the user has requested a change of the part number. The new part number is tested to determine whether it already exists in the file. (If the value already exists in the file, adding it would be an error.) The value of D1PN is reset to the original value, and the error indicator 88 is on. If the error indicator is off, the program chains into the physical file on the original value, which is stored in the hidden field.

The remainder of the ONSCHG subroutine is identical to the code in Figure 6.3 (page 112).

Figure 6.6

Pseudocode for ONSCHG Subroutine with Change of DIPN

```
ONSCHG Subroutine
     Turn off the error on part number change (indicator 88)
     If the subfile part number is not equal to the sbufile hidden part number
               (D1PN <> D1PNH)
               Test for the existence of a record in the physical file with the new part number
               If the new part number is equal to an existing part number
                    Turn on the error on part number indicator (indicator 88)
                    Reset the value of D1PN to the old value (D1PHN)
               Endif
     Endif
     If the error on part number indicator (indicator 88) is off
               Chain into the physical file on the old part number (D1PNH)
               Copy D1PN to the hidden field D1PNH and to INPN
               Update the physical file record
     Endif
     Compute the total price (quantity times cost)
     Update the subfile record (either with the new data or Indicator 88 *ON)
     If DPNFLG is on
               Update DSP01
     Else
               Update DSP03
     Endif
     Turn off the error on part number change indicator (indicator 88)
End subroutine
```

Exercise 6.1B Computers Are US Inventory Project

Purpose

To modify existing code to provide on-screen edit capabilities for all fields (including the Key field).

General Program Specifications

Create the maintenance program INV016B and the display file INVD016B.

3. Copy display-file member INVD016A to new member INVD016B. Modify the code to designate the subfile fields (including the Key field) as both. Add the CHANGE keyword for these fields.

4. Copy RPG program source member INV016A to new member INV016B. Change the ONSCHG subroutine to allow changing the part number.

Exercise 6.2B Purchase Order Line Project

Purpose
To design and code subfiles with on-screen change capabilities.

General Program Specifications
Create RPG program ORDL26B, which will let users make on-screen changes, including changes to the Key field.

3. Copy display-file source member ORDD026A to new member ORDD026B. Make the necessary modifications to prepare this display for on-screen changes, including changes to the Key field.

4. Copy RPG source member ORDL26A to new member ORDL26B. Make the necessary modifications to add the on-screen change capabilities to this program.

Prompting on Non-Subfile Fields

You've already seen prompting used on various AS/400 screens. You point at an entry field and press F4, the Prompt function key, and a window or screen appears with options, further information, and an entry field. In theory, this is fairly easy to do.

For our first experiment, let's develop a prompt window for the header field Locate on Part Number (SELPN). When the user points to the Locate on Part Number field, we will display the window shown in Figure 6.7.

```
              Locate Part Number
      Type in the Part Number
      or the first few digits of the Part Number:
      _____
```

Figure 6.7
Prompt Window for Locating on Part Number

This prompting should happen only when users point the cursor to the field and press F4. To know that F4 has been pressed, we need to activate the key in the display-file description with the CF04(04 'F4=Prompt') keyword. If prompting is to be used on all records, the CF04 keyword should be placed at the file level (before the first record declaration). If prompting is to be used for specific screens, the CF04 keyword should be placed at the record level, after the record declaration of a record for which prompting will be provided. Because the command function key-word cannot be included in a subfile record, it is defined in the subfile control record to provide prompting for fields on the control record and the subfile record.

To provide the correct prompt, we need to know what field the cursor is pointing to when F4 is pressed. The field name is available through the display-file keyword RTNCSRLOC (Return Cursor Location). The keyword actually returns two values: the activated format and the activated field. As is shown in Figure 6.8, I named these fields CSRFMT and CSRFLD, and both must be 10 characters long. When the fields are used in the command itself, they are preceded by an ampersand (&). The RTNCSRLOC keyword should be added to every display-file record for which prompting is provided.

In the subfile control record that defines variables, display-file keywords must come after the general subfile control commands. Because the SFLRCDNBR (Subfile

Record Number) keyword does both, it is the last subfile keyword. The RTNCSRLOC keyword must come after the general SFL commands but before SFLRCDNBR. Finally, the variable definitions must be added in the subfile control record variable definition area, which starts with the keyword SFLRCDNBR.

Figure 6.8

Part of the Subfile Control Record with the RTNCSRLOC (Return Cursor Location) Keyword and Its Related Field Definitions

```
*...1....+....2....+....3....+....4....+....5....+....6....+....7....+....8
A                                            RTNCSRLOC(&CSRFMT &CSRFLD)
A              SFLRCD        4S ØH           SFLRCDNBR(CURSOR)
A              CSRFMT       1ØA   H
A              CSRFLD       1ØA   H
```

In our experiments, we have two control records with different subfile column layouts. Because we want to provide the prompting on both screens, the CF04 and RTNCSRLOC keywords must be added to both subfile control records.

Finally, a window definition — as was shown in Figure 6.7 — must be added to the display file for the prompt window. The window can use the same field name as the control record field for Select Part Number (SELPN), and it should be designated both.

The RPG program must be modified to execute the new prompt window when indicator 4 is on and the field name returned from the RTNCSRLOC keyword matches the name of the field on the control record (SELPN).

In the RESPD subroutine (Figure 6.9), we can check the status of IN04. If it is *ON and CSRFLD contains the value SELPN, we can execute a DDS record format named PMTPN window, which you will design. If the user changed the part number in the PMTPN window, then the code for Locate on Part Number (developed in a previous chapter) will find that the SELPN no longer matches the SELPNH field and will proceed to locate the correct position in the file and reload the subfile.

Figure 6.9

Part of the RESPD Subroutine with Prompt Cases

```
....+....1....+....2....+....3....+....4....+....5....+....6....+....7....+....8

        ****************************************************************
        *  PROCESS RESPONSE TO SUBFILE
        ****************************************************************
        C     RESPD         BEGSR
A6C C                       If        *INØ4 = *on
A6C C                       Eval      *INØ4 = *off
A6C C                       Select
A6C *    Case 1 - prompt on Select Part Number Field.
A6C C                       When      CSRFLD = 'SELPN'
A6C C                       Exfmt     PMTPN
A6C *    Case 2 - prompt on Select Description Field.
A6C C                       When      CSRFLD = 'SELDES'
A6C C                       Exfmt     PMTDSC
A6C *    Insert other prompt fields cases here.
A6C C                       EndSL
A6C C                       EndIf
A6C *    The remainder of the subroutine as previously defined follows.
```

Exercise 6.1C Computers Are US Inventory Project

Purpose
To modify existing code to prompt for specific fields.

General Program Specifications
Create the maintenance program INV016C and the display file INVD016C to provide prompting on the Locate on Part Number and Locate on Description fields.

5. Copy display-file member INVD016B to new member INVD016C. Modify INVD016C to activate F4 for prompting. Add the RTNCSRLOC keyword to the control records. Add two new windows, one for prompting for part number and the other for prompting by description.

6. Copy RPG program source member INV016B to new member INV016C. Add the code to the RESPD subroutine shown in Figure 6.9.

Exercise 6.2C Purchase Order Line Project

Purpose
To design prompt screens.

General Program Specifications
Create RPG program ORDL26C, which provides prompting on the Locate on Order Number and Locate on Part Number fields.

5. Copy the display-file source member ORDD026B to a new member ORDD026C. Make the necessary modifications to prepare this display for prompting on Locate on Order Number as well as Locate on Part Number.

6. Copy the RPG source member ORDL26B to new member ORDL26C. Make the necessary modifications to add prompting on the two alternative selection fields.

F4=Prompt on Fields in the Subfile
Users might also need the prompt capability on fields in the subfile (as shown in Figure 6.10). As you will see in Chapter 7, prompts on these fields become more useful when the prompt window is changed to a list of values (a subfile in the window) that lets the user select the value instead of keying it.

Warehouse Code: STL   Enter Warehouse
Correct Values are:
STL, DLS, FTW

Figure 6.10
Prompt for
Warehouse Field

Just as in developing prompts for non-subfile fields, the RTNCSRLOC keyword returns the field that the cursor is on when the display file returns control to the program. However, when it works with the subfile, in addition to knowing which field is being prompted, the program must also know which subfile record is being prompted. The display-file keyword that identifies what subfile record the cursor is on — the SFLCSRRRN (Subfile Cursor Relative Record Number) keyword — was introduced in Chapter 4. SFLCSRRRN returns the number of the subfile record that the cursor is on, or a zero if the cursor is not pointing at a row of the subfile (Figure 6.11).

Figure 6.11

Extract from Subfile Control Record with the SFLCSRRRN Keyword

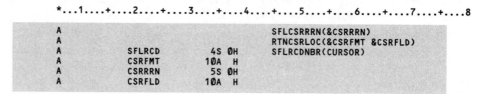

```
*...1....+....2....+....3....+....4....+....5....+....6....+....7....+....8
     A                                         SFLCSRRRN(&CSRRRN)
     A                                         RTNCSRLOC(&CSRFMT &CSRFLD)
     A            SFLRCD         4S  0H         SFLRCDNBR(CURSOR)
     A            CSRFMT        10A   H
     A            CSRRRN         5S  0H
     A            CSRFLD        10A   H
```

If indicator *IN04 is on and the value in CSRFLD is D1WH, we know that the cursor is pointing to the subfile record number stored in the variable CSRRRN and to the subfile field D1WH. Because we are likely to have a number of prompts to service, I have moved the prompt processing into a new subroutine, the Prompt (PROMPT) subroutine, shown in Figure 6.12. This subroutine is called from the RESPD subroutine whenever indicator 4 is on. Prompting of a subfile field requires chaining into the display file using the RRN returned by the SFLCSRRRN (Subfile Cursor Relative Record Number) keyword. Then the prompt window that uses the same field name as the field in the screen (i.e., D1WH) is executed. And unless the user presses F12 or F3, the value returned from the window is used to update the physical file and the display file.

Figure 6.12

Prompt Subroutine

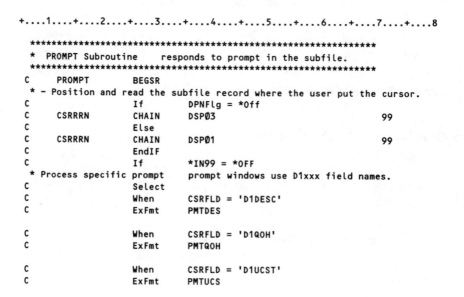

```
+....1....+....2....+....3....+....4....+....5....+....6....+....7....+....8

     ****************************************************************
     *  PROMPT Subroutine     responds to prompt in the subfile.
     ****************************************************************
     C     PROMPT        BEGSR
     * - Position and read the subfile record where the user put the cursor.
     C                   If        DPNFlg = *Off
     C     CSRRRN        CHAIN     DSP03                           99
     C                   Else
     C     CSRRRN        CHAIN     DSP01                           99
     C                   EndIF
     C                   If        *IN99 = *OFF
     * Process specific prompt     prompt windows use D1xxx field names.
     C                   Select
     C                   When      CSRFLD = 'D1DESC'
     C                   ExFmt     PMTDES

     C                   When      CSRFLD = 'D1QOH'
     C                   ExFmt     PMTQOH

     C                   When      CSRFLD = 'D1UCST'
     C                   ExFmt     PMTUCS
```

continued

+....1....+....2....+....3....+....4....+....5....+....6....+....7....+....8

Figure 6.12
Continued

```
C                     When      CSRFLD = 'D1WH'
C                     ExFmt     PMTWH

 * Process additional prompt fields.
C                     EndSL
 * Update physical file record and subfile record.
C                     If        *IN03 = *off and *IN12 = *OFF
C          D1PN       Chain     INVPF                              97
C                     If        *IN97 = *Off
C                     Eval      InDESC = D1Desc
C                     Eval      InQOH  = D1QOH
C                     Eval      InWH   = D1WH
C                     Eval      InWHL  = D1WHL
C                     Eval      InUCST = D1UCST
C                     UpDATE    INVPFR

C                     Eval      D1LTOT = D1QOH * D1UCST
C                     If        DPNFlg = *Off
C                     Update    DSP03
C                     Else
C                     Update    DSP01
C                     EndIF
C                     EndIF
C                     EndIF
C                     EndIF

C                     ENDSR
```

Exercise 6.1D Computers Are US Inventory Project

Purpose

To modify existing code to prompt for subfile fields.

General Program Specifications

Create the maintenance program INV016D and the display file INVD016D to provide prompting on the Description, Quantity, and Cost fields in the subfile.

7. Copy display-file member INVD016C to new member INVD016D. Modify INVD016D to add the keyword SFLCSRRRN (Subfile Cursor Relative Record Number) to the control records. Add new windows to prompt for description, quantity, and cost.

8. Copy RPG program source member INV016C to new member INV016D. Modify the RESPD subroutine to call the PROMPT subroutine when F4 is pressed. Put all prompt servicing into the PROMPT subroutine.

Exercise 6.2D Purchase Order Line Project

Purpose
To design prompt screens.

General Program Specifications
Create the RPG program ORDL26D, which will provide prompting on all of the subfile fields.

7. Copy display-file source member ORDD026C to new member ORDD026D. Make the necessary modifications to prepare this display for prompting on Locate on all of the subfile fields

8. Copy RPG source member ORDL26C to new member ORDL26D. Make the necessary modifications to add prompting on all of the subfile fields.

Positioning the Cursor

In the previous two sections of this chapter, you developed prompt capabilities that let the user point to a position on the screen and press F4. A prompt window appeared and users entered the required data. The program then updated both the screen and the physical file when appropriate. Finally, the screen was redisplayed. However, users may notice that the cursor has wandered from where it was when they pressed F4. For example, users may have pressed F4 to prompt on the third field of the fourth record on the screen. They would expect the cursor to return to the point of origin or perhaps move to the next field or the next record. In this section, we explore how to return the cursor to the point at which it was when the prompt was requested.

We can find out the exact row and column of the cursor's location when F4 was pressed by making just a few changes to the RPG program. The cursor position is passed from the display file to the program in the file data structure. The file data structure contains a wealth of data about the display file and is updated and returned to the program whenever the display returns control to the program. To link the program with the file data buffer, you add another continuation specification to the F-spec for the display file, as shown in Figure 6.13.

Figure 6.13

F-Spec with a Continuation Specification for the Data Structure

```
+....1....+....2....+....3....+....4....+....5....+....6....+....7....+....8

 *  Display File with subfiles DSP01 and DSP03 and Data Stru FILDS
FINVD016D  CF    E              WORKSTN
F                                         SFILE(DSP01:RRN)
F                                         SFILE(DSP03:RRN)
F                                         INFDS(FILDS)
```

The continuation file data structure (INFDS) declares the name of a structure that will be defined in the I-specs. The structure defined in the specification in Figure 6.13 is FILDS. Figure 6.14 shows the I-specs that define this structure.

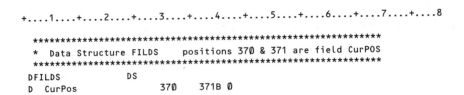

Figure 6.14
D-Spec for File Data Structure (FILDS)

```
+....1....+....2....+....3....+....4....+....5....+....6....+....7....+....8

************************************************************
*  Data Structure FILDS     positions 370 & 371 are field CurPOS
************************************************************
DFILDS          DS
D  CurPos           370    371B 0
```

The structure defined in Figure 6.14 extracts just 2 bytes of data from the large and complex structure that was passed from the display file to the program. These 2 bytes, representing a binary number, are in positions 370 and 371 of the structure. The binary number has zero decimal positions. In the example in Figure 6.14, the field mapped over these 2 bytes is named CURPOS. Whenever control is passed from the display file to the RPG program, the field CURPOS will contain a binary number that represents the cursor position and can be converted into the cursor row and column position.

A new subroutine will be added to the RPG program to compute the cursor location. The Locate Cursor (LOCCUR) subroutine, shown in Figure 6.15, extracts the row and column positions from the field that maps the display-file data structure, CURPOS.

```
+....1....+....2....+....3....+....4....+....5....+....6....+....7....+....8

************************************************************
*  LOCCUR Subroutine     Computes the row & column of the cursor
*                        from the file data structure field CurPOS
*                        Display File Keyword CSRLOC will locate
*                        the cursor at the computed Row and Column
************************************************************
         LOCCUR      BEGSR

                     Z-Add    CurPos         CurSA        5 0
         CURSA       DIV      256            RowPos
                     MVR                     ColPos
                     Eval     *In46 = *ON

                     ENDSR
```

Figure 6.15
The LOCCUR Subroutine Computes the Row and Column of the Cursor from the Field CURPOS

The LOCCUR subroutine should be called at the beginning of the Prompt subroutine. (If it is called after a prompt window has been displayed, it computes the cursor position on the prompt window instead of on the original screen.)

Notice that the LOCCUR subroutine turns on indicator 46. Indicator 46 conditions a new display-file keyword, CSRLOC (Cursor Location), shown in Figure 6.16. CSRLOC receives two fields of data from the program. Because they have the same field names as the fields computed in the LOCCUR subroutine — ROWPOS and COLPOS — the CSRLOC keyword will locate the cursor at the current values of those fields. ROWPOS and COLPOS must be signed (3 0) and hidden (note shaded lines in Figure 6.16). The CSRLOC keyword will only have an effect on the cursor when the conditioning indicator 46 is on. When indicator 46 is off, the values of ROWPOS and COLPOS have no effect.

Figure 6.16
CSRLOC Keyword
Added to Subfile
Control Record

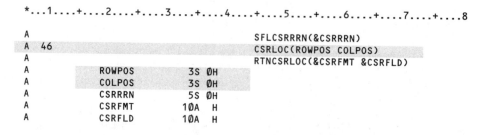

```
*...1....+....2....+....3....+....4....+....5....+....6....+....7....+....8
A                                              SFLCSRRRN(&CSRRRN)
A  46                                          CSRLOC(ROWPOS COLPOS)
A                                              RTNCSRLOC(&CSRFMT &CSRFLD)
A            ROWPOS       3S  0H
A            COLPOS       3S  0H
A            CSRRRN       5S  0H
A            CSRFMT      10A   H
A            CSRFLD      10A   H
```

Indicator 46 should be turned off after the screen that is being controlled is displayed. If the subroutine to recompute the value is called again, it will be turned on for the next time that the display is executed. In our current design, indicator 46 can be turned off at the top of the RESPD subroutine.

Exercise 6.1E Computers Are US Inventory Project

Purpose

To modify existing code to return the cursor to its original location when the program returns to the main screen after a prompt window has been displayed.

General Program Specifications

Create maintenance program INV016E and display file INVD016E to return the cursor to its location at the time the user requested the prompt.

9. Copy display-file member INVD016D to new member INVD016E. Modify INVD016E to add the CSRLOC keyword.

10. Copy RPG program source member INV016D to new member INV016E. Add the continuation specification for INFDS and the data structure for CURPOS (Figures 6.13 and 6.14). Modify the RESPD subroutine to turn off indicator 46 at the beginning of the routine. Modify the PROMPT subroutine to call the new LOCCUR subroutine at the beginning of the PROMPT routine.

Exercise 6.2E Purchase Order Line Project

Purpose

To develop the code necessary to use CSRLOC to control cursor location.

General Program Specifications

Create the RPG program ORDL26E to to return the cursor to its position at the time the user selected a prompt.

9. Copy the display-file source member ORDD026D to a new member ORDD026E. Make the necessary modifications to add the CSRLOC keyword.

10. Copy the RPG source member ORDL26D to new member ORDL26E. Make the necessary modifications to control the cursor location.

F1=Help

A feature of most on-line systems on the AS/400 is an extensive Help service. Typically, a user can point to the top of any screen, press F1, and access general Help about the screen. The user can also point to any field, press F1, and see a Help screen for that field. Users who rarely use printed manuals often are willing to press the Help key if the Help system is consistently available and easy to use. The information on the Help screens needs to be clear. I will introduce three different methods for handling requests for Help, which I refer to as HELP1, HELP2, and HELP3.

The HELP1 method is functionally similar to the prompt system. You create Help records in the display file and use the command action keyword CA01(01'F1=Help') to activate a function key to be used to request Help (usually F1).

If the program returns 01 on, the CSRFLD field is checked and the correct Help record displayed. This is not a bad solution, especially because the code is basically the same as the code that you developed for prompting. Because this method is functionally identical to the prompt system discussed earlier in this chapter, I will not explore it in this section.

The HELP2 method, like HELP1, calls Help records that have been included in the display-file description. However, with HELP2, new display-file keywords program the display file to display the Help record. With this method, there are virtually no changes to the RPG code. I will explain the new display-file keywords that HELP2 uses in the next few pages.

The HELP3 method uses some of the same display-file keywords as HELP2 but requires a few new keywords. The Help screens are not included in the display file but coded in a new type of object, a panel-group object (PNLGRP). The resultant Help screens look and act exactly the same as others used throughout the operating system (Figure 6.17).

Figure 6.17
Example of HELP3 Method

```
                    Print Key Output                        Page   1
     5763SS1 V3R2M0 960517          JEFFCIS1      08/03/99  11:36:07
     Display Device . . . . . :  TC10717S1
     User . . . . . . . . . . :  DEVELOPER
                    Work with Members Using PDM                JEFFCIS
 File . . . . . .  QDDSSRC
   Library . . . .  TEXTBOOK          Position to  . . . . .
 Type options, press Enter.
   2=Edit        3=Copy  4=Delete 5=Display      6=Print    7=Rename
   8=Display description  9=Save  13=Change text  14=Compile  15=Create module..
   ...............................................................
 Opt :                    Options - Help                           :
     :                                                             :
     : Use this column to perform different operations on individual :
     : members. Type the option number next to a member and press Enter or :
     : F4=Prompt. You can type the same option next to more than one :
     : member at a time, and you can also type different options next to :
     : different members at the same time.                         :
     :                                                             :
     : Choose from the following:                                  :
     :                                                             :
 Par :                                                      More... :
 === : F2=Extended help   F10=Move to top  F11=Search Index  F12=Cancel :
 F3= : F13=Information Assistant   F20=Enlarge   F24=More keys :
 F9= :...........................................................:
```

Changing Help text in panel groups is easy because it does not require changes to the program or the display file. The same panel group can contain Help panels for many programs and a help panel can be used by many programs. All that is required to change Help text is to type the changes into the "text" PNLGRP member and recompile it.

HELP2: Using Help Records

Using Help records is an efficient and simple way to create Help screens. The changes required are entirely in the display file. The display file itself manages the Help. The RPG program will not need to be modified and will not know that the Help screen was displayed.

The four display-file keywords that we will explore are the following:

- HELP (Help) is a file-level keyword that activates the Help system.
- ALTHELP (Alternate Help) is a file-level keyword that redefines the Help key from the Scroll Lock to a function key (e.g., ALTHELP(CA01)) and that defines Function key F1 as the Help key.
- HLPARA (Help Area) is a file and record-level keyword that defines the record, field, or area of the screen for which a Help definition will be created. Figure 6.18 shows samples of a Help area delared for 1) the area of the record footer, 2) the area of the field SELPN, and 3) the definition of a Help area of a rectangle. Remember that if the definition is at the record level, that definition exists only when that record is active.

Figure 6.18
Three Examples of HLPARA

HLPARA(*RCD FOOTER) — the area defined is the footer record
HLPARA(*FLD SELPN) — the area defined is the field SELPN
HLPARA(8 4 15 14) — the area defined is from row 8 column 4 to row 15 column 14

- HLPRCD (Help Record) is a file and record-level keyword that identifies the record to display for a specific Help request (e.g., HLPRCD(SPNHLP) displays the display-file record format SPNHLP; you must create the record SPNHLP).

One new display-file tool needs to be introduced: the Help specification. An H in the type field identifies a record as beginning a Help definition. Typically, a Help definition occupies two lines. The first line has the H type and the HLPARA keyword, which defines what area of the screen is to be defined. The next line has a blank type and the HLPRCD definition. The pair of keywords identifies what record to display when the cursor is within the specified area and the Help key is pressed.

Help specifications cannot be included in subfile records though they can be included in every other type of record. To provide Help for subfile fields, put the Help specifications in the control record for the subfile. These specifications must identify the rectangle of each Help area (not the field names of subfile fields).

Figure 6.19 shows the use of the ALTHELP keyword and contains the default declaration of a Help record. The default record GENERAL is displayed whenever Help is requested (F1) unless another definition is in effect for the specific part of the screen that the cursor is pointing to at the time of the request. These are file-level declarations that must appear before the first record declaration.

```
*...1....+....2....+....3....+....4....+....5....+....6....+...7....+....8

 *** added to File Level DDS
 **-- makes F1 the Help key and HELP activates the help system.
A                                       ALTHELP(CA01)
A                                       HELP
 **-- At the file level, this will display the DDS record General
 **-- whenever Help is called and no other further definition applies.
A                                       HLPRCD(GENERAL)
```

Figure 6.19

Example of File-Level Declaration of Help Key and a Default Help Declaration That Will Display the Record GENERAL

Figure 6.20 demonstrates Help specifications. When the user points the cursor to the SELPN field and presses F1, the Help specification for the field SELPN displays the screen HLPSPN. If the cursor is located anywhere in the rectangle from row 8 column 4 to row 15 column 14 and F1 is pressed, the display record format HLPDPN is displayed.

```
*...1....+....2....+....3....+....4....+....5....+....6....+....7....+....8

A      R DSP02                  SFLCTL(DSP01)
 *-- SFL keywords not shown
A                               RTNCSRLOC(&CSRFMT &CSRFLD)
A                               SFLCSRRRN(&CSRRRN)
A  46                           CSRLOC(ROWPOS COLPOS)

 *-- added to control record; must be after SFL keywords
 *-- and before variables are defined.
 *-- If Help is requested while pointing at SELPN field then
 *--    The record named HLPSPN is displayed.
A      H                        HLPARA(*FLD SELPN)
A                               HLPRCD(HLPSPN)

 *-- If Help is requested while pointing at rectangle row 8 col 4
 *--    to row 15 col 14. This is the area where the part number
 *--    is displayed. The record named HLPDPN is displayed.
A      H                        HLPARA(8 4 15 14 )
A                               HLPRCD(HLPDPN)

A      SFLRCD       4S 0H       SFLRCDNBR(CURSOR)
A      ROWPOS       3S 0H
```

Figure 6.20

Subfile Control Record Containing Help Specifications for the Field SELPN and the Area (8 4 15 14)

Exercise 6.1F Computers Are US Inventory Project

Purpose

To modify existing code to incorporate Help method HELP2.

General Program Specifications

Create maintenance program INV016F and display file INVD016F to provide general Help on the entire screen and specific Help on the fields SELPN and D1PN.

11. Copy display-file member INVD016E to new member INVD016F. Modify INVD016F to add the file-level and record-level Help keywords as shown in Figures 6.19 and 6.20. Create the display-file records GENERAL, HLPSPN, and HLPDPN, which give appropriate information about the purpose of the entire screen, the Locate on Part Number field, and the Part Number area of the subfile.

12. Copy RPG program source member INV016E to new member INV016F.

Exercise 6.2F Purchase Order Line Project

Purpose

To develop Help screens using the HELP2 method.

General Program Specifications

Create the RPG program ORDL26F. It should provide general Help on the entire screen, as well as specific Help on each field displayed and on the footer record.

11. Copy display-file source member ORDD026E to new member ORDD026F. Make the necessary modifications to add general Help on the entire screen, Help on each field, and Help on the footer record.

12. Copy RPG source member ORDL26E to new member ORDL26F.

HELP3: Using Help Panel Group

Only two new keywords beyond those used with the HELP2 are needed for the HELP3 method. The only change to the display-file description is replacing the HLPRCD with the HLPPNLGRP (Help Panel Group) keyword, as shown in Figure 6.21. The HLPPNLGRP keyword refers to records in the panel-group object not in the display file. Therefore, you can eliminate the Help records in the DDS.

Figure 6.21

Help Panel Group Keyword and Help Panel Group Title Replaces Help Record Keyword

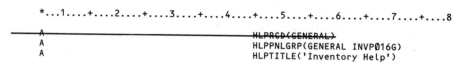

```
*...1....+....2....+....3....+....4....+....5....+....6....+....7....+....8
A                                      HLPRCD(GENERAL)
A                                      HLPPNLGRP(GENERAL INVP016G)
A                                      HLPTITLE('Inventory Help')
```

The HLPPNLGRP keyword identifies the record in the panel-group file and the name of the panel-group file. The HLPPNLGRP keyword identifies that the GENERAL record in the panel-group file INVP016G is to be called if Help is requested when no other Help applies.

The HLPTITLE (Help Panel Group Title) keyword provides a title to appear at the top of the Help screen. This will only be used if the panel definition has a blank panel title. The display-file description must contain at least one HLPTITLE keyword.

The Panel Group

You must create a new member of type PNLGRP, which will contain the Help text. You could create the source member in the file QDDSSRC or QUIMSRC. Members of type PNLGRP are text files with no prompting or syntax checking. Entries can be up to 80 characters long.

An example of a panel group is shown in Figure 6.22.

The panel-group definition begins with :PNLGRP. and ends with :EPNLGRP. The prefix E stands for End (e.g., End Panel Group, End Help).

The colons (:) and periods (.) are important. A colon (:) indicates a special panel-group command. A period (.) ends the command.

Each Help panel begins with the Help name, which is same as the name that was used in the HLPPNLGRP keyword in the display-file description:

```
:HELP NAME = D1PN.
```

Each panel ends with :EHELP.

The second line of each Help panel is the panel heading:

```
Part Number - Help Screen.
```

The third line of each Help panel is the highlighted topic name you'll find when you scan through expanded Help (F2) that identifies this as a topic heading:

```
:XH3.Part Number - Help
```

Figure 6.22
Panel Group INVP016G

```
:PNLGRP.
:HELP NAME = GENERAL.

:P.
The Inventory Inquiry/Maintenance screen is designed to allow you to
view and update inventory amounts by location. You should be
careful not to change product numbers if orders exist for the
products.
:P.
This system has been developed by _____ for class _____.
:EHELP.
.*******************************************************************
:HELP NAME = SELPN.
Select Part Number - Help Screen
:XH3.Select Part Number - Help
:P.
You can position the list to the part number that you need to view
by typing part of or the whole part number.
:EHELP.
```

continued

Figure 6.22
Continued

```
.****************************************************************************
:HELP NAME = D1PN.
Part Number - Help Screen
:XH3.Part Number - Help
:P.
You can change the part number in three ways.
:P.
 1. Move to the part number and type over it.
:P.
 2. Move to the part number and press F4 for prompting.
:P.
 3. Type a 2 in the option beside the record to be changed.
:P.
The number will not be changed if there is a current product with the
same number. You should not change the number if there are any
outstanding orders for the product.
:EHELP.
.****************************************************************************
:EPNLGRP.
```

The XH3 identifies the format that will be applied to the Part Number-Help. The panel-group system provides fourteen different "formats," each of which will be displayed differently. The formats are numbered XH1, XH2, and so forth, up to XH14.

Each paragraph begins with :P.

It's that easy. The body of the Help text is typed in a paragraph format. Each line is a maximum of 80 characters long. Lines of text can be copied, moved, and deleted, just as in other applications that use SEU.

Exit with F3 and use 14 (compile) to create the panel group. Obviously, check your messages for errors, then correct and recompile until you reach a normal completion of the compile.

Exercise 6.1G Computers Are US Inventory Project

Purpose
To modify existing code to incorporate Help method HELP3.

General Program Specifications
Create maintenance program INV016G and display file INVD016G to provide general Help on the entire screen and specific Help on the fields SELPN and D1PN.

13. Create the panel group INVP016G of type PNLGRP based on the sample in Figure 6.22. Compile the panel group.

14. Copy display-file member INVD016F to new member INVD016G. Modify INVD016G to add the file-level and record-level Help keywords as shown in Figure 6.21 and change all Help record keywords to Help panel group keywords. Remove the display-file records GENERAL, HLPSPN, and HLPDPN.

15. Copy RPG program source member INV016F to new member INV016G.

Exercise 6.2G Purchase Order Line Project

Purpose

To develop Help screens using the HELP3 method.

General Program Specifications

Create RPG program ORDL26G to provide general Help on the entire screen, as well as Help on each field displayed and on the footer record.

13. Create panel group ORDLP26F of type PNLGRP to hold Help definitions for the general Help, for each field on the display, and for the footer area. Compile the definition.

14. Copy display-file source member ORDD026F to new member ORDD026G. Make the necessary modifications to use a panel group to provide general Help on the entire screen, Help on each field, and Help on the footer record.

15. Copy RPG source member ORDL26F to new member ORDL26G.

Review

1. Discuss the problems associated with letting the user change the value in the key field.
2. What does the Change keyword do?
3. How do you add a hidden field to a display-file description and why would you do it?
4. Describe how you determine which field users are "pointing" to when they press F4 for prompt.
5. Describe how you can determine the RRN of the subfile record where your cursor is positioned.
6. Describe how you can control the positioning of the cursor.
7. Why do you need to know the subfile RRN when the prompt is requested on a subfile field, how is this number determined, and how is it used?
8. Which of the Help options would require changes to the RPG code? What changes?
9. A display-file record displays the field EMPNAM. EMPNAM is not a subfile field. You are to provide Help on this field based on the HELP2 method described in this chapter. Write the Help specifications necessary to display the format HLPENM when F1 is pressed and the cursor is positioned on that field.
10. A display file contains a subfile field named EMPNM2. This field is defined in the subfile record SFLR1, which is controlled by the subfile control record SFLCR1. This field is 15 characters long and begins in column 19. The first record of the subfile is displayed on row 9 and the subfile page value is 10. You are to provide Help on this field based on the HELP2 method described in this chapter. Write the Help specifications necessary to display the format HLPENM when F1 is pressed and the cursor is on that field.

continued

Review, *Continued*

11. A display-file record displays the field EMPNAM. (EMPNAM is not a subfile field.) You are to provide Help on this field based on the HELP3 method described in this chapter. Write the Help specifications necessary to display the panel-group record HLPENM in panel group EMPHELP when F1 is pressed and the cursor is on that field.

12. Write the panel-group code for the help record HLPENM in panel group EMPHELP. This should display the employee's last name. It must be the name that is on the employee's birth certificate, driver's license, or another legal document. If the name is longer than 25 characters, use the first 25 characters.

Chapter 7

Creating Window-Based Subfiles

Chapter Overview

When you complete Chapter 7, you will be able to create subfiles in windows that offer users an opportunity to make selections

- using the prompt option
- using the point-and-shoot feature

Subfiles in Windows

Windows are a great way to present popup information on a display screen and prompt users to make a choice. When the information to be presented is a list, subfiles are required. You will learn to display a subfile in a window and prompt users to make a selection among the options offered.

In the display-file description, the subfile record for a window is defined like any other subfile record. The width of the window, which is defined in the control record, must be enough to accommodate the left and right window borders. The subfile control record contains the window definition as well as optional window border commands. Adding a footer to a window containing a subfile is discussed later in this chapter. For now, the definition of function keys will appear above the subfile display. Remember to reserve one line at the bottom of the window as a message line as well as two rows, one for the top border and one for the bottom border, and two columns, one for the left border and the other for the right border.

In Chapter 6, you developed prompts for many fields, including the warehouse code (Figure 7.1). As you may recall, the warehouse code prompt window used in Chapter 6 had the valid values STL, DLS, and FTW hard-coded in it.

Warehouse Code: STL

Enter Warehouse
Correct Values are:
STL, DLS, FTW

Figure 7.1
Prompt for Warehouse
Field with Hard-Coded
Values

Although Computers Are US has a certain number of warehouses at present, the company may add more later. Therefore, instead of hard-coding the warehouse codes in the display, it would be better to load the values from a data file that contains up-to-date warehouse data. The warehouse file is shown in Figure 7.2.

Figure 7.2
Warehouse File

```
*...1....+....2....+....3....+....4....+....5....+....6

**********************************************************
* Phil Levinson   Jefferson College  11/16/99   WHPF
* Warehouse Physical File
**********************************************************
A                                         UNIQUE
A          R WHPFR
A            WHPWH         3A             TEXT ('WAREHOUSE ID')
A            WHPA1        20A             TEXT ('WH ADDRESS LINE 1')
A            WHPA2        20A             TEXT ('WH ADDRESS LINE 2')
A            WHPCT        20A             TEXT ('WH CITY')
A            WHPST         2A             TEXT ('WH STATE')
A            WHPZIP       11A             TEXT ('WH ZIP')
A          K WHPWH
```

Because Computers Are US has three warehouses at present, the warehouse files would contain the data shown in Figure 7.3.

Figure 7.3
Warehouse Data

```
WHPWH:  DLS
WHPA1:  2100 W 4TH STREET
WHPA2:
WHPCT:  DALLAS
WHPST:  TX
WHPZIP: 51233-1234

WHPWH:  FTW
WHPA1:  789 FIFTH STREET
WHPA2:
WHPCT:  FORT WORTH
WHPST:  TX
WHPZIP: 59191-1123

WHPWH:  STL
WHPA1:  9004 STATE STREET
WHPA2:
WHPCT:  SAINT LOUIS
WHPST:  MO
WHPZIP: 63511-1241
```

Two new records will replace the current warehouse prompt window in the display file: 1) the warehouse subfile record WHSF, shown in Figure 7.4, and 2) the subfile control record WINPWH, which contains the WINDOW definition, shown in Figure 7.5.

Figure 7.4
Warehouse Subfile

```
*...1....+....2....+....3....+....4....+....5....+....6

A***********************************************
A***  WHSF - WAREHOUSE SUBFILE
A      TO BE DISPLAYED IN WINPWH
A***********************************************
A          R WHSF                        SFL
A            WHWH          3A 0   4  5
A            WHCTY        20A 0   4  9
A            WHAD1        20A 0   4 30
A            WHST          2A 0   4 51
A            WHZIP        11A 0   4 54
```

```
*...1....+....2....+....3....+....4....+....5....+....6

**********************************************************
***    WINDOW subfile control record - WINPWH    ***
***    DISPLAYS WAREHOUSE SUBFILE    - WHSF       ***
**********************************************************
A
A          R WINPWH                    SFLCTL(WHSF)
A
 **** W I N D O W    C O N T R O L S    ***
A                                      WINDOW(8 6 12 70)
A                                      WDWBORDER((*COLOR RED)-
A                                      (*DSPATR HI -
A                                      RI) (*CHAR '        '))
 **** S U B F I L E    C O N T R O L S    ***
A                                      SFLSIZ(07)
A                                      SFLPAG(06)
A                                      OVERLAY
A 53                                   SFLDSP
A 53                                   SFLDSPCTL
A N53                                  SFLCLR
A 54                                   SFLEND(*MORE)
A
 **** S C R E E N    H E A D E R    *****
A                                    1  05'WAREHOUSE INFORMATION'
A                                    2   5'Enter=Exit Screen'
A                                    3   5'WHs'
A                                    3   9'City'
A                                    3  30'Address'
A                                    3  51'St'
A                                    3  54'Zip'
```

Figure 7.5
Warehouse Subfile
Control Record

Let's suppose that users have indicated that a display of all of the warehouse fields except Address 2 would help them select the correct warehouse. Figure 7.4 shows the subfile record definition. Although we will not need it in this example, subfile drop or subfile fold (covered in Chapter 4) can be used in window-based subfiles, just as in other subfiles.

The control record (Figure 7.5) is slightly more complex than previous control records because it contains the WINDOW (Window) and WDWBORDER (Window Border) keywords as well as subfile control keywords. The number of columns (70) in the window must be wide enough for all the fields of the subfile, and the number of rows (12) must accommodate the subfile, which starts at line 4 and continues for the number of lines defined in the SLFPAG keyword (6).

Conditioning indicator 53 controls the SFLDSP (Subfile Display), SFLDSPCTL (Subfile Control Display), and SFLCLR (Subfile Clear) keywords. Indicator 54 is used to indicate the End of File (EOF) of the warehouse file.

The changes required in the RPG program are also familiar. The F-spec for the display file needs another continuation record for the new subfile, as is shown in the shaded line in Figure 7.6.

```
+....1....+....2....+....3....+....4....+....5....+....6....+....7....+....8
 *  Display File with subfiles DSP01 and DSP03 and Data Stru FILDS
 *            and subfile WHSF
FINVD017A  CF  E              WORKSTN
F                                      SFILE(DSP01:RRN)
F                                      SFILE(DSP03:RRN)
F                                      INFDS(FILDS)
F                                      SFILE(WHSF:WHrrn)
```

Figure 7.6
F-Specs for the
Display File with the
Warehouse Subfile

The program also requires an F-spec for the warehouse file, WHPF. This specification (not shown) would access the file for input as a keyed file.

Because the warehouse file is a short file that probably will remain relatively short, it is appropriate to use subfile load option 1, loading the entire file before it is displayed. The subroutine to load and display the warehouse window, WINWH, is called from the PROMPT subroutine, developed in Chapter 6, whenever the F4 key is pressed while the cursor points to a warehouse code. The WINWH subroutine is shown in Figure 7.7.

Figure 7.7

Subroutine WINWH Loads and Displays the Warehouse Window

```
    +....1....+....2....+....3....+....4....+....5....+....6....+....7....+....8

    ********************************************************************
    *  WinWH Subroutine     Loads and Displays the Warehouse FIle
    ********************************************************************
    C     WinWH         BEGSR
    *                                         Clear subfile.
    C                   Eval      *IN53 = *OFF
    C                   Write     WinPWH
    C                   Eval      *IN53 = *ON
    C                   Eval      WHrrn = 0
    C     *LoVAL        SETLL     WHPF
    C                   Read      WHPF                                      54
    C                   DOW       *IN54 = *OFF and WHrrn < 9999
    C                   Eval      WHWH  = WHPWH
    C                   Eval      WHCTY = WHPCT
    C                   Eval      WHAD1 = WHPA1
    C                   Eval      WHST  = WHPST
    C                   Eval      WHzip = WHPZIP
    C                   Eval      WHrrn = WHrrn + 1
    C                   Write     WHSF
    C                   Read      WHPF                                      54
    C                   ENDdo
    C                   If        WHrrn = 0
    C                   Move      'No WHS '      WHCTY
    C                   Eval      WHrrn = 1
    C                   Write     WHSF
    C                   Endif
    C                   ExFMT     WINPWH
    C                   Endsr
```

Exercise 7.1A Computers Are US Inventory Project

Purpose

To develop a program to display a subfile in a window.

General Program Specifications

Create maintenance program INV017A and display file INVD017A. When users prompt on the Warehouse field, the program displays the warehouse list in a subfile in a window.

1. Create warehouse file WHPF (Figure 7.2).

2. Use Data File Utility (DFU) to add the records shown in Figure 7.3 to the warehouse file.

3. Copy display-file member INVD016G to new member INVD017A. Modify INVD017A to add the subfile record shown in Figure 7.4 and the subfile control record shown in Figure 7.5.

4. Copy RPG program source member INV016G to new member INV017A. Modify this program by adding the F-spec for the new file (WHPF) and the continuation F-spec for subfile WHSF (Figure 7.6). Modify the program to call the WINWH subroutine when F4 is pressed while the cursor points to the Warehouse field, and add subroutine WINWH (Figure 7.7).

Exercise 7.2A Purchase Order Line Project

Purpose

To develop a program to display a subfile in a window.

General Program Specifications

Create RPG program ORDL27A, which will display a subfile in a window when the user presses F4 while the cursor points to the Part Number field in the subfile display.

1. Create the physical file called Parts Master Physical file (PMPF) with two fields: the Part Number field (PMPN 11 A) and the Part Description field (PMDS 30 A).

2. Use DFU to enter the data in Figure 7.8 into the file PMPF.

Figure 7.8
Product Data

PMPN	PMDS
A123	COMPUTER X486
A124	COMPUTER PENT
A125	PRINTER — LASER
A213	PRINTER — INK JET
A214	PRINTER — DOT MATRIX
A215	SCANNER — HAND
A216	SCANNER — FLAT BED
A217	SCANNER/KEYBOARD
A319	CD-ROM
A320	CD-ROM 4X

3. Copy display-file source member ORDD026G to new member ORDD027A. Make the necessary modifications to add a subfile and a control record with a window definition to display the data in file PMPF.

4. Copy RPG source member ORDL26G to new member ORDL27A. Modify the member to display the subfile with the part numbers when F4 is pressed while the cursor is in either the part-number or the part-description area of the subfile.

Selection in a Window Subfile Using the Prompt Option

Although we've done well to show users our prompt window subfile, prompt screens are intended to let users add or change a value. To make our prompt screen really useful, we need to let the user pick one of the entries and update the main display subfile. In this section, we explore adding a pick field to the subfile. The pick field is much like the option column that was added to the display in Chapter 2. When a user makes an entry in this column, the RPG program uses a READC operation to locate the warehouse record that the user has selected. With the warehouse value from the subfile in the prompt window, the program can update the main display and the physical file INVPF.

Changes to the display file are minor: We will need to add a new field to the subfile record WHSF (Figure 7.9). We will also modify the control record to activate F12 for cancel, add the display F12=Cancel to the heading, and add the text SL (for selection) to be displayed above the new column.

```
*...1....+....2....+....3....+....4....+....5....+....6
A           WHPIC        1A  I  4  2
```

Figure 7.9
Pick Field to be Added to the Subfile Record WHSF

The changes to the RPG code are shown in Figure 7.10. After displaying the subfile/window, if IN12 is off, the processing continues. The program will use the READC operation to read the record selected in the warehouse prompt window. Once field D1WH is updated from the subfile field WHWH, processing returns to the PROMPT subroutine where the subfile (DSP01 or DSP03) is updated and the physical file record is updated with the new warehouse value.

```
+....1....+....2....+....3....+....4....+....5....+....6....+....7....+....8
   *
C                 ExFMT    WINPWH

 * Additional code added to  WinWH Subroutine to update file when
 * a record is picked.

C                 If       *in03 = *Off and *In12 = *Off
C                 ReadC    WHSF                                95
C                 If       *in95 = *off
C                 Eval     D1WH = WHWH
C                 EndIf
C                 EndIf
C                 Endsr
```

Figure 7.10
Additions to Subroutine WINWH

Exercise 7.1B Computers Are US Inventory Project

Purpose

To develop code to display a subfile in a prompt window and use the user's response to update the display and the physical file.

General Program Specifications

Create maintenance program INV017B and display file INVD017B. When users prompt on the Warehouse field, this program displays the warehouse list in a subfile in a window. When the user makes a selection, both the display and the physical files are automatically updated.

5. Copy display-file member INVD017A to new member INVD017B. Modify INVD017B to add a pick field to the subfile record, as shown in Figure 7.9.

6. Copy RPG program source member INV017A to new member INV017B. Modify this program by adding the changes (shown in Figure 7.10) to the WINWH subroutine to update the display and the physical file with the value selected from the prompt window.

Exercise 7.2B Purchase Order Line Project

Purpose

To develop a prompt using a subfile in a window.

General Program Specifications

Create RPG program ORDL27B to display a subfile in a window when users press F4 while the cursor points to either the Part Number field or the Description field in the subfile display. When users select a value from the prompt window, the program then updates both the Part Number field and the Description field on the subfile display and in the physical file.

5. Copy display-file source member ORDD027A to new member ORDD027B. Make the necessary modifications to add a selection field to the part number prompt subfile.

6. Copy RPG source member ORDL27A to new member ORDL27B. Modify the member so that it uses the selected record on the prompt screen to update the display and the physical file. Both the Part Number and Description fields should be updated.

Selection in a Window Subfile Using Point and Shoot

The inventory maintenance system we've been developing is becoming quite user friendly. Our new prompt screens, however, still require that the user type a letter and then press Enter to make a selection. We can save users a keystroke by adding what are often called point-and-shoot capabilities. Such capabilities let users select a subfile record, such as a warehouse record, on the prompt screen by simply placing the cursor anywhere on the record and pressing Enter. This technique does not require a selection column in the subfile record.

The subfile cursor RRN keyword, SFLCSRRRN (Figure 7.11), is added to the subfile control record of the prompt window. The field associated with this keyword returns the RRN of the record that the cursor was pointing to when the display returned control to the RPG program. If the return from this keyword is zero, the cursor was not pointing to any record in that subfile.

```
*...1....+....2....+....3....+....4....+....5....+....6
A                                        SFLCSRRRN(&CSWHRN)
A           CSWHRN        5S ØH
```

Figure 7.11

Additional Keyword Control Record for Prompt Window

Notice that a different variable (CSWHRN) is used to return the cursor position in the subfile because the WINWH subroutine needs to use the RRN in both the prompt window to retrieve the selection and the main subfile to retrieve the inventory record that is to be updated.

We have been using the value of SFLCSRRRN in our PROMPT subroutine to determine which record was active when F4 was pressed. The value of CSWHRN tells us which record the user pointed to in the prompt subfile. To use it, we replace the READC operation on the prompt subfile with a CHAIN (Random Retrieval from a File) operation into the prompt subfile using the field CSWHRN (note the shaded lines in Figure 7.12).

```
+....1....+....2....+....3....+....4....+....5....+....6....+....7....+....8
C             ExFMT     WINPWH
 * Additional code added to  WinWH Subroutine to update file when
 * a record is picked using point and shoot.
 * Field CSWHRN will return the subfile record number in the warehouse
 * subfile where the cursor was located when the enter key is pressed.

C             If        *inØ3 = *Off and *In12 = *Off
C                       and CSWHRN <> Ø
C   CSWHRN    Chain     WHSF                              95
C             If        *in95 = *off
C             Eval      D1WH = WHWH
C             endif
C             endif

C             Endsr
```

Figure 7.12

New Code to Replace READC in WINWH Subroutine

Exercise 7.1C Computers Are US Inventory Project

Purpose

To develop code to display a subfile in a prompt window and use the user's point-and-shoot response to update both the display and the physical file.

General Program Specifications

Create maintenance program INV017C and display file INVD017C. When users prompt on the Warehouse field, this program displays the warehouse list in a subfile in a window. After the user makes a selection using point and shoot, both the display and the physical file are updated.

7. Copy display-file member INVD017B to new member INVD017C. Modify INVD017C to delete the selection field from the prompt window, and add the subfile cursor RRN to the prompt subfile control record (Figure 7.11).

8. Copy RPG program source member INV017B to new member INV017C. Modify this program based on the code in Figure 7.12 to use the RRN of the record in the warehouse prompt window subfile to locate that record and update both the display and the physical files with the warehouse value.

Exercise 7.2C Purchase Order Line Project

Purpose

To develop a prompt in a subfile in a window using the point-and-shoot technique.

General Program Specifications

Create RPG program ORDL27C, which displays a subfile in a window if the user presses F4 while the cursor points to the Part Number or the Description field in the subfile display. When the user selects a value from the prompt window using the point-and-shoot method, the program then updates both the Part Number and the Description fields in the subfile display and the physical file.

7. Copy display-file source member ORDD027B to new member ORDD027C. Make the necessary modifications to remove the selection field in the part-number prompt subfile. Add the subfile RRN keyword SFLRRN to the control record for the window that prompts on part number.

8. Copy RPG source member ORDL27B to new member ORDL27C. Modify the member to use the RRN of the selected record on the prompt screen to update the display and the physical file. Both the Part Number and the Description fields should be updated.

Creating and Using a Window Definition Record

A window definition record contains the keywords that define a window and its border. Once the window definition record is written to the display, any number of display records can be overlayed in the window. Records to be displayed in the window reference the window definition record instead of containing detailed window and window border descriptions. Both subfiles and simple display records can be shown in a window defined by the window definition record.

Display records referencing the same window definition record and the OVERLAY keyword can be displayed simultaneously in the same window, provided they do not attempt to write in the same territory. This capability lets you design more complex and flexible displays within the window. The capability to display multiple records in the same window can also be used to add footer information displaying the text definitions of the function keys at the bottom of a window that contains a subfile.

Figure 7.13 shows the window definition record WDR1, which contains the WINDOW (Window) and WDBORDER (Window Border) definitions.

```
+....1....+....2....+....3....+....4....+....5....+....6....+....7....+....8

A****************************************
A**** WINDOW DEFINITION RECORD    - WDR1   ***
A****************************************
A
A         R WDR1
A                                         WINDOW(8 6 12 70)
A                                         WDWBORDER((*COLOR RED) -
+A                                        (*DSPATR HI RI) -
A                                         (*CHAR '        '))
```

Figure 7.13
Window Definition
Record

Figure 7.14 shows window reference record FOOTW1, which contains footer information.

```
+....1....+....2....+....3....+....4....+....5....+....6....+....7....+....8

A**********************************************************
A**** WINDOW FOOTER RECORD    - FOOTW1 ***
A**********************************************************
A
A         R FOOTW1
A                                         WINDOW(WDR1)
A                            11  5'F12=CANCEL'
```

Figure 7.14
Window Reference
Record FOOTW1

Figure 7.15 is the subfile control record for the prompt window. It is a window reference record that contains the OVERLAY keyword so that its information can be added to the window display without erasing the existing footer record.

Figure 7.15
Warehouse Subfile
Control Record
Defined as a Window
Reference Record

```
*...1....+....2....+....3....+....4....+....5....+....6

**********************************************
***    subfile control record - WINPWH      ***
***    DISPLAYS WAREHOUSE SUBFILE   - WHSF   ***
**********************************************
A           R WINPWH                  SFLCTL(WHSF)
**** W I N D O W   R E F E R E N C E    ***
A                                      WINDOW(WDR1)
**** S U B F I L E   C O N T R O L S    ***
A                                      SFLSIZ(07)
A                                      SFLPAG(06)
A                                      OVERLAY
A 53                                   SFLDSP
A 53                                   SFLDSPCTL
A N53                                  SFLCLR
A 54                                   SFLEND(*MORE)
A                                      SFLCSRRRN(&CSWHRN)
A           CSWHRN        5S 0H
 **** S C R E E N   H E A D E R          *****
A                                      1 05'WAREHOUSE INFORMATION'
A                                      3  5'WHs'
A                                      3  9'City'
A                                      3 30'Address'
A                                      3 51'St'
A                                      3 54'Zip'
```

Before a program can write or execute a window reference record, the window that is referenced must be on the display. As shown in Figure 7.16, the RPG program writes the window definition record, WDR1, then writes the footer record, FOOTW1, and then executes the format of the subfile control record, WINPWH.

Figure 7.16
RPG Code with Window
Definition Record

```
+....1....+....2....+....3....+....4....+....5....+....6....+....7....+....8
 *     Subroutine WINWH modified to use window definition record WDR1
 *        with footer record FootW1.
C                   Write     WDR1
C                   Write     FootW1
C                   ExFMT     WINPWH
```

Exercise 7.1D Computers Are US Inventory Project

Purpose

To display a subfile in a prompt window using a window definition record.

General Program Specifications

Create maintenance program INV017D and display file INVD017D. When prompted on the Warehouse field, this program displays the warehouse list in a subfile in a window. When the user makes a selection using point and shoot, the display and the physical file are automatically updated. The prompt window will be a window definition record and the footer and subfile will be window reference records.

9. Copy display-file member INVD017C to new member INVD017D. Modify member INVD017D as follows:

   - Add the window definition record, WDR1 (Figure 7.13).
   - Add the window reference record, FOOTW1 (Figure 7.14).
   - Modify the record WINPWH to be a window reference record (Figure 7.15).

10. Copy RPG program source member INV017C to new member INV017D. Modify this program based on the code in Figure 7.16 to write the window definition record, WDR1, and the window reference record, FOOTW1, before executing the window reference record, WINPWH.

Exercise 7.2D Purchase Order Line Project

Purpose

To develop prompt windows using window definition records and window reference records.

General Program Specifications

Create RPG program ORDL27D, which displays a subfile in a window when the user presses F4 while pointing to the Part Number field or the Description field in the subfile display. When the user selects a value from the prompt window using the point-and-shoot method, the program automatically updates both the Part Number and Description fields in the subfile display and the physical file. The prompt window should use window definition records and window reference records.

9. Copy display-file source member ORDD027C to new member ORDD027D. Add a window definition record and a footer record that is a window reference record. Modify the prompt subfile control to be a window reference record.

10. Copy the RPG source member ORDL27C to new member ORDL27D. Modify the member so that it will write the window definition record and the footer record before executing the subfile control record for the prompt window.

Review

1. If a window is defined as 10 6 10 50 and the subfile to be put in the window is defined for row 3, what is the maximum value for the SFLPAG? What would be the maximum value if the subfile provided FOLD onto row 4?

2. How do you define a footer record in a window that displays a subfile?

3. With the point-and-shoot technique, how can you tell which record the cursor was pointing to when Enter was pressed?

4. Why do you need to update both the subfile display and the physical file when you return from a prompt?

Subfile Bookstore Order Project 2

Project Overview
To further demonstrate that you can design, code, test, and debug a system with two subfiles.

The Bookstore Order System (Continued)

12. Modify SCREEN2 from the earlier Subfile Bookstore Order Project 1 (page 105), so that the header information (except for the order number) is input capable (Use=B). Upon returning to your program from that screen, if you find that these fields have been changed, update the record in the physical file.

13. Modify SCREEN2 so that the subfile fields (except for the line number) are also input capable (Use=B). If you find that these fields have changed when you do your READCs, update them in the physical file.

14. Use panel group technology to create Help text for all the fields on Screen 1 and Screen 2.

15. Create a prompt window for selecting a shipping method. First, create a physical file that contains shipping options, including the following data:

Ship By	Description
UPS	United Parcel Service
US-POSTAL	United States Postal Service
FED X	Federal Express
FASTEST WAY	
CHEAPEST	

Provide a prompt capability on Screen 1 and Screen 2 for the Shipping Instructions field. The prompt is to display the prompt window for selecting shipping method. Users will point and shoot to select a method or press F12 to cancel the request.

16. Provide a prompt capability on Screen 2 for the Ship To fields. First, create a physical file to contain the shipping information — the data that is shown in the Ship To area of the screen.

Put the following data in the shipping file to test the window:

        BOOKSTORE
        JEFFERSON COLLEGE
        1000 VIKING ROAD
        HILLSBORO, MO 63050

        MAIL ROOM
        JEFFERSON COLLEGE
        1000 VIKING ROAD
        HILLSBORO, MO 63050

continued

Subfile Project 2 *Continued*

MAINTENANCE DEPARTMENT
JEFFERSON COLLEGE
1000 VIKING ROAD
HILLSBORO, MO 63050

The prompt is to display a window containing the list of Ship To
addresses from the shipping file. User will point and shoot to select the
Ship To address or press F12 to cancel the request.

Section 2

Modular Programming Tools in RPG IV and ILE

The Integrated Language Environment (ILE) was introduced concurrently with the introduction of RPG IV. With the Original Program Model (OPM) environment, used with previous languages such as RPG III, modular design had been difficult and presented serious performance challenges. ILE includes a broader array of tools that encourages "modular" program design.

The Original Program Model

In the original program model (OPM), RPG programs are subdivided into subroutines and Cobol programs are subdivided into paragraphs.

Original Program Model

Program1	Program 2
Subroutine 1.1	Subroutine 2.1
Subroutine 1.2	Subroutine 2.2

These programs can call other programs written in languages such as RPG, Cobol, and CL. The advantages of separating the task into separate units such as programs include

- the development of reusable code that could be called by any number of programs, and
- the isolation of code, so that each program is an independent unit. All variables in each program are "local" variables that have a specific value within that program. Even if both Program 1 and Program 2 have variables named Counter, these variables are stored in different locations in memory. Changing one does not effect the value of the other.

In general, we would like to design small, simple, isolated code units that carry out a relatively simple task, units that can be easily tested and easily maintained. This type of design is referred to as modular design.

When implementing modular design, the OPM requires lots of simple programs which call other programs whenever necessary. Although we can design a system of programs in the older OPM, the design usually fails in practice because each OPM program call requires a significant amount of system overhead, causing the system of programs to run slower than large single programs. In the OPM, designers must choose between performance and code modularity, and, because performance is often critical, many large and complex programs exist. In the OPM, it's not at all unusual to encounter programs which create compiled listings of 400 to 600 pages processing data from 20 or more files. For additional information on modular design, see Chapter 14, "Program-to-Program Communication and Date Queues" and Appendix A, "A Matter of Style".

The Integrated Language Program Environment

The ILE program environment provides a range of tools to allow the implementation of modular programming techniques while avoiding the performance problems of multiple programs in the OPM. Programs in this environment are assembled from compiled modules. A single program can include modules written in RPG, CL, and Cobol. These modules must be written and compiled using the new types RPGLE, CLLE and CBLLE for RPG IV, CL for ILE, and COBOL for ILE. Chapter 8 describes the ILE model in detail.

The ILE environment and RPG IV offer a number of tools to build maintainable code. During the design phase you must determine what tasks will be contained in a specific program, module, procedure, or subroutine.

The RPG IV and ILE tools are introduced in Chapters 8 and 9. Chapter 8 focuses on RPG modules, programs and service programs. Chapter 9 focuses on procedures.

Chapter 8

RPG and ILE: Programs, Modules, and Service Programs

Chapter Overview

Chapter 8 focuses on the ILE module programming tools. In this chapter you learn to

- describe the ILE model
- code and compile RPG IV modules
- use the CALLB (Call Bound Module) operation in a module to call other modules within the program
- create ILE programs with two or more modules
- create service programs with one or more modules
- create programs with bound service programs
- use the CALLB operation in a module to call other modules in the service program

The Integrated Language Environment Model

The ILE program model (Figure 8.1) looks familiar but introduces a number of new terms and appears to change our basic concept of a program.

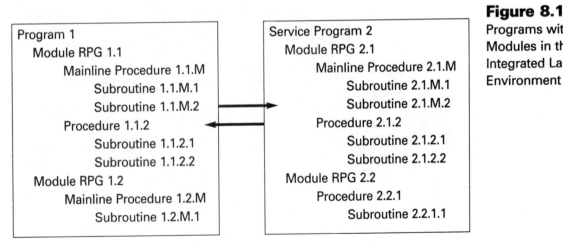

Figure 8.1
Programs with Internal Modules in the Integrated Language Environment

The table on the following page introduces definitions that apply in the ILE environment.

Program	One or more compiled modules that have been assembled into a callable object. When the program is called, the call is always passed to the module designated as the entry procedure module.
Module	Roughly equal to an Original Program Model (OPM) program, a module represents a source member that has been compiled. Modules provide the type of code isolation that is necessary to meet our design requirements and must be assembled into a program to be used.
Procedure	A tool that was not present in OPM. Modules are made up of one or more procedures. Most modules will contain a "mainline" procedure. Procedures can be isolated from other procedures within a module by using local variables. Global variables are shared by all procedures within a module. Procedures can be called with a CALLP. Procedures that return a value can also be used as "functions" in RPG EVAL commands and in other operations where a function would be permitted. Procedures will be discussed in detail in Chapter 9.
Subroutine	Like OPM subroutines, ILE subroutines are not isolated. All variables in a subroutine are shared with all other subroutines in the procedure.
Service Program	This program contains a set of "utility" modules and procedures that may be used by many different programs. When a program is assembled, a service program can be identified that is loaded whenever the program is loaded. Although calls to modules and procedures in the service program require slightly more overhead than calls within the main program, these calls take considerably fewer resources than OPM calls. Placing common utilities in service programs reduces the amount of memory used because the service program code can be used by multiple programs once it is loaded. Service programs also simplify maintenance of the frequently used modules because they only need to be updated in one object: the service program.
Call	Just as in the OPM, the CALL operation is used to Call other programs.
Call Bound Programs	The CALLB (Call Bound Program) operation is used to call other modules within the program object or within a service program that is bound to the program.
Call Procedure	The CALLP (Call Procedure) operation is used to call procedures within the module, program, or in a bound service program. The CALLP operation will be discussed in detail in Chapter 9.

Creating a Program with Two Modules

This section discusses and demonstrates creating a program object (PGM8A) with two modules (MOD8A and MOD8B). Figure 8.2 shows PGM8A.

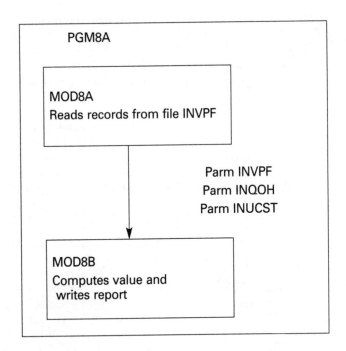

Figure 8.2
PGM8A Comprises Two
Modules: MOD8A and
MOD8B

Entering the Modules

MOD8A and MOD8B source code is entered the same way as source code for a
standalone program. The source code for MOD8A and MOD8B is shown in Figures
8.3 and 8.4.

```
****************************************************************
*  Phil Levinson Jefferson College 12/28/99                  *
*  Creating a program with two members.                      *
*  MOD8A calls bound program MOD8B.                           *
****************************************************************
+....1....+....2....+....3....+....4....+....5....+....6....+....7....+....8


FINVPF     IF   E           K Disk
 *    Process all records in the file.
C                    Read      INVPF                                    90
C                    DoW       *IN90 = *OFF
C                    CallB     'MOD8B'
C                    Parm                    INPN
C                    Parm                    INQOH
C                    Parm                    INUCST

C                    Read      INVPF                                    90
C                    EndDO

 *    Pass a value to MOD8B to indicate that it can close
 *    output file Qprint.
C                    Eval                    INPN = 'EOF'
C                    CallB     'MOD8B'
C                    Parm                    INPN
C                    Parm                    INQOH
C                    Parm                    INUCST

C                    Move      *on           *INLR
C                    Return
```

Figure 8.3
Source Code for MOD8A:
Reads Records from File
INVPF and Calls the
Bound Module MOD8B

Figure 8.4

Source Code for MOD8B:
Receives Data from
MOD8A, Computes
Extended Cost, and Writes
Records to a Printer File

```
*****************************************************************
 *   Phil Levinson Jefferson College 12/28/99                  *
 *   Creating a program with two members                       *
 *   Mod8B called by module Mod8A                              *
 *****************************************************************
+....1....+....2....+....3....+....4....+....5....+....6....+....7....+....8


FQprint    O    F  132        Printer OFLIND(*InOF)

DExtendedCost    s            7P 2
DPN              s           11A
DQOH             s            5P 0
DUCst            s            6P 2
DFirstTime       s            1A   INZ(*On)

C      *Entry        Plist
C                    Parm                    PN
C                    Parm                    QOH
C                    Parm                    UCST


C                    If       PN = 'EOF'
C                    Eval     *INLR = *ON
C                    Return
C                    EndIf

C                    If       FirstTime = *On
C                    Eval     FirstTime = *Off
C                    Except   Heads
C                    Endif

C                    Eval                    ExtendedCost = Qoh * Ucst
C
C
C                    If       *InOF = *ON
C                    Eval     *InOF = *OFF
C                    Except   Heads
C                    EndIf

C                    Except   Detail

C                    Return
OQprint    E         Heads        02 02
O                    udate        y    10
O                                      80 'Computers are US'
O                                     122 'Page'
O                    Page         z   127
O          E         Detail       01
O                    PN               12
O                    QOH          1   24
O                    UCST         1   36
O                    ExtendedCost 1   48
```

Module MOD8A (Figure 8.3) uses the CALLB operation to call MOD8B and pass parameters to it. The module named MOD8B in the CALLB operation must be capitalized for the system to recognize it when the program object is created.

MOD8B (Figure 8.4) normally processes using the passed data, prints a line, but does not set on the last record indicator (*INLR). When this module ends processing without turning on the last record indicator, the printer file is left open so that subsequent records can be written to it. Once MOD8A (Figure 8.3) encounters the end of file (EOF) condition, it calls MOD8B one last time and passes it the special value of 'EOF' in the part number field. When MOD8B receives this special value, it turns on the last record indicator, which closes the print file, and ends.

If a module like MOD8B ends without setting on *INLR, the following things happen:

- All files including the printer file remain open, the file pointers remain where they were, and locked records remain locked.
- When the module is subsequently called, variable initialization is not repeated.
- When the module is subsequently called, *INZSR is not executed.
- Values from one call of MOD8B still exist. In MOD8B, for example, variable FirstTime retains its value, causing the headings to be printed on the first page when the program is subsequently called.

Unlike MOD8B, most modules set on the last record indicator before they end. If you are coding a module with that needs to have files remain open or variables retrain values, code it like MOD8B, so that it does not turn on the last record indicator until your design no longer needs that special condition.

In the file INVPF (Figure 8.3) both INQOH and INUCST are signed numeric variables; however, as MOD8A reads records, the values are converted to packed numeric. Therefore, when you define the variables in module MOD8B to receive the passed values of the variables INQOH and INUCST, you must define them as packed (refer to the D-specs in Figure 8.4).

Compiling the Modules

Each module that is assembled into the program must be compiled using the CRTRPGMOD command. One easy way to create modules is to use option 15 in WRKMBRPDM (Work with Members using Program Development Manager).

When you create the modules, you may want to change the compile parameter to provide a listing (Debug Views=*SOURCE) which is used with the debugger. You may also want to change the Source Listing Indention value of 'I', which makes the compiler listing easier to read by indenting loops and if structures. Both of these tools are described in Appendix B. To alter the compile parameters in WRKMBRPDM, type 15 beside the source member and press F4 (Prompt).

All modules must be successfully compiled before you can create the program. Modules themselves are not programs and cannot be called. The modules must be assembled into a program before logic testing can begin.

Assembling the Program

You create program PGM8A using the CRTPGM command. To get the complete set of parameter options for the CRTPGM command, type CRTPGM, press F4, and press F10 (Additional parameters). Figure 8.5 shows the CRTPGM command with all parameters.

Some important parameters in the CRTPGM command follow:

- The program name and library name are entered in the first two lines.
- The list of modules follows. In Figure 8.5, these are MOD8A and MOD8B. However, this can be a much longer list of modules, or could include a wildcard value such as MOD8* (all modules which begin with the characters MOD8).

- The Text 'description' adopts the entry module text unless you enter specific text on this line.
- The program entry procedure module identifies the module that is to be called when the program is called. The default is *FIRST, which indicates that the first module in the module list is actually called when the program is called. In Figure 8.5, the first module in the module list is MOD8A, so that module is called and that module's text is the default text for the program object.
- The bind service program is discussed later in this chapter.
- The binding directory is an object that contains a list of the modules and service programs. It provides an excellent way to keep track of the modules and service programs. When the binding directory is used, you don't need to enter module or service program names in the CRTPGM command.
- Activation group is an ILE management unit. Many environmental parameters can be changed for the entire activation group, which can contain multiple jobs. I recommend that you use the program name, job name, or *CALLER value for the activation group. Leaving the default value of *NEW may increase the overhead of starting the program.

Figure 8.5
CRTPGM Command
for PGM8A

```
                                  Create Program (CRTPGM)

Type choices, press Enter.

Program  . . . . . . . . . . . . > PGM8A        Name
  Library  . . . . . . . . . . . >   YourLib    Name, *CURLIB
Module . . . . . . . . . . . . . > MOD8A        Name, generic*, *PGM, *ALL
  Library  . . . . . . . . . . . >   YourLib    Name, *LIBL, *CURLIB...
               + for more values > MOD8B
                                 >   YourLib
Text 'description' . . . . . . .   *ENTMODTXT


                                Additional Parameters

Program entry procedure module    *FIRST       Name, *FIRST, *ONLY, *PGM
  Library  . . . . . . . . . .     _____       Name, *LIBL, *CURLIB...



                                                                   More...

Create Program (CRTPGM)

Type choices, press Enter.

Bind service program . . . . . .   *NONE        Name, generic*, *NONE, *ALL
  Library  . . . . . . . . . .     _____       Name, *LIBL
             + for more values     _____
                                   _____
Binding directory  . . . . . . .   *NONE        Name, *NONE
  Library  . . . . . . . . . .     _____       Name, *LIBL, *CURLIB...
             + for more values

Activation group . . . . . . . . > PGM8A        Name, *NEW, *CALLER
```

continued

```
Creation options . . . . . . . .    _____    *GEN, *NOGEN, *NODUPPROC...
            + for more values       _____
Listing detail . . . . . . . . .    *NONE       *NONE, *BASIC, *EXTENDED...
Allow update . . . . . . . . . .    *YES        *YES, *NO
User profile . . . . . . . . . .    *USER       *USER, *OWNER
Replace program  . . . . . . . .    *YES        *YES, *NO
Authority  . . . . . . . . . . .    *LIBCRTAUT  Name, *LIBCRTAUT, *CHANGE...
                                                                  More...


Create Program (CRTPGM)

Type choices, press Enter.

Target release . . . . . . . . .    *CURRENT    *CURRENT, *PRV, V3R0M5...
Allow reinitialization . . . . .    *NO         *NO, *YES
```

Figure 8.5
Continued

Exercise 8.1 Creating Multiple-Module Programs

Purpose
To create and manipulate multiple-module programs with necessary commands.

Instructions
1. Enter RPGLE modules MOD8A and MOD8B as shown in Figures 8.3 and 8.4.
2. Create modules MOD8A and MOD8B by using the CRTRPGMOD command (option 15 WRKOBJPDM). Set the parameter Debug View to *SOURCE.
3. Create the program PGM8A using the command CRTPGM (Figure 8.5).
4. Call the program.
5. View the output of the CL command DSPPGM (Display Program) with Detail = *ALL. Issue the command with the output value *PRINT to create a listing.
6. View the output of the CL command DSPPGM with Detail = *MODULE. Issue the command with the output value *PRINT to create a listing.
7. Modify the module MOD8B to accumulate a total of the Extended Cost field. This total should be printed when the module receives the part number value of 'EOF' just before the last record indicator is turned on.
8. Create the updated module MOD8B (CRTRPGMOD or Option 15 in WRKMBRPDM).
9. Use the UPDPGM (Update Program) command to replace module MOD8B in the program PGM8A.
10. Run the program again to confirm that the total now prints.

Service Programs

Modules that many programs use can be stored in service programs. Including these modules in a service program provides the following two advantages over including these modules in specific program objects:

- Only one copy of the object code exists on the system (in the service program), and only one copy must be corrected if a change is made.
- Less computer memory is used because the service program is loaded once to service any number of requests.

Figure 8.6 shows an example program that uses a service module in Service Program SRV8D.

Figure 8.6

MOD8B2 Shown with CALLB to MOD8D (in Service Program SRV8D) to convert currency from Canadian to US dollars

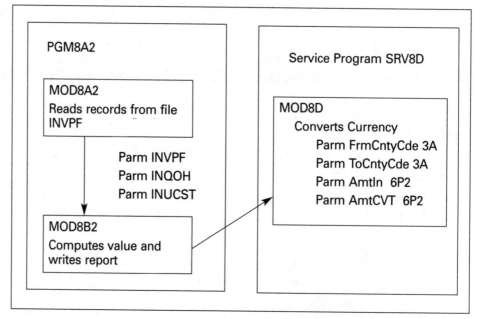

Service Program SRV8D could contain any number of modules. Modules in SRV8D can only be called with the CALLB operation from an ILE program that identifies this service program in the bind service program parameter. For purposes of this demonstration, the conversion program converts currency from Canadian (CAN) to US (USA) dollars by multiplying the value by .800. In an actual application, the conversion program would probably draw the multiplier from a file updated periodically from reported conversion data.

Table 8.1 describes the process of creating a service program and an ILE program that uses modules in it. If the service program already exists, only steps 3 and 4 are required. The specific tasks are described in the text that follows the table.

General Step	Command	As Demonstrated in Exercise 8.2
1. Compile all modules of the service program	CRTRPGMOD	Compile module MOD8D which will be used in service program SRV8D.
2. Create the service program	CRTSRVPGM	Create the service program SRV8D.
3. Compile all modules of the program	CRTRPGMOD	Compile modules MOD8A2 and MOD8B2.
4. Create the program.	CRTPGM	Create program PGM8A2.

Table 8.1
Creating a Program that
Uses a Service Program

Figure 8.7 shows the source code (RPGLE) for module MOD8D, which converts currency. The code shown is much too simple for the final release. However, because of the modular design, a module such as CVTCUR can be updated without impact to the calling programs unless the passed parameters must be changed.

```
******************************************************************
*    Phil Levinson Jefferson College 12/28/99              *
*    Converts data from one currency to another.           *
*    Mod8D called by module Mod8B2.                        *
******************************************************************
+....1....+....2....+....3....+....4....+....5....+....6....+....7....+....8

DAmtIn            s              6P 2
DAmtCVT           s              6P 2
DFrmCntyCde       s              3A
DToCntyCde        s              3A

C     *Entry      Plist
C                 Parm                         FrmCntyCde
C                 Parm                         ToCntyCde
C                 Parm                         AmtIn
C                 Parm                         AmtCVT

**   This code demonstrates how to use a service program.
**   This code is much simpler than would be used in production.

C                 Eval                         AmtCVT = AmtIn * .800
C                 Eval       *InLR = *ON
C                 Return
```

Figure 8.7
Source Code for
Module MOD8D

After module MOD8D (Figure 8.7) is created, the service program is created using the CRTSRVPGM (Create Service Program) command shown in Figure 8.8.

```
                    Create Service Program (CRTSRVPGM)

Type choices, press Enter.

Service program  . . . . . . . . > SRV8D      Name
   Library  . . . . . . . . . . >    YourLib  Name, *CURLIB
Module . . . . . . . . . . . . . > MOD8D      Name, generic*, *SRVPGM, *ALL
   Library  . . . . . . . . . . >    YourLib  Name, *LIBL, *CURLIB...
               + for more values   _
                                   *LIBL
Export . . . . . . . . . . . . . > *ALL       *SRCFILE, *ALL
Export source file . . . . . . .   QSRVSRC    Name, QSRVSRC
   Library  . . . . . . . . . .    *LIBL      Name, *LIBL, *CURLIB
Export source member . . . . . .   *SRVPGM    Name, *SRVPGM
Text 'description' . . . . . . .   *BLANK
```

Figure 8.8
Create Service Program
Command to Create the
Service Program SRV8D

When creating the service program you must

- identify the service program and the library in which it will be stored
- identify the modules that are to be included in the service module
- identify the Export listing that identifies the modules and procedures that are available to calls from other programs (Export *ALL makes all modules and procedures in the service file available to the calling programs)

Module MOD8B2 (Figure 8.9) has been modified to call the bound program MOD8D. The CALLB operation is the same for calling modules within the program object, referred to as statically bound modules, and objects in the bound service modules, referred to as dynamically bound modules. The binding between the program and service module occurs when the program first calls a module in the service program. When that call is made, the program receives a map of the service program and becomes "bound" to it. Because this happens "on-the-fly" it is referred to as dynamic binding. The first call to any module in a service program incurs some additional overhead but subsequent calls to any module in that service program will be processed with little additional overhead.

Figure 8.9
MOD8B2

```
******************************************************************
*   Phil Levinson Jefferson College 12/28/99                    *
*   Creating a program with two members.                        *
*   Mod8B2 called by module Mod8A2.                             *
******************************************************************
* Modification A81      adds totals.
* Modification A82      adds call for currency conversions.
******************************************************************
+....1....+....2....+....3....+....4....+....5....+....6....+....7....+....8

     FQprint    O   F  132          Printer OFLIND(*InOF)

     DExtendedCost     s            7P 2
A8B1DTotExtCost        s            7P 2
     DPN               s           11A
     DQOH              s            5P 0
     DUCst             s            6P 2
     DFirstTime        s            1A   INZ(*On)
A8B2DUCstCVT           s            6P 2
A8B2DFrmCntyCde        s            3A
A8B2DToCntyCde         s            3A

     C     *Entry      Plist
     C                 Parm                    PN
     C                 Parm                    QOH
     C                 Parm                    UCST

     C                 If        FirstTime = *On
     C                 Eval      FirstTime = *Off
     C                 Except    Heads
     C                 Endif

     D8B2C*            Eval                ExtendedCost = Qoh * UCst
     A8B2C             Eval                FrmCntyCde = 'CAN'
     A8B2C             Eval                ToCntyCde = 'USA'
     A8B2C             CALLB     'MOD8D'
     A8B2C             PARM                FrmCntyCde
     A8B2C             PARM                ToCntyCde
     A8B2C             PARM                UCst
     A8B2C             PARM                UCstCVT
     A8B2C             Eval                ExtendedCost = QOH * UCstCVT
     A8B1C             Eval                TotExtCost =
```

continued

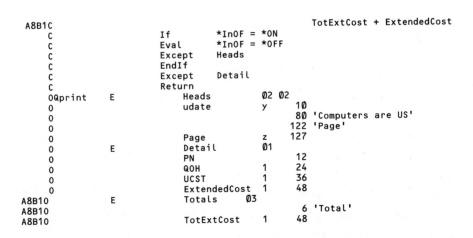

Figure 8.9
Continued

```
A8B1C                                              TotExtCost + ExtendedCost
    C                    If        *InOF = *ON
    C                    Eval      *InOF = *OFF
    C                    Except    Heads
    C                    EndIf
    C                    Except    Detail
    C                    Return
    OQprint     E        Heads           02 02
    O                    udate           y       10
    O                                           80 'Computers are US'
    O                                          122 'Page'
    O                    Page            z      127
    O           E        Detail          01
    O                    PN                      12
    O                    QOH             1       24
    O                    UCST            1       36
    O                    ExtendedCost    1       48
A8B10           E        Totals       03
A8B10                                            6 'Total'
A8B10                    TotExtCost      1       48
```

Module MOD8B2 contains minor changes from the previous version of the module. MOD8B2 contains a CALLB operation to MOD8D which will convert currency value. Module MOD8A2 (not shown) has the CALLB altered from MOD8A (Figure 8.2) to call MOD8B2 instead of MOD8B.

Once these modules (CRTRPGMOD or option 15 in WRKMBRPDM) and the service program SRV8D are created, then the program PGM8A2 can be created.

Debugging sessions using the debugger can include the service program modules as well as the initial program modules. Remember each module must be compiled with Debug Views = *SOURCE. Once the debugger is started, select F14, Work with Module List, shown in Figure 8.10. To add a service program, on the first line type **1**, type the service program name, and identify the type as ***SRVPGM**. The service program and its modules are shown in the program/module list. To view a module and add break points in a module, use option 5 on this screen.

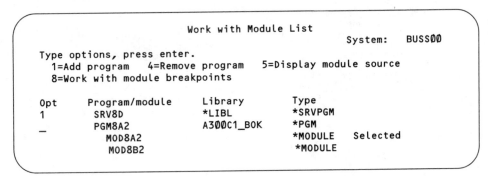

```
                        Work with Module List
                                          System:   BUSS00
   Type options, press enter.
     1=Add program    4=Remove program    5=Display module source
     8=Work with module breakpoints

   Opt    Program/module     Library       Type
   1      SRV8D              *LIBL         *SRVPGM
          PGM8A2             A300C1_BOK    *PGM
   _        MOD8A2                         *MODULE    Selected
            MOD8B2                         *MODULE
```

Figure 8.10
Work with Modules
(F14) in Debugger

Exercise 8.2 Learning to Create Service Programs

Purpose

To create and use service programs.

Instructions

1. Enter the RPGLE module MOD8D as shown in Figure 8.7.
2. Create the module MOD8D. Set the parameter Debug View to *SOURCE.
3. Create the service program SRV8D using CRTSRVPGM (Figure 8.8).
4. Enter the RPGLE module MOD8A2. Refer to MOD8A in Figure 8.2, and make the CALLB operation refer to MOD8B2 instead of MOD8B.
5. Enter the RPGLE module MOD8B2 as shown in Figure 8.9.
6. Create the modules MOD8A2 and MOD8B2 by using the CRTRPGMOD command (option 15 WRKOBJPDM). Set the parameter Debug View to *SOURCE.
7. Create the program PGM8A2 using the command CRTPGM (Figure 8.5). For Bind service program name, type **SRV8D**.
8. Call the program CALL PGM8A2.
9. View the output of the CL command DSPPGM (Display Program) with Detail = *ALL. Issue the command with the output value *PRINT to create a listing.
10. View the output of the CL command DSPPGM with Detail = *MODULE. Issue the command with the output value *PRINT to create a listing.
11. Create the physical file Currency shown in Figure 8.11.

Figure 8.11
Physical File Currency

```
....+....1....+....2....+....3....+....4....+....5....+....6....+....7....+....8
      *  PHYSICAL FILE CURRENCY
     A         R CURREC
     A           FRMCTY          3A           TEXT('FROM COUNTRY')
     A           TOCTY           3A           TEXT('TO COUNTRY')
     A           CONVF           6S 3         TEXT('CONVERSION FACTOR')
     A         K FRMCTY
     A         K TOCTY
```

Figure 8.12
Data for File Currency

```
w....+....1....+....2....+....3....+....4....+....5....+....6....+....7....+....8
      *  PHYSICAL FILE CURRENCY
     A         R CURREC
     A           FRMCTY          3A           TEXT('FROM COUNTRY')
     A           TOCTY           3A           TEXT('TO COUNTRY')
     A           CONVF           6S 3         TEXT('CONVERSION FACTOR')
     A         K FRMCTY
     A         K TOCTY
```

continued

Exercise 8.2 Learning to Create Service Programs, *Continued*

12. Load the data shown in Figure 8.12 into this file (UPDDTA CURRENCY).
13. Modify the module MOD8D to
    - Use the file Currency.
    - Chain to this file using the fields from the *Entry Plist if found.
    - Multiply the passed value by the field CONVF else.
    - Put *HiVAL into the return value endif.
14. Create the updated module MOD8D (CRTRPGMOD or Option 15 in WRKMBRPDM).
15. Use the UPDSRVPGM (Update Service Program) command to replace module MOD8D in the program SRV8D.
16. Run the program again to confirm that the total now prints.

Review

1. Identify which of these modules should be included in a program and which should be included in a service module.

    - Compute the number of working days between two dates.
    - Print report of open orders.
    - Convert from cubic meters to cubic feet.
    - Select the next order to fill.

2. Determine whether the following statements are true or false based on information in Figure 8.2.

    - PGM8A must be created before MOD8A can be created.
    - Syntax checking occurs when modules are created.
    - The CRTRPGMOD is used to compile MOD8A
    - Both MOD8A and MOD8B must use the variable names INVPF, INQOH, and INUCST.

3. When a program is called, how does the system determine which module within the program should be run?

4. Why must the service program exist prior to creating the program that is to be bound to it?

5. What is dynamic binding and how does it apply to service programs?

Chapter 9

Procedures

Chapter Overview

Chapter 9 focuses on RPG IV procedures. In this chapter you learn to

- code and compile RPG IV modules that contain a mainline procedure and subprocedures
- use the CALLP (Call Prototyped Procedure) operation to call procedures
- code and compile RPG IV modules that contain procedures but do not contain a mainline
- create procedures with the EXPORT keyword
- create service programs with procedures

The modular approach to program design and development was introduced in the Section 2 introduction and Chapter 8, and is further discussed in Appendix A. Using modules in programs and subprograms makes all your code easier to debug and maintain because the small program units operate independently. Unless the interface between the modules is altered, changes can be made to the code in any of the modules without requiring changes to other modules.

Until the introduction of procedures, modules comprised a mainline routine and any number of subroutines. Now modules can be divided into any number of named procedures, and procedures are divided into subroutines (Figure 9.1). The program entry procedure module (described in Chapter 8) and modules called by name must contain mainline code, referred to as a mainline procedure. Modules that do not contain a mainline procedure can be created, as described later in this chapter in the "A Module of Procedures" section (page 173).

```
Program1
  Module RPG 1.1
    Main Procedure 1.1.M
      Subroutine 1.1.M.1
      Subroutine 1.1.M.2
    Procedure 1.1.2
      Subroutine 1.1.2.1
      Subroutine 1.1.2.2
  Module RPG 1.2
    Main Procedure 1.2.M
      Subroutine 1.2.M.1
```

```
Service Program 2
  Module RPG 2.1
    Main Procedure 2.1.M
      Subroutine 2.1.M.1
      Subroutine 2.1.M.2
    Procedure 2.1.2
      Subroutine 2.1.2.1
      Subroutine 2.1.2.2
  Module RPG 2.2
    Procedure 2.2.1
      Subroutine 2.2.1.1
```

Figure 9.1
Program 1 Comprises Multiple Modules, Modules Can Comprise Multiple Procedures, and Procedures Can Comprise Multiple Subroutines

Unless a procedure is declared with the EXPORT keyword, the procedure is considered local and can be called only from within that module. Procedures with the EXPORT keyword can be called from other modules in the program or service program.

Procedures can be further divided into subroutines. Subroutines offer no isolation capabilities. If one subroutine in a procedure alters the value of a variable, that value is changed for all subroutines in that procedure. When a local variable with a D-spec in a procedure changes, the change has no effect on variables with the same name in other procedures in the same module. The isolation of procedures lets procedures in the same module contain subroutines with the same name.

Starting with a Simple Example

Fig.9.2 presents a module that contains two procedures.

Figure 9.2
Program PGM9A:
One Module (MOD9A)
That Comprises
Two Procedures

PGM9A

   MOD9A

      Mainline Procedure

      Procedure WriteOut

Procedures that are called from a mainline procedure in the same module are referred to as subprocedures. These subprocedures can use files, fields, and other procedures declared in the mainline F-specs and D-specs. Such files, fields, and other procedures are referred to as global because they are visible and can be used (or, in the case of variables, changed) within any procedure.

Variables and subroutines declared within a subprocedure are, however, local. These exist only within the procedure that declares them. If a procedure declares a local variable with the same name as a global variable, the local one is used within the procedure. It doesn't have the value of the global variable, and changes to the local variable do not change the value of the global variable with the same name.

Our first example, MOD9A (Figure 9.3), uses the global definitions of variables FirstTime and *InOF and of the exception names Heads and Detail.

Figure 9.3
MOD9A Contains
Procedure WriteOut

```
*****************************************************************
*   Phil Levinson Jefferson College 12/28/99                  *
*   Creating a program with a subprocedure                    *
*   MOD9A                                                      *
*****************************************************************
..
+....1....+....2....+....3....+....4....+....5....+....6....+....7....+....8

FINVPF     IF   E           K Disk
FQprint    O    F 132         Printer OFLIND(*InOF)
 *-- procedure prototype
DWriteOut       PR

DExtendedCost   s             7P 2
DFirstTime      s             1A   INZ(*On)
 *-- Mainline Procedure ------------------------------------------
C                   Read      INVPF                              90
C                   DoW       *IN90 = *OFF
C                   CallP     WriteOut
C                   Read      INVPF                              90
C                   EndDO
C                   Move      *on           *INLR
```

continued

```
+....1....+....2....+....3....+....4....+....5....+....6....+....7....+....8
C               Return

OQprint     E           Heads           02 02
O                       udate           y    10
O                                           80 'Computers are US'
O                                          122 'Page'
O                       Page            z   127
O           E           Detail          01
O                       inpn                12
O                       inqoh           1   24
O                       inucst          1   36
O                       ExtendedCost    1   48
 *-- begin procedure WriteOut
PWriteOut        B
 *-- procedure interface
DWriteOut        PI

C               If      FirstTime = *On
C               Eval    FirstTime = *Off
C               Except  Heads
C               Endif

C               Eval                    ExtendedCost = inqoh*inUcst

C               If      *InOF = *ON
C               Eval    *InOF = *OFF
C               Except  Heads
C               EndIf

C               Except  Detail
C               Return
PWriteOut        E
```

Figure 9.3
Continued

Prototype

The compiler must be informed that a procedure exists. Prototyping identifies the procedure, its type if applicable, and the structure of the variables that are "passed" to the procedure. In MOD9A, procedure WriteOut is declared in a D-spec (Figure 9.4). This specification identifies the procedure with the declaration type of PR (Prototype). Throughout this chapter, we explore prototyping further.

```
+....1....+....2....+....3....+....4....+....5....+....6....+....7....+....8
DWriteOut       PR
```

Figure 9.4
Prototype Declaration for the Procedure WriteOut

Calling a Prototyped Procedure

The CallP (Call Prototyped Procedure) operation is used to call the procedure as shown in Figure 9.5. Later in this chapter we discuss calling the procedure with passed parameters (page 171) and using the procedure as a function (page 174).

```
+....1....+....2....+....3....+....4....+....5....+....6....+....7....+....8
C               CallP   WriteOut
```

Figure 9.5
CallP Operation Used to Call the Procedure WriteOut

The Subprocedure

The subprocedure code follows the mainline procedure code; in MOD9A, the subprocedure WriteOut appears after the O-specs of the mainline procedure. Procedure WriteOut is shown in Figure 9.6.

Figure 9.6

Procedure WriteOut

```
+....1....+....2....+....3....+....4....+....5....+....6....+....7....+....8

 *-- begin procedure WriteOut
PWriteOut        B
 *-- procedure interface
DWriteOut        PI

C                    If        FirstTime = *On
C                    Eval      FirstTime = *Off
C                    Except    Heads
C                    Endif

C                    Eval                       ExtendedCost = inqoh*inUcst

C                    If        *InOF = *ON
C                    Eval      *InOF = *OFF
C                    Except    Heads
C                    EndIf

C                    Except    Detail

C                    Return
PWriteOut        E
```

The WriteOut procedure in Figure 9.6 begins with a P-spec (created in SEU using the PR prompt) that contains the procedure name. The letter B in column 24 indicates the beginning of the procedure. The procedure ends with another P-spec containing the procedure name and an E in column 24 indicating the end of the procedure.

The prototype D-specs from the mainline are repeated in the procedure. These are referred to as the procedure interface. The D-specs in the mainline (Figure 9.4) used to prototype the procedure must have the declaration type PR columns 24 and 25. The D-specs in the procedure have the declaration type PI (Procedure Interface). As discussed later in this chapter, the prototype and procedure interface are more complicated when variables are passed to the procedure.

Creating a Program with a Procedure

Program PGM9A contains only one module. However, because it contains a procedure, you must go through the same two steps to create it that you used to create multiple-module programs in Chapter 8. First, the module must be created with the command CRTRPGMOD or option 15 in WRKMBRPDM (Work with Members using Program Development Manager). (CRTBNDPGM or option 9 in WRKMBRPDM does not create a single member program that contains a procedure.) Remember that if you want to debug this code you must change the debug view to *SOURCE. Once the module is created, use the command CRTPGM (Create Program) to create the program PGM9A with the module MOD9A.

Exercise 9.1 Creating a Module with Subprocedures

Purpose

To develop a working knowledge of subprocedures.

Instructions

1. Enter the RPGLE module MOD9A shown in Figure 9.3.
2. Create the module (CRTRPGMOD or option 15 in WRKMBRPDM). Set the parameter Debug View to *Source.
3. Create the program PGM9A using the CRTPGM command.
4. Test the program.

Multiple Procedures in a Module and Subroutines in a Procedure

MOD9B (Figures 9.7 and 9.8) is an example of a module with two procedures, both of which contain subroutines. Both procedures are identified with prototype information in the D-specs of the mainline procedure. In this example procedure, ProcessRcd is called by the mainline procedure, and procedure WriteOut is called by the procedure ProcessRcd.

To demonstrate the code isolation that occurs within procedures, we have coded each procedure with a subroutine named DoProcess. This coding reveals the advantage of using procedures. Variables and subroutines introduced in a procedure are referred to as local because their scope or existence is limited to the procedure. When subroutine DoProcess is called within procedure ProcessRcd, only the DoProcess subroutine in the procedure ProcessRcd is used. This isolation frees procedure designers to use variable names and subroutine names without having to check other parts of the program for possible name or use conflicts and is especially useful when assembling programs out of predefined procedures.

```
*****************************************************************
 *   Phil Levinson Jefferson College 12/29/99               *
 *   Creating a program with a subprocedure                 *
 *   MOD9B                                                  *
*****************************************************************
+....1....+....2....+....3....+....4....+....5....+....6....+....7....+....8

FINVPF     IF   E           K Disk
FQprint    O    F  132        Printer OFLIND(*InOF)
 *-- procedure prototype
DWriteOut          PR
DProcessRcd        PR

DExtendedCost    s             7P 2
DFirstTime       s             1A   INZ(*On)

 *---Mainline Procedure ------------------------------
C                   CallP     ProcessRcd
C                   DoW       *IN90 = *OFF
C                   CallP     ProcessRcd
C                   EndDO
C                   Move      *on           *INLR
```

Figure 9.7

Module 9B Comprises Procedures WriteOut and ProcessRcd

continued

Figure 9.7
Continued

```
+....1....+....2....+....3....+....4....+....5....+....6....+....7....+....8
C                       Return

OQprint     E           Heads          02 02
O                       udate          y     10
O                                            80 'Computers are US'
O                                           122 'Page'
O                       Page           z    127
O           E           Detail         01
O                       inpn                 12
O                       inqoh          1     24
O                       inucst         1     36
O                       ExtendedCost   1     48
    * procedure section (Figure 9.8 follows this line.)
```

Figure 9.8
Procedure Section of
MOD9B with
Subroutines

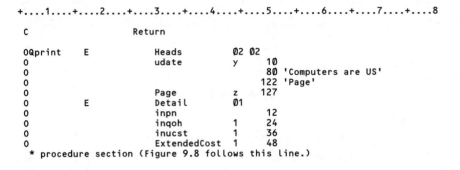

```
+....1....+....2....+....3....+....4....+....5....+....6....+....7....+....8
    *-- subprocedure ProcessRcd
PProcessRcd    B
    *-- procedure interface
DProcessRcd    PI

C                       ExSR      DoProcess
C                       Return
C           DoProcess   Begsr
C                       Read      INVPF                              90
C                       If        *In90 = *Off
C                       CallP     WriteOut
C                       EndIf
C                       EndSR

    * procedure ProcessRcd ends
PProcessRcd    E

    *-------------------------------------------------------------
    *-- subprocedure WriteOut
PWriteOut      B
    * -- procedure interface
DWriteOut      PI
c
C                       Exsr      TestFirstTime
C                       Exsr      DoProcess
C                       Exsr      TestOverFlow
C                       Exsr      WriteDetailLn
C                       Return
C
C           TestFirstTime Begsr
C                       If        FirstTime = *On
C                       Eval      FirstTime = *Off
C                       Except    Heads
C                       Endif
C                       Endsr

C           DoProcess   Begsr
C                       Eval                     ExtendedCost = inqoh*inUcst
C                       Endsr

C           TestOverFlow Begsr
C                       If        *InOF = *ON
C                       Eval      *InOF = *OFF
C                       Except    Heads
C                       EndIf
C                       Endsr

C           WriteDetailLn Begsr
```

continued

```
+....1....+....2....+....3....+....4....+....5....+....6....+....7....+....8
 C                    Except    Detail
 C                    Endsr

  * procedure WriteEnds
 PWriteOut            E
  *-----------------------------------------------------------------
```

Figure 9.8
Continued

Exercise 9.2 Adding a Procedure to a Module

Purpose

To develop a further understanding of procedures.

Instructions

1. Enter the RPGLE module MOD9B shown in Figures 9.7 and 9.8.
2. Create the module (CRTRPGMOD or option 15 in WRKMBRPDM).
3. Create the program PGM9B using the CRTPGM command.
4. Test the program.
5. Add a procedure to MOD9B and accumulate the total extended cost.
6. Add a procedure to print the total line.
7. Add O-specs for the total line.
8. Create the module.
9. Update program PGM9B using the UPDPGM command.
10. Test and debug the program.

Passing Parameters to Procedures

The procedures that have been introduced so far use global variables to send values between procedures. This method is only available to the procedures within a module. Parameters are usually passed to a procedure in a more formal manner (Figure 9.9). The prototyped call (CALLP) to the procedure ComputeTotal passes the memory location of the values of the fields ExtendedCost and TotalCost. The format of the CallP operation includes the procedure name followed by the parameter list, with parameters separated by colons and enclosed in parentheses. The order, type, and size of the parameters must match the order of the prototype (Figure 9.10) and the procedure interface (Figure 9.11). In effect, the list of parameters takes the place of the PARMs or PLIST used in calling a program or module.

Figure 9.9

Calling a Prototyped
Procedure (CALLP) with
Parameters

```
+....1....+....2....+....3....+....4....+....5....+....6....+....7....+....8

 *-- Procedure Call -------------------------------------
C                      CallP                   ComputeTotal(
C                                                 ExtendedCost : TotalCost)
```

The prototype for a procedure with parameters requires additional D-specs that show the structure of each parameter. These D-specs can use arbitrary names (as in Figure 9.10, where the D-specs are named with the letters *a* and *b*) or the D-specs can use actual field names. However, the actual fields passed to the procedure are determined by the CALLP operation, not by the prototype. The order of these field specifications must match the order used in the CALLP and the program interface (Figure 9.11).

Figure 9.10

Including the
ComputeTotal
Procedure Prototype

```
+....1....+....2....+....3....+....4....+....5....+....6....+....7....+....8

 *-- Procedure Prototypes -------------------------------------
DWriteOut         PR
DProcessRcd       PR

DComputeTotal     PR
D a                             7P 2
D b                             8P 2
```

The procedure interface for a procedure with parameters (Figure 9.11) requires D-specs that define the structure of each field. These fields must be in the same order as in the procedure prototype and the CallP operation. The fields can have local names within the procedure that are different from the names in the calling procedure. The first field in the CallP (Figure 9.9), ExtendedCost, has the local name EC in the procedure interface, and therefore in the procedure itself (Figure 9.11). The CALLP passes the memory locaton of the variable ExtendedCost to the procedure, which internally refers to the same memory location as EC. If the value of EC is changed in the procedure, the value in the shared memory location is also changed, and that new value is the value in the ExtendedCost field when the procedure ends. Thus, the TotalCost, field or TC in the procedure ComputeTotal, is given a new value in the Eval operation. That new value is placed in the shared location of TC and TotalCost, and the new value is available in the field TotalCost when processing returns to the calling program. In effect, the procedure interface takes the place of the *ENTRY PLIST used in a called program or module.

Figure 9.11

Procedure
ComputeTotal

```
+....1....+....2....+....3....+....4....+....5....+....6....+....7....+....8

 *---Subprocedure ComputeTotal-------------------------------------
PComputeTotal     B

 * -- procedure interface
DComputeTotal     PI
D EC                            7P 2
D TC                            8P 2

C                      Eval      TC = TC + EC

PComputeTotal     E
 *-------------------------------------------------------------
```

Exercise 9.3 Passing Parameters

Purpose

To develop further understanding of passing parameters to procedures.

Instructions

1. Copy RPGLE module MOD9B to MOD9C.
2. Modify your procedure to compute the extended total cost, the prototype for the procedure, and the call to the procedure to pass parameters as shown in Figures 9.9, 9.10, and 9.11.
3. Create module MOD9C and program PGM9C.
4. Test the program.

Using Procedures in Other Modules

To make a procedure available beyond the limits of the module in which it resides, the keyword EXPORT is added to the procedure-begin P-spec (Figure 9.12). Including the keyword EXPORT indicates that when the program or service program is created, it should map the procedure so that it is visible to calls from other modules.

Variable declarations can also include the EXPORT keyword. However, I don't recommend doing so because its use reduces the modularity and isolation of the code units (modules and procedures).

Any procedure in the program and/or the bound service programs can call a module with the keyword EXPORT. The prototype and call do not change if the procedure is in another bound module. Both the prototype in Figure 9.10 and the call in Figure 9.9 are exactly the same whether the procedure ComputeTotal is in the same module as the call or in another bound module.

```
+....1....+....2....+....3....+....4....+....5....+....6....+....7....+....8

  *---Subprocedure ComputeTotal-------------------------------
PComputeTotal     B                    Export

  * -- procedure interface
DComputeTotal     PI
D EC                            7P 2
D TC                            8P 2
  * procedure code would follow here (see Figure 9.13)
```

Figure 9.12
Procedure
ComputeTotal

A Module of Procedures

Procedures are a great tool for creating general purpose utilities such as the currency conversion program in Chapter 8. One module included in the program, or more likely in the service program, might be devoted exclusively to procedures for a specific category of problems such as computing dates. Such a module does not need a main-line procedure. The module is never called; rather the procedures within the module are called. Figure 9.13 shows module MOD9D2. The H-spec keyword NOMAIN declares that this module does not have a mainline procedure. This module can still have F-specs to provide linkages to files and D-specs to provide prototype, global field, and global data structure information. The procedures that are available to external call are identified with the keyword EXPORT on the procedure-begin P-spec.

Figure 9.13
Module9D2 with
NOMAIN Keyword

```
+....1....+....2....+....3....+....4....+....5....+....6....+....7....+....8

*************************************************************
*  Phil Levinson Jefferson College 12/29/99                *
*  Service Program SRV14D -- Module MOD9D2                  *
*  Procedure ComputeTotal -- Export, makes procedure        *
*                          visible to external modules.    *
*************************************************************
*- H-Specification declares that this module has no Mainline procedure
HNoMain

DComputeTotal     PR
D a                             7P 2
D b                             8P 2

 *---Subprocedure ComputeTotal-------------------------------
PComputeTotal     B                       Export

 * -- procedure interface
DComputeTotal     PI
D EC                            7P 2
D TC                            8P 2

C                 Eval     TC = TC + EC
PComputeTotal     E
 *----------------------------------------------------------
```

Exercise 9.4 Creating a Module without a Mainline

Purpose

To develop a NoMain service module.

Instructions

1. Copy RPGLE module MOD9C to MOD9D1.
2. Remove procedure ComputeTotal from the module.
3. Create module MOD9D1.
4. Create module MOD9D2 (Figure 9.13).
5. Create service program (CRTSRVPGM) SRV9D, which contains one module MOD9D2 with EXPORT value of *ALL.
6. Create program PGM9D, which contains module MOD9D1 and is bound to service program SRV9D.
7. Call PGM9D and check the results.

Procedures as Functions

You can create procedures that can be used as functions. Procedures that are used as functions return either the result of the activity or an indication of the success or failure of the task. Figure 9.14 shows a call to procedure CurrencyCvt, which returns the result.

```
+....1....+....2....+....3....+....4....+....5....+....6....+....7....+....8

 * procedure CurrencyCvt adjusts the value in inUcst
C                   Eval      inUcst = CurrencyCvt(FrmCntyCde :
C                                                  ToCntyCde  :
C                                                  inUcst)
```

Figure 9.14
Eval (Evaluation Operation) Calls Procedure CurrencyCvt, Passes it Three Values, and Receives the Results into Field inUcst

```
+....1....+....2....+....3....+....4....+....5....+....6....+....7....+....8

 *---Subprocedure CurrencyCvt --------------------------------
PCurrencyCvt      B                   Export

 * -- procedure interface
DCurrencyCvt      PI              6P 2
D FrmCntyCde                      3A
D ToCntyCde                       3A
D AmtIn                           6P 2

C                   Return    AmtIn * .800

PCurrencyCvt      E
```

Figure 9.15
Prototype of CurrencyCvt Procedure

Figure 9.15 shows the prototype of the CurrencyCvt procedure. Unlike earlier procedures, the CurrencyCvt procedure has a length, type, and number of decimals. These values represent the structure of the return value that is provided to the calling program.

The procedure shown in Figure 9.16 ends with a return operation. Factor 2 of the return operation defines the value that is returned when this statement is processed. Although this is a very simple procedure, much more complicated procedures can still return a value.

```
+....1....+....2....+....3....+....4....+....5....+....6....+....7....+....8

 *---Subprocedure CurrencyCvt --------------------------------
PCurrencyCvt      B                   Export

 * -- procedure interface
DCurrencyCvt      PI              6P 2
D FrmCntyCde                      3A
D ToCntyCde                       3A
D AmtIn                           6P 2

C                   Return    AmtIn * .800

PCurrencyCvt      E
```

Figure 9.16
Procedure CurrencyCvt Returns the Result of AmtIn * .800

Exercise 9.5 Returning a Value

Purpose
To develop a procedure that returns a value.

Instructions

1. Copy RPGLE module MOD9D1 to MOD9E1.
2. Add the procedure prototype and call to use the CurrencyCvt procedure (Figures 9.14 and 9.15).
3. Create module MOD9E1.
4. Copy RPGLE module MOD9D2 to MOD9E2.
5. Modify this module by adding the prototype and the procedure CurrencyCvt (Figures 9.15 and 9.16).
6. Create module MOD9D2 (Figure 9.13).
7. Create service program (CRTSRVPGM) SRV9E, which contains one module, MOD9E2, with EXPORT value of *ALL.
8. Create program PGM9E, which contains module MOD9E1 and is bound to service program SRV9E.
9. Call PGM9E and check the results.
10. Modify the CurrencyCvt procedure to get the conversion factor from file CURRENCY (Exercise 8.2 in Chapter 8). This requires an F-spec in MOD9E2 for the file Currency, which should include the keyword USROPN. In the procedure the file must be opened, the record found with a chain operation, the value computed, the file closed, and the value returned.
11. Update the service program SRV9E and the program PGM9E.
12. Call PGM9E and check the results.

Review

1. Describe the relationship of the prototype D-specs, the CallP, and the procedure interface.
2. Write a module that contains a single procedure named WRKDAYS. Make WRKDAYS globally available. The WRKDAYS procedure receives startdate and enddate (datetype), a field number of days (signed 5 0). The program opens a file named WRKDAY01. It chains into the file on the startdate field. Until the field in the file WRKDAYF is equal to or greater than the field enddate, add 1 to the number of days and read another record from the file. If the EOF is encountered before the enddate, then move *HIVAL to number of days.
3. Modify the WRKDAYS procedure in the previous exercise so that it can be used as a function. It should receive two parameters, startdate and enddate, and return the result, number of days.

continued

Review, *Continued*

4. Write a module that computes the average number of days until orders are shipped. The program

    - reads records from the file orders
    - passes the date fields orderdt and shipdt to the procedure WRKDAYS (#2 above)
    - adds the number of days to the total number of days and counts the order

5. Modify the program described in question 4 to perform the following at the end of orders file:

    - compute the average
    - print a line with the number of orders and the average number of work days

6. Modify the program described in question 5 to use the procedure WRKDAYS as a function (the procedure was created in question 3).

Section 3

Advanced Topics in RPG

Section 3 (Chapters 10 through 14) of *Essentials of Subfile Programming and Advanced Topics in RPG IV* covers selected advanced programming techniques and tools. This section provides in-depth information on accessing files, file and program data structures, error handling, journaling and commitment control, and methods of program-to-program communication.

Chapter 10 introduces advanced concepts in linking RPG programs and database files. It explores access paths and teaches you to use the record format level identifier, the OVRDBF (Override with Database File) command, the OPNQRYF (Open Query File) command, and file and record locks, as well as file security with RPG programs.

Chapter 11 presents an in-depth study of the file-information and program-status data structures that are used in normal processing and error handling. You will learn to use the file-information data structure to extract file status and other file-related data and the program-status data structure to extract program status and other program-related data.

Chapter 12 then explores error handling in greater depth. When you have completed Chapter 12, you will be able to use the *PSSR subroutine to capture general program errors and the INFSR keyword and LO indicators to capture file errors. You will also learn to use the file-information data structure for error information, send an error message, and develop an error log.

Chapter 13 examines journaling and commitment control, which provide both Control Language (CL) and RPG tools to improve data integrity. You will learn to create a journal and a journal receiver, start and stop the journaling of physical files, change a journal, and add commitment control at the program and transaction levels.

Finally, Chapter 14 explores program-to-program communication, then focuses on data queues, a powerful AS/400 tool for program-to-program communication.

As in previous sections, frequent exercises and summary reviews strengthen your knowledge of the concepts presented. After reading the Section 3 chapters and successfully completing the exercises in these advanced topic areas, you will be prepared for a solid launch into the world of AS/400 programming.

Chapter 10

The RPG Program and the Data File

Chapter Overview

In your previous studies, you have written RPG programs that access physical files, identifying the file by name in the F-spec and having the system search your library list for the specific file. You have also written RPG programs that access data in a physical file via a logical file. Chapter 10 expands your understanding of how programs and files are linked and of the Control Language (CL) tools that can redirect the link to create the equivalent of a logical file whenever needed. You will also be introduced to how RPG programs react to file and record locks and file security. Chapter 10 explores

- the importance of the record format level identifier
- the concept of access paths
- the concept and use of the OVRDBF (Override with Database File) command
- the concept and use of the OPNQRYF (Open Query File) command
- the impact and use of file and record locks with RPG programs
- the impact and use of file security with RPG programs

Programming Perspectives

A good programmer should to be able to look at a process or problem from a number of different perspectives, including those of the user, the programmer, the program, and the database. The range of perspectives that programmers can encompass will, in part, determine their effectiveness.

In an interactive system, users see certain screens and data, make certain entries, and then see new screens and data. One example of a design tool that helps programmers understand the *users' perspective* is storyboarding. Storyboarding uses sketches of screens and descriptions of what leads from one screen to the next to provide the users' view of what occurs. Understanding the users' perspective helps you design screens that are clear and easy to use.

The *programmer's perspective* includes multiple elements, such as sets of programs, database files, programming tools such as RPG and CL, and utilities. When that perspective is broad, it includes the whole "system" — the group of tools that meets enterprise-wide challenges. When it is focused, it might be concentrated on a single process, program, or data file.

In your programming courses, you have most likely been developing a *program perspective*. The program takes in data, manipulates data, and outputs data. The program may display screens and wait for a user response to determine its next action. From this perspective, you will look at the processes of a single program, a single subroutine, or a single statement and its effect on the data. You may think about one statement as various data flows by it, or about one data set as it flows through a section of code.

However, you can also view a computer process from the perspective of the *database* itself. The database management system (DBMS) is a set of programs that receives requests from a program, such as an RPG program, and attempts to fulfill the requests. The database perspective provides a distinctly different and useful view.

In this chapter, we will explore how the database and the operating system combine to meet your programs' data requests. You will be introduced to CL program commands that affect how the operating system and DBMS react to a program's data request. I will also introduce the **OPNQRYF** (Open Query File) command. Although a complete study of this powerful and complex tool is beyond the scope of this book, you should understand its effect on RPG programs. Elsewhere in your studies, you should gain a broader knowledge of the OPNQRYF command.

Connecting RPG Programs and Data Files

When an RPG program starts, it attempts to open all files listed in the F-specs except those that are under user control. The program demands access to these files by file name and access requirements, such as input, output, or update. OS/400 receives these requests and attempts to fill them. Unless otherwise directed, OS/400 searches the job's library list for each named file and uses the first type *FILE object with that name that it finds within this list. The search for each file occurs in the following sequence:

- the system section of the library list
- the product section of the library list
- the current library
- the user section of the library list

You can see your interactive job's library list with the DSPLIBL (Display Library List) command. The system and product portions of the library list are the same for every user and job.

The **CHGCURLIB** (Change Current Library) command changes your job's current library. The **EDTLIBL** (Edit Library List), **ADDLIBLE** (Add Library List Entry), and **DLTLIBLE** (Delete Library List Entry) commands change the job's user section of the library list. A permanent change to the user section of the library list requires a change to the job description that is being used by that job.

The **DSPOBJD** (Display Object Description) command provides a method to find the objects in your library list that have a specific name and a type of *FILE. To respond to this command, the system must make the same search through the library list for the object that it will make when the file is opened. If the system finds more than one file with the requested name, the DSPOBJD command reports that the screen will allow access to detailed information about the first file and the number of files found. When you press Enter, you will see the screen that provides access to information about the second, and so on. When your RPG program runs, it will access the first file it finds in the library list that has the requested name.

A batch job will start with the library list of the interactive job that submitted it — unless it has a particular library list specified in that job's job description.

Exercise 10.1 Learning to Use Files and Library Lists

Purpose

To experiment with library lists, particularly to see how a library list behaves when a program searches for a file.

Instructions

1. Display your library list with the DSPLIBL command and print it. Most CL display commands, including DSPLIBL, provide a neatly formatted printout that is available if you type the command name, press F4 (for prompt), and select *PRINT as the output type.

2. Copy one of your files to library QTEMP. (Every job, including your current interactive job, has a temporary library named QTEMP.)

3. Use the DSPOBJD command to find the file you copied. The command will probably find two copies of the object. (If it doesn't find two copies, use EDTLIBL to add the original library that the file was in as well as QTEMP to your job's library list.) Make note of the order of the two libraries that the file is in. Remember that your program will use the first occurrence of the file.

4. In seeking objects such as our experimental file, OS/400 will search your current library before it searches the libraries listed in your library list. This experiment on the effect of the position of libraries in the library list will not work if you have QTEMP or your library designated as the current library. To ensure that the current library doesn't impact this experiment, remove the category of current library from your library list by issuing the CL command CHGCURLIB *CRTDFT (Change Current Library) with the predefined value of *CRTDFT (Create Default), which removes the current library entry from your library list. (The value *CRTDFT lets OS/400 use the default library QGPL as the current library if necessary.) Now use EDTLIBL to put QTEMP at the "top" of your user list. Make sure that the original library of the file that you copied is below QTEMP. Use WRKOBJ to see the order of the two files.

5. Use EDTLIBL to move QTEMP below the other library. Now use WRKOBJ to look at the order.

Review

1. What control does the RPG program have over what files are used?
2. What control does the library list have over what files are used?
3. How can you test a program using data in a test library named TESTLIB, and, once it's operating correctly, have the same program use the data in another library named PRODLIB?

Record Format Level Identifier

The format information for externally defined files is critical to the correct operation of RPG programs. This information provides the record length, as well as the names, sizes, and types of the fields in the file. When RPG programs are compiled, the compiler incorporates structural information for files identified as externally defined. The RPG compiler obtains the necessary information on the file and fields directly from the data file. (Because the RPG compiler does not access the source member used to create the data file, the source member of the physical file does not need to exist on the system when the program is compiled.)

If an RPG program were allowed to open a file that has the wrong format, the input or output data to the file would almost certainly be wrong. Because this is critical, the system checks each file when it is opened.

Whenever a file is compiled, a record format level identifier is computed for each record format. The record format level identifier is a number that corresponds to the structure of a record format. It is computed using the record length and the sizes and types of all of the fields in the file. If you were to add a field, change a field, or change the record length, the system would generate a different record format level identifier.

When an RPG program is compiled, it saves the record format level identifiers of the record formats of externally defined files used in the program. As noted above, if a field is changed in length or type or is added to a record format, the identifier changes. A physical file has only one record format and, therefore, only one identifier. A multiformat logical file has one record format level identifier for each record format. For example, if the multiformat logical file defines a record format for the order header file, another record for the order detail file, and a third record for the order comments file, it will have three record format level identifiers, one for each record format.

A display file or a print file has an identifier for each record format. Typically, display files and print files define a number of record formats, and, like logical files, each record format will have a record format level identifier.

As the RPG program starts, it requests that the system open each file described in the F-specs except those that are user controlled. The system checks the record format level identifier of each record in each file with the identifiers that are stored with the program object. The program will abort if the values do not match. You can get a list of the files and the record format level identifiers that a program needs with the **DSPPGMREF** (Display Program References) command. You can obtain a file's record format level identifier (along with a wealth of other information) with the **DSPFD** (Display File Description) command.

By checking the level identifiers of a program against the level identifiers of the files to be used, you can determine whether a change to the file requires that the program be recompiled. This comparative information will also be useful in tracking down the cause if a program aborts due to a difference in the record format level identifier.

Exercise 10.2 Learning to Use Record Format Level Identifiers

Purpose
To examine the record format level identifier of physical files, logical files, and display files, and to compare these values to the identifiers an RPG program needs.

Instructions
1. Use the DSPPGMREF command on one of your subfile programs, directing the output to the printer (use F4 to fill in the command information). Note that even the display-file record identifiers are included and must match those from the display file. Circle or highlight the record format level identifiers for each record.
2. Use the DSPFD command on each of the files listed in the last step. Circle or highlight the record format level identifiers for each record.

Review
4. What happens if the system attempts to open a version of a file that has a different record structure from the one that was used when it was compiled?

Access Paths

An *access path* is a map that connects your program to the data. Physical data files can have two access paths — arrival sequence and keyed sequence. With arrival sequence access paths, READ operations access the records in the sequence of the relative record number (RRN). The CHAIN, SETLL, and SETGT operations use RRN values to position the file.

With keyed sequence access paths (i.e., if the physical file has been keyed), READ operations access data based on a map or index that the key defines. The access path used is based on the value in the access method field of the RPG program's F-specs. Logical files provide a single-access path. With a simple logical file, the access path connects the program to some or all of the records in a single physical file. The key values of the logical file define the map or index used to access these records.

Multiformat logical files provide a single-access path that splits to map or index records from all of the physical files included in the logical file.

Join-logical files provide a map of composite records comprising fields from different physical files. Join-logical files are input only.

In the case of a multirecord logical file, the key or index is based on the composite key value. In multirecord logical files in which the READ operation specifies the logical file name, the DBMS delivers the next record based on the composite key from any of the physical files. However, if the READ operation specifies a record format name, the database reads through the file until it finds the next record with that format name.

The SETGT and SETLL operations reposition the access path pointer based on the value in factor 1.

All of the access paths except join-logical files support input, update, delete, and write operations.

Alternative Access: OVRDBF (Override with Database File)

CL commands that precede the file OPEN operation in the job stream can alert the system to present an alternative access path when an RPG program demands file access. File opens generally occur immediately after the program is called, except in the case of user-controlled files. With user-controlled files, an OPEN operation must be performed to open the file, and the file can be closed with a **CLOSE** operation or when the last record indicator is set on at the program end. You can "trick" the system into attaching your program to a different physical or logical file from the one that it would normally choose. You also can force the program to use a specific member of a multimember file instead of using the data from all members. The command to make this happen is OVRDBF (Override with Database File).

With the OVRDBF command, you can direct the system to use a file of the same or a different name in the library list or from a specific library.

Figure 10.1 shows a short CL program. The OVRDBF command redirects file operations targeted for FILEA to FILEB in the library MYLIB3. Whenever the program RPGPGM1 does a file operation on FILEA, the operating system redirects the operation to FILEB in the library MYLIB3. The program will, of course, immediately abort if the record format level identifier of FILEB does not match the record format level identifier that was used when the program was compiled.

Figure 10.1

Override Database File
Command

```
PGM
    OVRDBF   FILEA    MYLIB3/FILEB    SHARE(*YES)
        Call RPGPGM1
ENDPGM
```

The SHARE(*YES) causes that one path to remain open throughout this job stream or until the override is deleted with **DLTOVR** (Delete Override), shown in the shaded area in Figure 10.2.

As long as the override is in effect, the same access path and pointer are used. This can sometimes create a problem if the CL program calls two RPG programs while the OVRDBF command is in effect (Figure 10.3A). If the first program processes FILEB to the end of the file (EOF), the second program opens the file with the record pointer at the same point that the first program left it, at the EOF. The **POSDBF** (Position Database File) command can be used to reposition the file pointer to the top or bottom of a file (Figure 10.3B).

```
PGM
    OVRDBF    FILEA    MYLIB3/FILEB    SHARE(*YES)
    Call RPGPGM1
    DLTOVR FILEA
ENDPGM
```

Figure 10.2
Delete Override
Command

```
PGM
    OVRDBF    FILEA    MYLIB3/FILEB    SHARE(*YES)
    Call RPGPGM1
    Call RPGPGM2
    DLTOVR FILEA
ENDPGM
```

Figure 10.3A
A CL Program Calling
Two Programs with a
File Override in Effect
for Both Programs

```
PGM
    OVRDBF    FILEA    MYLIB3/FILEB    SHARE(*YES)
    Call RPGPGM1
    POSDBF FILEA *TOF
    Call RPGPGM2
    DLTOVR FILEA
ENDPGM
```

Figure 10.3B
Position Database File
Command Used to
Reposition the Pointer
to FILEA Before It Is
Used by RPGPGM2

Exercise 10.3 Learning to Use the OVRDBF Command

Purpose

To experiment with the OVRDBF command.

Instructions

1. Select a program that you know works.
2. Copy one of the data files for this program to QTEMP, giving it the name TEMP1.
3. Use the command UPDDTA TEMP1 to modify the data so that you can verify that your program is using TEMP1 instead of the original file.
4. Use OVRDBF to redirect calls to the original file to QTEMP/TEMP1.
5. Call the program. Which file did it use?
6. Issue the command DSPJOB. Use option 15 to see what overrides are in effect for this job.
7. Use the DLTOVR command to eliminate the override of this file.
8. Repeat step 6 to make sure that the override has been removed.
9. Run your RPG program again. Which file did it use this time?

Review

5. Your RPG program PAYROLL opens the files TIMEKP and EMPLOY for input and PAY for output. A CL program contains the following commands:

```
OVRDBF TIMEKP        COMPANYA/TIME03        SHARE(*YES)
OVRDBF EMPLOY        COMPANYA/EMPLOY        SHARE(*YES)
OVRDBF PAY           COMPANYA/PAY03         SHARE(*YES)
CALL PAYROLL
DLTOVR TIMEKP
DLTOVR EMPLOY
DLTOVR PAY
```

What files does the program PAYROLL actually use?

The OPNQRYF (Open Query File) Command

This section provides a brief introduction to the OPNQRYF command and explores the impact of this command on RPG programs. More complete discussions of this command are available in the *Desktop Guide to CL Programming* (29th Street Press, 1994), by Bryan Meyers; the *Starter Kit for the AS/400, Second Edition* (29th Street Press, 1994), by Wayne Madden; *Database Design and Programming for DB2/400* (29th Street Press, 1996), by Paul Conte; *OPNQRYF by Example* (29th Street Press, 1999), by Mike Dawson and Mike Manto; and *Control Language Programming for the AS/400*, Second Edition (29th Street Press, 1997), by Bryan Meyers and Dan Riehl.

Using the OPNQRYF (Open Query File) command, a CL program can create the on-the-fly equivalent of logical files (Figure 10.5). Just as you can with a logical file, you can use the OPNQRYF command to provide an alternative key structure and/or select records by specific rules. The OPNQRYF command is particularly powerful because the key fields, selection rules, and other features can be altered programmatically. For example, if we have a receivables file with a due date, you can use OPNQRYF to select only those records with due date < today's date and status = OPEN and with the primary key field as Due Date and secondary key field as Amount Due. The RPG program to print the aged receivables report would be a simple reporting program because the OPNQRYF command has done most of the work.

Figure 10.5
CL Program with Open Query File

```
PGM
    DCL &VALUE1 *CHAR 100
    DCL &TODAY   *CHAR 6
    RTVJOBD DATE(&TODAY)
    CHGVAR &VALUE1 ('DUEDTE <= ' *CAT &TODAY)
    OVRDBF   RECP        SHARE(*YES)
    OPNQRYF RECP QRYSLT(&VALUE1) KEYFLD( DUEDTE, AMTDUE)
    CALL RPGPGM1
    DLTOVR RECP
ENDPGM
```

Exercise 10.4 Learning to Use the OPNQRYF Command

Purpose
To experiment with the OPNQRYF command.

Instructions
1. Create a short CL program that uses the commands that you used in Exercise 8.3. The CL program should include the OVRDBF command, the CALL (Call Program) command (to call an RPG program), and the DLTOVR command. Run the program.
2. Add an OPNQRYF command to select only specific records and rerun the program.

Review

6. Your RPG program PAYROLL opens the files TIMEKP and EMPLOY for input and PAY for output. A CL program contains the following commands.

```
OVRDBF TIMEKP  COMPANYA/TIME03       SHARE(*YES)
OVRDBF EMPLOY COMPANYA/EMPLOY        SHARE(*YES)
OVRDBF PAY        COMPANYA/PAY03     SHARE(*YES)
OPNQRYF TIMEKP QRYSLT('EMPST = "A" *AND EMPTY = "HOURLY"')
CALL PAYROLL
DLTOVR TIMEKP
DLTOVR EMPLOY
DLTOVR PAY
```

What records will be available to the program PAYROLL?

File and Record Locks

When the system links the RPG program and file together, it checks to see whether that file is locked by another job at a level that prevents the request from linking with the file. For example, the request will fail if another job has an exclusive lock on the file.

The commands used to detect and control locks can be found on the menu CMDLCK. To view this menu, type **GO CMDLCK.**

The CL command ALCOBJ (Allocate Object) is used to lock objects, including, of course, files. The object then remains locked until the job ends or the DLCOBJ (Deallocate Object) command is issued.

If the job has not previously locked the file, the file will be locked when the RPG program establishes its link to the file with access rights of Shared Read, for an input-capable file, or Shared Update, for an update- or add-capable file. If the RPG program locks the file, the lock ends when the RPG program turns on the last record indicator, *INLR.

The CL command WRKOBJLCK (Work with Object Locks) displays all of the jobs that currently lock a specific object (or file) and provides the option of working with any specific job. By working with specific jobs, you can determine the user, status, start time, and date of that job — and you can end that job (if you have job control authority). Ending a job will, of course, remove its locks from the object file of interest.

The DSPRCDLCK (Display Record Locks) CL command can be used to determine which job has a specific record locked. Remember, if an RPG program executes any of the READ operations (including READ, READP, READE, and READPE) or CHAINs into an update-capable file, it normally locks that record until an update or delete changes the record, the program reads or chains into another record, or the program closes the file.

The record can also be unlocked with an UNLOCK command or by adding an N (Not Locked) in the Operation Extender field (column 53 of the CHAIN or READ operation).

Exercise 10.5 Learning to Use Object Locks on Files

Purpose
To experiment with object locks on files.

Instructions

1. Sign on to two sessions on your AS/400 (this may require two terminals). Remember that each session is a separate job.
2. In session 1, issue the command to acquire an exclusive lock on a file in your library.
3. In session 2, issue the same command on the same file and note the error message.
4. Use the CL command WRKOBJLCK to determine which job has a lock on the file.
5. In session 1, deallocate the lock on the file.
6. In session 2, use the WRKOBJLCK to determine whether the object is unlocked.

Review

7. When does an RPG programmer need to be concerned about file locks?
8. When does an RPG programmer need to be concerned about record locks?
9. Attempting to lock all resources needed for a multiple-program job before beginning the first program is a common feature of many job-controlling CL programs. Why? What would happen if the first program ran successfully and the second one crashed because of a locked file?
10. Exclusive locks guarantee that no other jobs can lock records within a file. When the lock level is Exclusive Allow Read, other jobs can lock the file in shared read mode, which allows the file to be read but not updated. But when the lock level is Exclusive, no other job can access the file for any purpose. When would each lock level be important?

File Security

When the system links the file to the program, the system does not check to make certain that the user has authority to perform the update, add, and delete processes on that file. Instead, the system sends a file error condition to the program if it attempts to actually perform a process on a record for which it lacks authority. To determine the authorization necessary to access a file, use the **DSPOBJAUT** (Display Object Authority) command. To change the authorization required to access an object, use the **EDTOBJAUT** (Edit Object Authority) command.

The job that controls your program can only do things that the job's USER is authorized to do. The profile of the user may be tied to a group profile. (You can use the **DSPUSRPRF** (Display User Profile) and **CHGUSRPRF** (Change User Profile) commands to determine or change the group profile.) To determine a user's authority to an object, the security system uses the specific authority granted to that user. If no specific authority to the object is granted to the user, then the security system will use the authority granted to that user's group profile. If no specific authority to the object is granted to the user or the user's group profile, then the security system will use the authority granted to *PUBLIC (all other users).

To run a program, the user must have *USE authority to the program object. The description of the program object identifies whether that program will run with the user's authority or the program object owner's authority. If the owner authority is used, the security system will test the owner's authority or the owner's group authority to subsequent objects that the program needs. The owner's authority can be set so that it is used by the program at the time of compile or accessed via the CHGPGM command. Only the program object owner or security officer has the authority to change a program to use the owner's authority.

Exercise 10.6 Learning to Use File Security

Purpose

To experiment with file security.

Instructions

1. Use the EDTOBJAUT command to give a fellow student *ALL authority to your library and the program and files of one of your subfile projects that includes update, add, and delete options.
2. Let your fellow student experiment with your program, including doing adds, deletes, and updates.
3. Now remove your fellow student's authority to delete records from the file and have him or her attempt all the program options again.
4. Now remove your fellow student's authority to add records to the file and have him or her attempt all the program options again.
5. Now remove your fellow student's authority to change records in the file and repeat the test.
6. Now remove your fellow student's authority to read records in the file and repeat the test.
7. Now use the CHGPGM command to change the program to use the user profile *OWNER and test it again. Use the DSPOBJAUT to determine who is the owner of the program and the file.

Review

11. If a file has the following authorities

User	
MIS	*ALL
*PUBLIC	*EXCLUDE

name two ways that an individual could run a program that uses this file without changing the object authorities.

Chapter 11

File-Information and Program-Status Data Structures

Chapter Overview

Chapter 11 helps you understand and use the file-information data structure and the program-status data structure, including

- accessing the data in the file-information data structure
- extracting and using file-status and other file-related data
- accessing the data in the program-status data structure
- extracting and using program-status and other program-related data

---

What Is the File-Information Data Structure?

Every file that an RPG program accesses has a buffer of critical data that is "handed" to the RPG program. This file-information buffer is available for all file types, including physical files, logical files, display files, and printer files. The data in this file-information buffer (also called the Open Feedback Area or I/O Feedback Area) is updated whenever the RPG program accesses the file. RPG programs use this data internally in many ways. For example, when the RPG program executes a READ operation, the associated indicator is turned *ON or *OFF, based on the value in a specific location in the file-information buffer.

The data in the file-information buffer is also used when a formatted dump is requested. A formatted dump can be requested at the time of a runtime error or requested via a DUMP operation in the RPG program. The formatted dump contains file-status information, program-status information, and the values of all variables. It is valuable in debugging a program with a runtime error. (The formatted dump is discussed further in Chapter 12.)

With the additional information available in this buffer, you can take more control of your program. The following list offers just a few examples of how the information can be used:

- To determine the cursor position in a display file.
- To determine the current line number on a print file.
- To determine the number of the current page on a print file.
- To determine the record name when accessing a multiformat logical file.
- To determine the number of records in a file.
- To determine why an input or output process failed.

- To ensure that an update or delete is not attempted unless the program has a record from that file locked by a previous successful READ or CHAIN operation. (If such an update or delete is attempted, the program issues the following message: Program name issued update or delete in file name without prior READ or CHAIN.)

- To create an error-handling routine that can determine the cause of the error, report an error, and, in some cases, correct an error and continue, so the program can continue. (For further discussion of error handling, see Chapter 12.)

Figure 11.1 shows an example of the file-information buffer for the file INVPF. In Exercise 11.1, you will learn how to retrieve this data.

Figure 11.1

528-Byte File-Information Buffer for File INVPF After a READ Operation

```
Column    1         2         3         4         5         6         7         8
12345678901234567890123456789012345678901234567890123456789012345678901234567890
INVPF   1000000READ F*DETC   605     INVPFR                                0000000000
DBINVPF     A300C1_BOK                              INVPF
UUNs                                   0                      _
                         INVPFR
D511      0                                  0      $ §            ny   h   aa
              £E                             0

Column    4         5         5         5         5
BottomRow9          0         1         2         2
12345678901234567890123456789012345678901234567890123456789012345678
```

This file-information buffer contains 528 bytes of data. To use this information, you will need to 1) provide a link within your program to the file-information buffer and 2) structure this data into subfields of the correct types and lengths. It is obvious that without some division of the data shown in Figure 11.1 into subfields of the correct type, the buffer will be fairly useless. The result of the restructuring is the file-information data structure.

We provide a linkage to the file-information buffer in the File Specification (Figure 11.2), by using the keyword INFDS (INFormation Data Structure). This keyword links the file-information buffer for the file INVPF to the data structure named in parenthesis with the keyword, INVDS. If data from the information data structures of more than one file is required, then each file must have a separate data structure. In Figure 11.2 file INVPF uses the data structure INVDS and file INVDSP uses the data structure DSPDS.

Figure 11.2

F-Spec for File INVPF and Display File INVDSP Defining File Information Structures INFDS and DSPDS

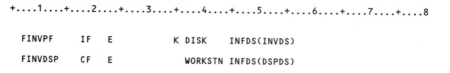

```
+....1....+....2....+....3....+....4....+....5....+....6....+....7....+....8

    FINVPF    IF   E           K DISK     INFDS(INVDS)

    FINVDSP   CF   E             WORKSTN INFDS(DSPDS)
```

Applying a Data Structure to the File-Information Buffer

The data structure defines the structure (comprising subfields) that is mapped over the file-information buffer. You define this structure in the D-specs. The subfields are defined in the following sections of this chapter.

Positions 1 through 8 of the buffer contain the "internal" file name that the RPG program uses to refer to the file. The internal file name is also the actual file name unless a CL program redirects the file selection with an OVRDBF (Override with Database File) command. (See Chapter 10 for more information on the OVRDBF command.) Later, we will find where the file-information buffer defines the actual file that is being used.

The keyword INFDS in the file specification shown in Figure 11.2 links the file-information buffer for the file INVPF with the data structure INVDS. Figure 11.3 shows the D-specs that define the data structure INVDS. This definition is what maps the subfield FILNM1 over the first 8 bytes of the file-information buffer. These 8 bytes contain the name — the internal file name just introduced — that the RPG program uses for the file throughout the program.

```
+....1....+....2....+....3....+....4....+....5....+....6....+....7....+....8


 DINVDS          DS
 D FILNM1              1       8
```

Figure 11.3

D-Specs that Map the Subfield FILNM1 over the First 8 Bytes of Data Structure INVDS

Figure 11.4 shows the result of the data structure definition. FILNM1 is mapped over the first 8 bytes of the buffer. The value currently in this location is INVPF; therefore, the value in FILNM1 is INVPF.

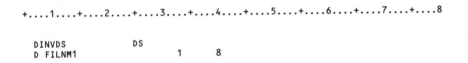

Figure 11.4

Data Structure Applied to the File Data Buffer of the File INVPF that Maps the Subfield FILNM1

Positions 11 through 15 of the file-information buffer contain the file status. In the example in Figure 11.1, the status value is 00000. Figure 11.5 lists many of the file status values and their descriptions. Status 00000, for example, indicates that no exception or error has occurred.

Figure 11.5

File Status Codes with Descriptions

Status	Description
00000	No exception/error occurred
00011	End of file
00012	No record found in a CHAIN operation
00013	A WRITE operation to a subfile resulted in subfile full; no record was added
00099	Error
01021	Attempt to write a record with a duplicate key
01211	Input or output operation attempted on a closed file
01215	Open operation attempted on file that was already open

01216	Error on implicit file open — file is not under user control (UC)
	    Open occurs automatically based on RPG cycle
	    File may not exist, may be locked, may exceed user authority

01217	Error on explicit file open — file is under user control (UC) Open attempt occurs at OPEN opcode
01218	Unable to allocate record (record is locked by another program)
01221	Update attempted without prior successful read
01299	Miscellaneous input/output error detected
01331	Wait-for-record time exceeded for READ or EXFMT operation

In Figure 11.6, you see the data structure INVDS with the subfield STAT1 mapped over the file status bytes.

Figure 11.6

D-Specs to Map Subfields over the Data Structure INVDS

```
+....1....+....2....+....3....+....4....+....5....+....6....+....7....+....8

    DINVDS           DS
    D FILNM1                   1      8
    D STAT1                   11     15 0
    D OPCD1                   16     21
    D FILRC1                  38     45
```

Figure 11.7 shows the buffer and the mapping of the subfields FILNM1, STAT1, OPCD1, and FILRC1, defined in Figure 11.6.

Figure 11.7

Data Structure Applied to File Data Buffer of the File INVPF

```
Column    1         2         3         4         5         6         7         8
12345678901234567890123456789012345678901234567890123456789012345678901234567890
INVPF   1000000READ F*DETC    605      INVPFR                          0000000000
|FILNM1| |STAT1|OPCD1|                 |-FILRC1|
```

Positions 16 through 21 contain the last operation executed on the file. In Figure 11.1, the value in positions 16 through 21 is READ F, which indicates that the last operation on this file was a read of the file. Figures 11.6 and 11.7 show this value mapped into the subfield OPCD1. The subfield that shows the last operation executed will contain values such as OPEN F, READ F, and WRITE F.

The internal record name is the name that our program will use for the record. It is occasionally different from the actual record name because internal record names must be unique. A program that accesses the same file via two or more access paths (e.g., via logical files) will have to rename the record for all but one access path using the keyword Rename with another name in parentheses in the F-spec.

Being able to determine the internal record name proves especially useful when a program reads from a multiformat logical file. Once the READ operation is accomplished, the program can use the value from the data structure to determine which record was accessed and therefore select the appropriate processing. The internal record name is in positions 38 through 45 of the file-information buffer; in Figures 11.6 and 11.7, this subfield is named FILRC1.

Notice that I have used 1 as the last digit of all of the file's data structure variables. In the data structure of the next file, I would use the same subfield names, but the names would end in the suffix 2. If there were third and fourth files, the subfields would end in 3 and 4, respectively.

The four parts of the data structure that we've mapped into our program are used so frequently that IBM has provided the keywords *FILE, *STATUS, *OPCODE, and *RECORD to represent the positions of these items in the file-information buffer. Figure 11.8 uses these keywords to define the equivalent structure (as was defined in Figure 11.6 with field positions).

```
+....1....+....2....+....3....+....4....+....5....+....6....+....7....+....8

DINVDS          DS
D FILNM1          *File
D STAT1           *STATUS
D OPCD1           *OPCODE
D FILRC1          *RECORD
```

Figure 11.8
D-Specs to Map Variables over the Data Structure INVDS Using Keywords

Exercise 11.1 Accessing the File-Information Data Structure

Purpose

To develop an understanding of data structures in general and the file-information data structure in particular. You will experiment with extracting the data from the file information and with mapping subfields for the file's internal name, status, operation code, and record name, using position and keyword definitions.

Instructions

1. Write the program PGM11A to READ each record in INVPF. It should map the 528 bytes of data in the file-information buffer into seven fields; each of the first six should be 80 characters long (the seventh should comprise the remaining 48 characters). Before the program performs the initial READ operation, as well as after each READ, it should print out the contents of the seven fields. Each time it prints, the output should look similar (but it won't be identical) to the data in Figure 11.1. We'll discuss the differences later in this chapter.

2. Create the program PGM11B to READ each record from the file INVPF. Before it performs a READ operation on the first record and after each READ, it should print out a line that contains the file name, status, operation code, and record name. Use the actual locations for these fields in the D-specs.

3. Create program PGM11C to READ each record from the file INVPF. Before it performs a READ operation on the first record and after each READ, it should print out a line that contains the file name, status, operation code, and record name. Use the keywords for these fields in the D-specs.

More on the File-Information Data Structure

In the previous section of this chapter, you learned about four subfields of the file-information data structure. There are, in fact, a large number of values that can be extracted from the file-information buffer. In Figure 11.9, a more complete list of available subfields is defined. As you see in the figure, some of the subfields apply exclusively to printer or workstation files.

To use any of these values, subfields are defined in the file-information data structure over the correct location. You can see the data type: C indicates character, N indicates numeric, and B indicates binary data. Most of the subfields should be defined as character type. The status field can be defined as either character or numeric. When you create the D-specs, binary fields must be identified with a B in the type field.

Type	From	To	Dec	Description	Values	Keyword	Type of File
C	1	8		Internal file name		*FILE	PF
C	9	9		Open	1=Open		PF
C	10	10		EOF	1=EOF		PF
N	11	15	0	Status		*STATUS	PF
C	16	21		Opcode		*OPCODE	PF
C	22	29		Routine — What part of RPG cycle was access in (meaningful for RPGII)			PF
C	30	37		Statement number of last access			PF
C	38	45		Internal record name		*RECORD	PF, DSPF
C	81	82		Type of open data path — DS=display file, DB=database file, SP=spool file			ALL
C	83	92		External file name — up to 10 characters long			PF
C	93	102		External file library name			PF
C	103	112		SPNAME — spool file name			Printer
C	113	122		SPLIBR — spool file library			Printer
B	123	124	0	SPNBR — spool number			Printer
B	125	126	0	Record length			PF
C	129	138		Member name of external file This can be really useful when processing multimember files.			PF
B	147	148	0	File type			
B	152	153	0	Number of lines per page (page length)			Printer Workstn
B	154	155	0	Number of columns			Printer Workstn
B	156	159	0	Number of records in file when it was open			PF
C	160	161		Type of database file access	KU=Keyed Unique, KF=Keyed FIFO, KL=Keyed LIFO, AR=Arrival sequence		PF
C	162	162		Duplicate keys allowed	D=Yes U = No (Unique)		PF
C	163	163		Is file a source physical file?	Y=Yes		PF
B	188	189	0	Overflow line			Printer
B	367	368	0	Current line number			Printer
B	370	371	0	Workstation cursor position	Z-ADDCURPOS CURSA 50 / CURSA DIV 256 ROWPOS / MVR COLPOS		Workstn

Figure 11.9
Subfield Definitions for the File-Information Data Structure

Figure 11.10 shows the data structure for the display file. In Figure 11.2, the file-information data structure DSPDS was linked to the file-information buffer of the display file INVDSP. (The cursor position subfield was introduced in Chapter 6.) Because the value is binary, the type is shown as binary.

Figure 11.10
F-Specs and I-Specs to
Map Vaiables over the
Display-File Data
Structure DSPDS

```
+....1....+....2....+....3....+....4....+....5....+....6....+....7....+....8

DDSPDS             DS
D FILNM2              *File
D STAT2               *STATUS
D OPCD2               *OPCODE
D FILRC2              *RECORD
D CurPos2                 370    371B 0
```

Exercise 11.2 Using Subfields in File-Information Data Structures

Purpose

To develop a further understanding of the file-information data structure, as well as of data structures in general. You will experiment with extracting the data from the file-information buffer and mapping subfields.

Instructions

1. Copy and modify PGM11C and call the new program PGM11D. Make the file opens user controlled. Add the open, end of file (EOF), record count, statement number, external file name, external file library name, external member name, file type, type of database file access, and duplicate key allowed to the file structure. Print out the values in these subfields before you open the file, after you open the file, after every read, and before and after you close the file. Modify the F-specs in one run to use the keyed access to INVPF and in another to use arrival sequence.

Exercise 11.3 Accessing a Printer File's File Information

Purpose

To develop a further understanding of the file-information data structure and data structures in general. You will experiment with extracting the data from the file-information buffer and mapping subfields for a printer file.

Instructions

1. Copy PGM11D to PGM11E. Modify PGM11E if necessary to use a printer file. Add a data structure to the printer file F-specs. You will want to capture the spool file name, the spool file library, the spool file number, the external file and external library names, as well as the number of lines per page, the number of columns per page, the overflow line number, and the current line number. Output this data to a second printer file. Print a detailed line every time a line is written to the first printer file.

Exercise 11.4 Accessing a Display File's File Information

Purpose

To develop a further understanding of the file-information data structure, as well as of data structures in general. You will experiment with extracting data from the file-information buffer and mapping subfields for a display file.

Instructions

1. Modify one of your subfile programs to print a line of the file-information data structure to a report after every EXFMT. Use a file-information data structure to capture information about the display file, including the file name, record name, status, operation code, statement number, external file name, external file library, file type, and workstation cursor position (row and column).

Review

3. Go through the list of data structure subfields and identify what value each would have during normal and abnormal operations of a program.

4. Go through the list of status codes and identify how each could be of value during normal operations (and whether each could occur then) and during abnormal operations.

5. The order form shown in Figure 11.11 should print detail lines until all the lines of the order have been printed. Detail lines should be printed only between lines 10 and 14 of the order form. If more lines are needed, then the program must print another page. The overflow line number is 17 — the line on which the totals print. Although the overflow indicator will come on when the line number is greater than 17, this is of little value when you print detail lines because you need to know whether the printer is positioned beyond line number 14. Your program should use the line number from the file-information data structure to determine whether the line number is greater than 14. If it is, the headings and the next detail will print on the following page. Write the F-spec, the data structure, and the C-specs to test for the need to print a new page.

Order Form	Order: 12345		Page 1

	TO:	Duke Press	FROM:	Jefferson College
		221 E. 29th Street		1000 Viking Road
		Loveland, CO 80538		Hillsboro, MO 63050

Quantity	Item	Unit Cost	Extended Price
50	Subfile Programming Essentials	60.00	3,000.00
100	RPG/400	60.00	6,000.00
		Total	**9,000.00**

Figure 11.11
Order Form

What Is the Program-Status Data Structure?

While an RPG program is running, OS/400 maintains 333 bytes of data about the job and the program. This data is available to the program through a special data structure called the program-status data structure. This data structure provides some useful data during normal program operations and a wealth of information if the program fails.

The complete data structure is shown in Figure 11.12. The program-status data structure is declared with an option value of S in column 18. Usually, programmers define only the subfields of the program-status data structure that apply to their specific needs. The program-status data structure contains a wealth of information that will be valuable if the program encounters an error. It also contains information that can be useful during normal operations. Job and user information can be used, for example, in sending messages and controlling spool files; program information can be printed on reports and shown on display screens.

Figure 11.12

Program-Status Data
Structure

```
+....1....+....2....+....3....+....4....+....5....+....6....+....7....+....8

*               SDS     declares this as the program data structure.

DProgramDS          SDS
D ProgramName            1      10
D ProgramStatus       *STATUS
D PreviousStatus        16      20   0
D LineNumber            21      28
D SubRoutine            29      36
D Parms                 37      39   0
D ErrorType             40      42
D ErrorCode             43      46
D InstructionNBR        47      50
D MessageWRK            51      80
D ProgramLibrary        81      90
D MessageText           91     170
D ExcMbr               171     174
D ErrorInFile          201     208
D ErrINF               209     243
D JobName              244     253
D User                 254     263
D JobNum               264     269   0
D JobDate              270     275   0
D SystemDate           276     281   0
D SystemTime           282     287   0
D PgmCreateDate        288     293   0
D PgmCreateTime        294     299   0
D CompileLevel         300     303
D SourceFile           304     313
D SourceLibrary        314     323
D SourceMember         324     333
```

Operational Data in the Program-Status Data Structure

Figure 11.13 defines the subfields of the program-status data structure that are most frequently used to gather data that is valuable during normal program operation.

Type of data	Typical Operational Uses
User ID	Can be used to route reports to the correct queue or printer.
	Can be used to send messages to the user.
	Can be used on displays, and so forth.
Job name	For a batch job, the job name is the line ID or terminal ID and is sometimes shown on displays and printed in reports. It can be used in sending break messages.
	Can be shown on displays or printed on reports.
	Can be used to send break messages.
System century date & time	Can be used on reports, displays, and messages. Century is in CC format and date in YYMMDD format for the time when the program started running.
Job date	In YYMMDD format, gives the date when the job became active.
Program name	Can be placed on reports and displays.
Program library	Can be placed on reports and displays.
Program date & time	Date in YYMMDD format.
	Time when program was compiled.
Program source	The library, file, and member names of the program source.
Compiler level	Revision of the compiler that was used to compile code.

Figure 11.13
Operational Data Available in the Program-Status Data Structure

Exercise 11.5 Getting Operational Data from the Program-Status Data Structure

Purpose

To access the program-status data structure to obtain operational data.

Instructions

1. Write the program PGM1105, which uses a program-status data structure and outputs all the available operational data with appropriate headings to a spool file.

Review

6. Why do many AS/400 systems include the user ID, display ID, and time and date on all the DSPF displays?
7. When would the program library, compile date and time, and source data be particularly important?

Error-Related Data in the Program-Status Data Structure

The program-status data structure contains all of the operational information plus the error-related data shown in Figure 11.14. If a program fails, this information is often invaluable in discovering the cause.

Figure 11.14
Error-Related Data in the Program-Status Data Structure

Type of Data	Typical Operational Uses
Status Code	Defines the type of error that occurred (see the program status code table, Figure 11.15)
Previous Status	Shows the status prior to the error
Source Statement	Identifies the source line number that caused the error
MSGID	Shows system error message ID
MSGTXT	Contains an error message if the status code is 09999
ERRFIL	Identifies the last file accessed
ERRINF	Shows the status of last file accessed + operation code + RPG

Figure 11.15 contains the values of the program-status codes, which are located in columns 11 through 15 of the program-status data structure. As was shown in Figure 11.12, the status can be defined using the keyword *STATUS.

Figure 11.15
Program Status Codes

Status	Description
00000	No exception/error
00001	Called program ended with LR indicator on
00101	Square root of a negative number attempted
00102	Divide by zero attempted
00121	Invalid array index
00122	OCCUR operation outside of data-structure occurrence range
00211	Program specified in CALL or FREE operations not found
00221	Program accessed a parameter that was not passed to it
00401	Data area specified in IN or OUT operation code not found
00411	Attributes of data area specified in IN or OUT operation do not match those of the actual data area
00412	Data area specified in the OUT operation was not locked
00413	Error occurred during IN or OUT operation to the data area
00414	Security violation while attempting to read a data area
00415	Security violation while attempting to write to a data area
00421	Error occurred during UNLCK operation to a data area
00431	Data area lock detected by another process while attempting to access a data area in this program
00432	Data area lock detected by another program in this job stream while attempting to process a data area in this program
00907	Decimal data error; packed or zoned field is blank or corrupt
09998	Internal failure in RPG
09999	Program exception in an operating system routine

Review

8. Describe at least three scenarios in which the error status and other program-status data structure error-related fields could be of use.

Chapter 12

Error Handling

Chapter Overview

Chapter 12 explores RPG tools and methods used to capture errors and determine their cause. A useful subroutine — *PSSR — will execute whenever errors occur. File errors can be captured by a subroutine that runs automatically if access to that specific file encounters an error. Errors in file input/output operations can be monitored with an indicator in the LO indicator column and used to branch to error-handling code. Further, the chapter will demonstrate how to use a single file-information structure for multiple files, how to send error messages, and how to keep an error log. Finally, you'll learn how to avoid the endless-error condition.

When you have completed Chapter 12, you will be able to

- describe when the *PSSR subroutine will run and use it to capture general program errors
- link error-handling subroutines to files using the INFSR keyword
- use the Input/Output operation error indicator to detect I/O errors
- use the file-information data structure with multiple files
- send an error message from an RPG program
- log errors to an error log
- avoid the endless-error condition in *PSSR

General Error-Handling Concepts

Without special error-handling code, your programs will eventually "crash." When a program crash occurs, the operators and/or users will be left with cryptic error messages. They may have to respond to these messages with a response such as G(o), I(gnore), R(etry), C(ancel), or D(ump). Unless you have given instructions on how to respond to a particular message for a specific job or program, they may choose any of the above — or call you at home at 2 a.m. for clarification.

The error might not have a serious impact, or it might wreak havoc with the data. But without special error-handling code, you may never even know that an error occurred — or you may not know about the error until it is too late to easily correct whatever problems it created.

Error-handling tools in RPG let your program detect an error and determine its cause. The program-status data structure will contain the type of error and the RPG statement number that was in error. If the error is a file-related error, the file-information data structure for that file will contain a wealth of information about the file and the error.

Error-handling subroutines in RPG programs can include code for dealing with frequently encountered errors. These error-handling subroutines can send messages to system operators or users informing them of the error, can log the error to an error log or execute an RPG-formatted DUMP, and can print every file's status and every variable's value at the time of the error.

Program Errors

There are two basic types of errors — syntax errors and runtime errors. Syntax errors, violations of the of RPG grammar rules, are detected by the compiler and must be corrected before a program object can be created. Therefore, a program cannot be run until all syntax errors have been corrected. Runtime errors occur when the program is running.

Runtime errors can be divided into two types: A program with logic errors will run but not produce the correct results. An example of a logic error is a program that adds pay rate to hours worked to compute gross pay. The program runs, but the results are wrong. Fatal runtime errors will, unless a program contains error-handling code, cause the program to terminate (see the sidebar "Avoidable Program Errors").

Any program can encounter an error. Errors can occur when the program is requested to perform in ways outside its design parameters or when it receives bad data. Errors can also occur when the program attempts to call or use an object that is not in the job's library list or when the program or user does not have the necessary authority to the object.

Using the *PSSR Subroutine
to Capture Program Errors

Fatal errors caused by file operations require specific file error-handling tools introduced in the next section of this chapter. All other fatal errors can be captured with a special subroutine called the *PSSR subroutine. This subroutine does not have to be called; it is called automatically whenever a non-file error occurs. The *PSSR subroutine can include all of your non-file error-handling code, or it can call other subroutines to handle specific types of errors. Many programmers also put their file error code in the *PSSR subroutine. If you want the program to terminate at the end of the *PSSR subroutine, it should end with the Last Record indicator on.

Figure 12.1 shows the simplest *PSSR subroutine. The H-spec is required with the DUMP operation code. The H-spec contains the keyword DEBUG(*Yes) which activates the debug capabilities needed for the DUMP operation. The H-spec can be preceded by comments, but it must be the first active specification in your program.

Figure 12.1

H-Spec with DEBUG(*Yes) and *PSSR Subroutine That Creates a Formatted RPG DUMP and Ends the Program

```
+....1....+....2....+....3....+....4....+....5....+....6....+....7....+....8

H    Debug(*YES)
 .
 :
 :
C    *PSSR          BEGSR
C                   DUMP
C                   Move      *ON           *INLR
C                   RETURN
C                   EndSR
```

Avoidable Program Errors

Three common runtime errors that can be avoided by adding preventive code follow:

• 00102 Divide by zero — Every divide operation involving a denominator that is a variable can end in a divide-by-zero situation. This common error can be avoided with the sample code in Figure 10.2.

```
*...1....+....2....+....3....+....4....+....5....+....6
* The never-divide-by-zero code --
C          DIV2      IFEQ *ZERO
C                    Z-ADD*LOVAL    RES1
C                    ELSE
C          DIV1      DIV  DIV2      RES1
C                    ENDIF
```

Figure 12.2
Code to Avoid the Divide-by-Zero Error

You can avoid the divide-by-zero error by performing the division only when the denominator is not equal to zero.

• 00101 Square root of a negative number — In business processing, we don't get much call for the SQRT (Square Root) operation code. But you can avoid the square-root-of-a-negative-number error by using code similar to the code used to avoid the divide-by-zero problem. In this case, the SQRT operation would not be used if the variable contains a negative number.

• 00907 Decimal data error — A decimal data error occurs when a decimal field is blank or corrupt. This error crops up most often when you move data to decimal fields from other decimal or character fields. This type of error can be eliminated by the use of the TESTN operation code to confirm that the character string contains a true numeric before it is moved to a numeric field. Remember: you should always use the Z-ADD operation to move values from one numeric field to another.

When a non-file error occurs, the program will terminate after it creates a program dump. The termination of this program will not appear to be abnormal. Users and the calling program may not realize that the program "abended" (ended abnormally).

Exercise 12.1 Error Handling Using *PSSR and the DUMP Operations

Purpose

To demonstrate file error handling using the *PSSR subroutine and the DUMP operation.

Instructions

Create program PGM12A, which initiates a dump when an error occurs.

1. Create the program PGM12A, which contains the DUMP - *PSSR subroutine as shown in Figure 12.1.

2. The program should contain the following C-specs, which will create a runtime error by attempting to divide by zero.

```
*. 1 ...+... 2 ...+... 3 ...+... 4 ...+... 5 ...+... 6 ...+... 7


C                   z-add     *zero          Field1            2 0
C          10        Div       Field1         Result            2 0
```

> **Note:** This program error occurs because FDL1 is equal to zero when it is used as a denominator for division. The sidebar "Avoidable Program Errors" presents the code to avoid divide-by-zero errors.

Exercise 12.2 Using the *PSSR Subroutine to Print Program Information to a Spool File

Purpose

To develop a program that demonstrates error handling using the *PSSR subroutine to extract error status code, program name, job, and user from the program-status data structure and print it to a spool file.

Instructions

Create program PGM12B, which will print the line number of the error, the program name, the program status code, the job name, and the user ID when an error occurs.

1. Copy PGM12A to PGM12B.

2. Add the program-status data structure from Chapter 11, including error-related fields.

3. Add O-specs or a print file to print the fields from the program-status data structure.

4. Remove the H-Spec and the DUMP.

5. Add output operations to the *PSSR subroutine to print the fields of the program-status data structure.

Exercise 12.2, *Continued*

6. Run the program. What is the program-status code? Is it consistent with what you would expect according to the list of program-status codes shown in Figure 11.15?

7. Copy PGM12B to PGM12C. Replace the operations that cause the program to divide by zero with the operations that cause it to take the square root of a negative number. Run the program. What is the program-status code? Is it consistent with what you would expect according to the list of program-status codes shown in Figure 11.15?

8. Copy PGM12B to PGM12D. Replace the operations that cause the program to divide by zero with code that will cause it to call a nonexistent program. Run the program. What is the program-status code? Is it consistent with what you would expect according to the list of program-status codes shown in Figure 11.15?

Review

1. What advantages are there to using the DUMP code in the *PSSR subroutine?
2. What advantages are there to using formatted output in the *PSSR subroutine?
3. What problems do you anticipate if the program ends without an error message?

File Errors

File errors include

- an attempt to update, delete, or add a record to a file without authority
- an attempt to access a record locked by another job
- an attempt to delete or update a record when the program does not have a current record lock on that file

File errors can be trapped in two ways. First, all file errors for a specific file can be trapped by assigning a subroutine to be used if any access to that file encounters an error.

Using the INFSR Keyword

The INFSR keyword is coded by adding another continuation F-spec to the file with the keyword INFSR and the name of the subroutine to be run in case of error. In Figure 12.3, the subroutine FILSR1 will be run if a file error is encountered when the program accesses the file INVPF. The file-information data structure (FILDS1) will contain information about that file and its status at the time of the error. The file-information data structure was defined in Chapter 11 and contains

- the internal file name
- the actual file, library, and member accessed; the file status; the last operation performed

- the RPG statement number of the last operation that accessed the file
- the record name of the last record accessed

Figure 12.3

File INVPF Opened with Informational Data Structure FILDS1 and Error Routine FILSR1

```
+....1....+....2....+....3....+....4....+....5....+....6....+....7....+....8

 FINVPF     UF   E          K Disk    INFDS(FILDS1) INFSR(FILSR1)
```

Using the Input/Output Operation Error Indicator

File errors can be trapped as specific file operations occur. This method is coded by putting an indicator in the LO position of the specific file operation for which you want to catch errors (Figure 12.4). (This indicator position was the LO/Minus/Less Than/Error indicator position on old RPG II coding sheets.)

Figure 12.4

Using an Indicator in the LO Position to Trap an Operational File Error (Program Code Tn Tests the Value of the Indicator and Executes the BadReadINVPF Subroutine)

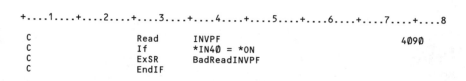

```
+....1....+....2....+....3....+....4....+....5....+....6....+....7....+....8
 C                   Read      INVPF                                  4090
 C                   If        *IN40 = *ON
 C                   ExSR      BadReadINVPF
 C                   EndIF
```

If a file operation with an indicator identified in the LO position fails, the indicator is turned on and no other response to the error occurs. In this case, the program does not abort, the *PSSR (if it exists) is not automatically called, and the INFSR subroutine for the file (if it exists) is not automatically called. Code should be added to the program to test the indicator and process the error as shown in Figure 12.4.

Exercise 12.3 Using the Keyword INFSR and a Subroutine to Capture File Input/Output Errors

Purpose
To demonstrate file error-handling techniques.

Instructions
Create program PGM12E, which will open a file, read a record from it, and issue an update of the record. If the user does not have the authority to update the file, the program prints error information from the file-information data structure.

1. Create a simple program, PGM12E, that opens the file INVPF for update, reads a record from the file, and then issues an update on it.
2. Run your program. It should run without error.
3. Use the EDTOBJAUT command to remove your update authority to the file.

continued

Exercise 12.3, *Continued*

4. Run your program again and dump the results.
5. Add a file description continuation line to associate the subroutine FILSR with the file. This subroutine should run only if an error occurs during file access. The FILSR subroutine should contain the code to display the value 'Err Bad Updt'.

```
+....1....+....2....+....3....+....4....+....5....+....6....+....7....+....8

C        FiLSR         Begsr
C        'Err Bad Updt'DSPLY
C                      EndSR
```

6. Run the program again; it should display the error message whenever an error occurs.
7. Add the file-information data structure from Chapter 11. When an error occurs, print out the relevant status data.
8. Add the program-status data structure from Chapter 11. When an error occurs, print out the relevant status data.

Exercise 12.4 Using the LO Indicator to Detect File Errors

Purpose
To demonstrate file error handling using the LO indicator to detect file access errors.

Instructions
Create program PGM12F, which will detect file operation errors via the LO indicator.

1. Copy PGM12E to PGM12F.
2. Add an indicator in the LO indicator field of the UPDAT operation.
3. Run the program. What happened? Why?
4. After the UPDAT operation, add code to test the value of the new indicator and if it is on, call the subroutine BADUPD. BADUPD should print the file-information and program-status data structures.
5. Change the object authority on the file to what it was originally.

Review

4. If you were to route all errors to the *PSSR subroutine instead of to individual subroutines, how could you determine whether the error was file-based as well as which file was in error?

5. What would happen if you coded an indicator in the LO field of every I/O operation but did not check the indicator status?

Reusing the File-Information Data Structure

If you code the file-information data structure with subfields for every file, you discover the following:

- Your code is really long.
- The data structure subfields for each file must have unique names, which makes subsequent reporting cumbersome because it would require a separate set of O-specs for each file-information data structure.

Figure 12.5 demonstrates how error handling with multiple files can be simplified by using a general file-information data structure, and, at the time of error, moving the specific data structure of the file in error to the general data structure. The compiler will only recognize the keywords *FILE, *STATUS, *OPCODE, and *RECORD for a data structure that is associated with a file, and, because the data structure FILEDS is not associated with any specific file, all field definitions must be coded with the field's positional values.

In the *PSSR subroutine shown in Figure 12.5, the file that caused the error is determined from the program-status data structure subfield ErrorInFile. The data structure of the file in error is moved to the general file data structure FILEDS; then the subfields within that structure can be used to report the error.

The printer file for error reporting — ERRRPG — is identified in the F-specs as user controlled because it is needed only when an error occurs. Before writing to the error printer file in the *PSSR subroutine, the printer file must be opened with the OPEN operation code. Making the error-reporting printer file user controlled will save the program the overhead of opening this printer file except on the occasions when it is needed.

Figure 12.5

Using a General File Data Structure and a Printer File (ERRRPG) Designed to Handle the Reporting of All Errors from All Files

```
+....1....+....2....+....3....+....4....+....5....+....6....+....7....+....8
   *- File invpf datastructure is FILED1 and error subroutine *PSSR.
 FINVPF    UF   E          K Disk    Infds(FILED1) Infsr(*PSSR)

   *-- Printer file for error reporting, is only open if needed.
 FErrRPG   O    E                    Printer OFLIND(*IN39) USROPN

   *-- File specific data structure contains no fields, but is long
   *    enough to accomodate the part of the data structure of interest.
 DFileD1          DS            21

   *-- General data structure contains field definitions for the file
   *    data structure but, since it is not associated with a file, cannot
```

continued

Figure 12.5
Continued

```
+....1....+....2....+....3....+....4....+....5....+....6....+....7....+....8
     *   use symbolic names *FILE, *STATUS, *OPCODE, *RECORD.
DFileDS          DS
D FILNM1                   1      8
D STAT1                   11     15  0
D OPCD1                   16     21

     * The program data structure would include all the fields of specific
     *-- interest, but especially the ErrorInFile field which identifies
     *   the file name of the file in error.
DProgramDS       SDS
D ProgramName              1     10
D ProgramStatus     *STATUS
D PreviousStatus          16     20  0
D LineNumber              21     28
D ErrorType               40     42
D ErrorCode               43     46
D InstructionNBR          47     50
D ErrorInFile            201    208
C                 Read      INVPF                                        90
C                 Write     INVPFR
C                 Eval      *INLR = *ON
C                 Return

C       *PSSR     BegSR
     *-- Determine which file is in error and move that file's data
     *   structure to the general file data structure.
C       ErrorInFile   IFEQ    'INVPF'
C                 Move      FILED1         FILEDS
C                 EndIF
C                 OPEN      ErrRPG
C                 Write     ErrHds
C                 Write     ErrDtl
C                 Close     ErrRPG
C                 Eval      *INLR = *ON
C                 Return
C                 EndSR
```

Exercise 12.5 Reusing the File-Information Data Structure

Purpose

To demonstrate file error handling that incorporates the code to reuse the file-information data structure.

Instructions

Create program PGM12G, which will detect file operation errors through the use of the LO indicator and utilizes the concept of a reusable file-information data structure.

1. Copy PGM12F to PGM12G. Modify your code to change the error handling to use the general file-information data structure.

2. Open and use the external printer file ERRRPG. This printer file should create the report shown in Figure 12.6

continued

Exercise 12.5, *Continued*

Figure 12.6
Output from ERRRPG Printer
File (Lowercase/Shaded
Denotes Where Values Are
To Be Provided from the
Program-Status or File-
Information Data Structure)

```
RPG ERROR REPORT                                        DATE: mm/dd/yy
PROGRAM: pgmlib/pgmname                                 TIME: 00:00:00

JOB: jobname  USER: user              JOBNUM: jobnum
JOBDATE: mm/dd/yy

PROGRAM HISTORY: SOURCE: pgmsrclib / pgmscrfil ( pgmsrcmbr )
      COMPILE: pgmdat pgmtim cmplvl


PROGRAM ENDED WITH STATUS program status
AT STATEMENT # 031001 error type/code
MESSAGE: msgwrk
         msgtxt

FILE: File name from program data structure WAS IN ERROR.
FILE STATUS: 000000   OPERATION: opcode
```

Review

6. What is the advantage of using a printer file over O-specs for error reporting? How many programs could use this printer file?
7. What is the advantage of using a single data structure when you develop the report?

Sending an Error Message

Sometimes you'll need to send the operator or user a message that clearly defines the problem and resolution. Perhaps the easiest way to manage this is to write a short CL program that sends an inquiry message to the specified message queue.

Figure 12.7
CL Program to Send a
Message

```
+....1....+....2....+....3....+....4....+....5....+....6....+....7....+....8

/*******************************************************/
/* PHIL LEVINSON  1/15/99  ADVANCED RPG                */
/* PROGRAM SMSG                                        */
/*                                                     */
/* This program sends a break message to the display   */
/* or a message to the user or messageQ.               */
/*******************************************************/
PGM Parm(&WRKSTNQ &USER &MSGQ &MESSAGE)

DCL &USER       *CHAR   10
DCL &MSGQ       *CHAR   10
DCL &WRKSTNQ    *CHAR   10
DCL &MESSAGE    *CHAR   180

If (&WRKSTNQ > ' ') THEN (SNDBRKMSG MSG(&MESSAGE) TOMSGQ(&WRKSTNQ)
If (&USER    > ' ') THEN (SNDUSRMSG MSG(&MESSAGE) TOUSR(&USER)
If (&MSGQ    > ' ') THEN (SNDUSRMSG MSG(&MESSAGE) TOUSR(&MSGQ)

ENDPGM
```

The CL program shown in Figure 12.7 will

- send a break message to the specified workstation
- send a message to the specified user
- send a message to the specified message queue

It will send the message to each of these locations only if the appropriate variable — &WRKSTNQ , &USER, or &msgQ , respectively — contains a value. The message destinations are passed to the program when it is called in the first three parameters.

The message to be sent is passed to the program as the fourth parameter.

The RPG program that sends a message would compose the message from data collected from the program-status data structure and/or the file-information data structure (or it could use this data to access a record in a data file that contains a list of errors and related message text). The program would call the CL program shown in Figure 12.7 and pass it the necessary parameters, including at least one destination for the message and the message text. If the RPG program passes a workstation message queue to the CL program in Figure 12.7, the CL program sends a break message to that queue. A break message appears immediately on the display station to which it is sent, temporarily interrupting other processes on that screen. Break messages can be sent only to display stations' message queues, not to other message queues.

Exercise 12.6 Sending an Error Message

Purpose
To develop a program that demonstrates file error handling, including sending an error message.

Instructions
Create program PGM12H, which will send the user an error message.

1. Copy PGM12G to PGM12H.
2. Create the CL program in Figure 12.7.
3. Add the necessary code to your error-handling subroutine to call the CL program that sends a message to your display with the program name and a message to check the spool file for further data if the program has failed. The call to the CL program should pass four variables with widths of 10, 10, 10, and 180. The value of the first variable should be the job name as indicated in the program-status data structure. The second and third variables should be blank. The fourth should contain the desired message.

Review

8. If you are creating a spool file that reports the problem, why is it necessary to send a message?

Logging Errors to a Data File

An excellent way to keep a record of errors is to create an error log, which is a database file that is written to every time that any program encounters an error. The error log contains fields for the program name, job name, time, date, program status code, statement in error, file name (if one was in error), last operation on the file and file status code, and job user. The error log should be checked periodically or when errors are suspected.

Additional fields in the error log can be used to manage problem resolution. These fields would identify to whom the problem was assigned, when it was assigned, when it was resolved, and how it was resolved. With this additional information, the error log becomes a resource that records past problems and their solutions.

Exercise 12.7 Logging Errors to a Data File

Purpose

To demonstrate file error handling that incorporates logging errors to a data file.

Instructions

Create program PGM12I, which will log errors to a data file.

1. Copy PGM12H to PGM12I.
2. Create a data file named ERRFILE with the correct structure to hold all the field data reported on the error report. The field names and structures should be the names you use in your data structures.
3. Add the F-specs to make ERRFILE user controlled.
4. In the error-handling subroutine add code to
   - open ERRFILE
   - write a record to the file
   - close the file

Using *PSSR to Avoid the Endless-Error Condition

When a program that contains the *PSSR subroutine detects an error, the *PSSR subroutine is executed. If an error is detected while the *PSSR subroutine is executing, the subroutine is called again. If the error is encountered again, the subroutine is called again. You can see that an error in the error-handling subroutine can lead to an endless series of calls to it.

In the *PSSR subroutine as shown in Figure 12.8, the variable ERRTST is *OFF when the program begins. The first time that the error subroutine *PSSR is reached, ERRTST is still off. Therefore, the test is true — ERRTST is changed to *ON, and the operational code is processed. If an error occurs in the error-handling code, *PSSR is called a second time; because ERRTST is now on, the operational code is skipped, the last record indicator is turned on, and processing returns to the parent program.

```
+....1....+....2....+....3....+....4....+....5....+....6....+....7....+....8

C        *PSSR         BegSR

C                      If        ErrTST <> *ON
C                      Eval      ErrTST = *ON

*     The operational error handling code is placed here.
*     This code can be run only once. If an error occurs in
*     this code, *PSSR is called again, but since ErrTST is now
*     ON, the If test prevents this code from being run a second time.

C                      EndIf
C                      Eval      *INLR = *ON
C                      Return
C                      EndSR
```

Figure 12.8
Error-Handling Code
That Avoids the
Endless Loop Error

Exercise 12.8 Avoiding the Endless-Error Condition

Purpose
To demonstrate file error handling that incorporates the code to avoid the endless-error condition.

Instructions
Create program PGM12J, which incorporates the code to avoid the endless-error condition.

1. Copy PGM12B to PGM12J.

continued

Exercise 12.8, *Continued*

> **Note:** The following experiment will lock up your terminal. To end the request, press ALT-SysRq. A line should appear at the bottom of your display. Press 2 to "End the Previous Request."

2. Modify your *PSSR subroutine to include a divide-by-zero situation after the call to the CL program.

3. Run your program. Your program will keep sending you messages and printing reports until the cows come home. Abort the job using the system request key.

4. Add code to avoid the endless-error condition and retest.

Review

10. Why is it necessary to include code to avoid the endless-error condition in your *PSSR subroutine?

Chapter 13

Journaling and Commitment Control

Chapter Overview

When you have completed Chapter 13's exploration of journaling and commitment control —
two tools that help you protect the integrity of your database and recover from abnormal
system termination — you will be able to

- describe journaling and understand its purposes
- describe commitment control and understand its purposes
- create a journal receiver and a journal
- start and stop the journaling of physical files
- change a journal
- add commitment control at the program level
- add commitment control at the transaction level

Introduction to Journaling and Commitment Control

This chapter introduces two tools that are used to maintain the integrity of the data
in data files — that is, to ensure that stored data is valid.

Programs that update, add, or delete records from data files can corrupt the
records if

- bad data is supplied to the program
- operations errors cause the program to run at the wrong time or in the wrong way
- programming errors cause the program to execute improper changes
- the program ends without completing all of the required processes

The first tool, **journaling**, can record all changes to a file or files. The database
of the AS/400 contains built-in journaling tools, including tools to

- record all changes to the data file or files
- back out selected changes from the data file or files
- apply selected changes to an earlier version of the data file

Journaling is a database function, not a programming function. It requires no
special techniques when you program the application. Journaling is introduced in
this book because it is the basis for the second tool, **commitment control**, which is a
programming tool.

Commitment control is a programming tool that holds a series of updates, deletes, and adds until the program issues a command related to these changes. The set of changes is held until

- the program issues a command to commit, which causes the current set of changes to become permanent
- the program issues a command to roll back, which causes the current set of changes to be removed from the database
- the program ends or aborts without issuing a commit, which causes the current set of changes to be removed from the database

Commitment control can protect a set of database files from an incomplete update, add, or delete. Exercise 13.1 demonstrates what can happen to a set of data files if an update program without commitment control ends abnormally.

Exercise 13.1 The Inherent Risks of Update Programs

Purpose
To develop an appreciation for the risks inherent in updating data and demonstrate the need for commitment control.

Instructions
You will analyze how data changes under different scenarios that use the logic in the pseudocode shown in Figure 13.1A and the data files shown in Figure 13.1B for a program to post shipments to inventory and to order detail.

The program posts shipments to our customers. It will update the inventory file by subtracting the quantity shipped and update the order detail by adding date and quantity shipped.

Figure 13.1A
Pseudocode for a Program to Post Shipments to Inventory and to Order Detail

Read the first record from the shipping file (step 1)
Do until end of file (EOF)
   If shipping record has not been posted (Posted = 'N') do
      Find the correct inventory record based on product number (step 2)
      Subtract the quantity shipped from the quantity on hand and update the inventory record (step 3)
      Find the order detail (line) record (step 4)
      Update the customer's order record to reflect the shipment date and shipment quantity (step 5)
      Create a record in the billing file for the billing program (step 6)
      Mark the shipping record as posted (step 7)
   End if
Read next record from the shipping file (step 8)
End do

continued

Exercise 13.1, *Continued*

Shipping File

Date	Ord No	Ord Ln	ProdNo	Quantity	Posted
971207	100140	3	A154	15	N
971207	100140	4	A155	7	Y
971207	100140	5	A156	11	N
971207	100140	6	A157	15	N

Figure 13.1B

The Shipping, Inventory, Order Line, and Billing Files

Inventory File

Prod No	QOnH
A153	250
A154	17
A155	3
A156	15
A157	19
A158	150
A159	300

Order Line File

Ord No	Ord Line	Prod No	QOrd	QShip	QNet
100140	1	B1201	430	215	215
100140	2	C1501	3	3	0
100140	3	A154	15	0	15
100140	4	A155	13	6	7
100140	5	A156	21	10	11
100140	6	A157	15	0	15
100141	1	A155	17	0	17

Billing File

OrderN	LineN	Date	Quantity

Case 1 — Program runs successfully. Create a copy of these files as they should appear after the Post Shipments program finishes, using the shipping records above. Remember: Post only records with an N in the posted flag.

Case 2 — Program ends before completion.

1. Beginning with the original data, the operator makes an error and stops the program when it is processing the third shipping record (order 100140, line 5). Just before it is stopped, the program executes pseudocode step 6 for this record. Show the files as they would look at this point.

2. When you realize what has happened, you restart the program (step 1). Show how the files look after processing completes.

If you do this exercise correctly, the third record has been posted twice. This transaction was partially processed in the first run (Case 2, step 1) and posted a second time in the second run (Case 2, step 2).

This kind of error is unacceptable. I might be happy about this error if it were made when deposits were being posted to my checking account but not when withdrawals were being posted. Bank examiners take a dim view of any error.

A program can abort for a number of different reasons, including system problems, security problems, file contention problems, operator errors (as in our example), data errors, and programmer errors. The system may also halt (this is extremely unlikely with an AS/400, but it can happen).

When a program is changing one or more files and failure will make recovery difficult, special controls have to be put in place. The program's design can be altered to remove some of the possible problems. For each transaction, for example, we could lock all the necessary records before the first file change is done. Although this ensures that we have access to all the records that we need for the transaction before we begin it, it increases the length of time that the records are locked — potentially causing problems for other programs.

We can add a *PSSR subroutine (see Chapter 10) to avoid the program crashing. However, its subsequent recovery or soft ending would leave the transaction partially posted. The *PSSR subroutine can detect a great deal about the program at the time of error and could be designed to back out the steps that were completed before the error, but this would be a difficult program to develop. You can imagine the difficulties if the records that you changed and need to revert to their former status were changed in the interim or deleted by another process. (Interim changes are possible because as your program changes a record, it is unlocked and therefore available to other processes.)

There is also potential for logical errors. Inventory should never be negative, the quantity shipped should not exceed the quantity ordered, and so forth. Each of these rules would require more checks before beginning the processing.

Commitment control keeps all the steps of the transaction in limbo — a state of near completion with all the updated records locked — until the transaction is either committed or rolled back. If the program aborts, the transaction is rolled back. If a rollback occurs, all the changes in the "protected" files revert to their status before the transaction and are then unlocked.

The whole process takes only a few lines of code in RPG and a few lines in CL. However, commitment control considerably increases the work that the system has to do, and this causes the program to run slower. The additional load may also slow down other processes on the system. Therefore, commitment control should be used only when

- files are being changed
- recovery will be difficult or impossible if the process fails
- the quality of the data is critical

About half the work load that commitment control puts on the system is actually created by a function that operates at a level below commitment control: journaling. Before we continue our discussion of commitment control, let's discuss journaling.

Journaling

It is relatively simple to imagine a system that records changes to many database files. In this system, if any records are written to the database, a copy of each record would be added to another database. To ensure that all changes were recorded, the implementation of this system would have to be a part of the database management system (DBMS) software. We might want the system to capture the type of change, before and after images of the data, the date and time a change occurred, who authorized the change, and what program made the change.

With such a system, it would be rather simple to find a specific change to a record and undo it, in effect removing a change to the database file. Further, if a backup of the database file were restored to the system, selective changes could be applied to the database to bring it up to the exact date and time desired — perhaps just before a program ran that destroyed data. The system could audit who used or updated the files and what changes were made.

The journaling tools on the AS/400 contain all the features of our imagined system. Every AS/400 includes a complete set of journaling tools as part of the built-in database, DB2/400. Journaling isn't "free," however. Its two "costs" are system overhead and disk consumption. Because the system writes the data twice — to the file and to the journal — the programs that use journaled files run slower and use more system resources. Because we will be in effect keeping the copy of the database file plus the copy of the changes, we will need more disk. Of course, we don't need to keep the record of the changes forever. We can move them to tape. But until we do, they take up disk space.

Exercise 13.2 Experiments in Journaling

Purpose
To experiment with AS/400 journaling tools toward a clear understanding of the why and how of journaling.

Instructions
Journal the file INVPF, make changes to the file, view the history of the changes, then remove the changes.

This project requires that each student have a separate library that is the first library in the student's library list containing the file INVPF. (Each student's library must have a copy of the file INVPF that contains records.) In the following instructions, wherever I specify YOURLIB, substitute the name of your data library.

Issue the CL commands described in the eight steps that follow at any command line.

1. Create a journal receiver. The command CRTJRNRCV (Create Journal Receiver) creates an object much like a physical file. When it is full, you can tell the system to "roll" to the next receiver. The system will compute that the next receiver should be INVJRN0002.

   CRTJRNRCV   yourlib/INVJRN0001

2. Create a journal. A second object, created with the command CRTJRN (Create Journal), contains the journaling rules, including which files are journaled, what data is captured for each file, and what journal receiver is in use. These rules will be defined after the journal is started with the STRJRNPF (Start Journal Physical File) command (step 3).

   CRTJRN   and press F4 for prompting

   The prompt screen for CRTJRN is shown in Figure 13.2.

   Fill in journal, journal library, journal receiver, and journal receiver library, as shown in Figure 13.2.

continued

Exercise 13.2, *Continued*

Figure 13.2
Create Journal
Command
Prompt Screen

```
                              Create Journal (CRTJRN)

Type choices, press Enter.

Journal  . . . . . . . . . . . . .   INVJRN         Name
   Library  . . . . . . . . . . .    yourlib        Name, *CURLIB
Journal receiver . . . . . . . .     INVJRN0001     Name
   Library  . . . . . . . . . .      yourlib        Name, *LIBL, *CURLIB

                                     *LIBL
Auxiliary storage pool ID  . . .     *LIBASP        1-16, *LIBASP
Journal message queue  . . . . .     QSYSOPR        Name
   Library  . . . . . . . . . .      *LIBL          Name, *LIBL, *CURLIB
Manage receivers . . . . . . . .     *USER          *USER, *SYSTEM
Delete receivers . . . . . . . .     *NO            *NO, *YES
Receiver size options  . . . . .     *NONE          *NONE, *RMVINTENT
Text 'description' . . . . . . .     *BLANK

                                                                  Bottom
F3=Exit    F4=Prompt   F5=Refresh   F10=Additional parameters  F12=Cancel
F13=How to use this display         F24=More keys
Parameter JRN required.                                               +
```

The CRTJRN prompt screen also defines which set of disks (called an auxiliary storage pool, or ASP) is to be used for the journal receivers. For insurance, it makes sense to locate the receiver in a different storage pool from the physical file. If the disk with the physical file fails, the journal receiver, which is on a different disk, will probably be available with a history of all the lost changes.

When you create the journal, you can define the journal message queue. You can define whether the user or the system should generate and attach the journal to the new receiver via the Manage Receivers option (see Figure 13.2). The *USER value indicates that the user must generate and attach new receivers to the journal when the receivers are full. The *SYSTEM indicates that OS/400 will generate and attach new receivers when receivers are full.

If the value for the Manage Receivers option is *SYSTEM and the value for the Delete Receivers option is *YES, the system will delete the old receiver as soon as it generates and attaches the journal to a new receiver.

3. Start journaling the file. The STRJRNPF command identifies a data file that will be journaled to a specific journal as well as what data should be collected for that file. The command itself will be journaled along with any other activity to that physical file until and including the ENDJRNPF (End Journaling Physical File) command. Any number of files can be journaled. All files in a commitment control set must be journaled.

STRJRNPF   and press F4 for prompting

Fill in the name and library of the file to be journaled, as well as the journal and the images to be captured, as shown in Figure 13.3. Set the image value to *BOTH, which captures what a record looks like both before and after a change. Both images will be required for commitment control.

continued

Exercise 13.2, *Continued*

```
                  Start Journal Physical File (STRJRNPF)
Type choices, press Enter.

Physical file to be journaled  .  INVPF       Name
   Library . . . . . . . . . . .    YOURLIB    Name, *LIBL, *CURLIB
               + for more values
                                    *LIBL
Journal . . . . . . . . . . . .  INVJRN       Name
   Library . . . . . . . . . . .    *LIBL      Name, *LIBL, *CURLIB
Record images . . . . . . . . .  *BOTH        *AFTER, *BOTH
Journal entries to be omitted  .  *NONE        *NONE, *OPNCLO


                                                              Bottom
F3=Exit    F4=Prompt    F5=Refresh    F12=Cancel    F13=How to use this display
F24=More keys
```

Figure 13.3
Start Journal Physical File Command Prompt Screen

Other frequently used journaling commands include ENDJRNPF, mentioned above, and CHGJRN (Change Journal). You can get a complete list of journaling commands by entering the command GO CMDJRN and a list of journal receiver commands by entering the command GO CMDJRNRCV.

4. Use the DSPFD (Display File Description) command to determine whether a file is journaled as well as to which journal.

   DSPFD INVPF

   Figure 13.4 shows part of the DSPFD display. The Page down key should be pressed until the journaling information is displayed.

```
File is currently journaled . . . . . . . :         Yes
Current or last journal . . . . . . . . . :         INVJRN
   Library . . . . . . . . . . . . . . . . :         YOURLIB
Journal images  . . . . . . . . . . . . : IMAGES   *BOTH
Journal entries to be omitted . . . . . . : OMTJRNE  *NONE
Last journal start date/time  . . . . . . :         12/14/98  10:51:50
```

Figure 13.4
Part of the DSPFD Display Showing Journaling Status

The information in Figure 13.4 shows that the file is journaled to the journal INVJRN in the library YOURLIB. Both images are captured. The value *NONE in the option Journal Entries to be Omitted causes the journal to include a record of every file open and file close as well as all changes to the data. (There is a value that would omit the record of the file opens and closes.)

5. Display journal entries. Journal entries can be viewed by using the DSPJRN (Display Journal) command, which includes the option of seeing journal entries based on time and date, physical file being journaled, job, and so forth. So far, there are only a few entries to the journal, as shown in Figure 13.5.

   DSPJRN INVJRN

continued

Exercise 13.2, *Continued*

Figure 13.5
Display Journal
Entries for the
Journal INVJRN

```
                            Display Journal Entries

 Journal  . . . . . . :    INVJRN          Library  . . . . . . :    YOURLIB

 Type options, press Enter.
   5=Display entire entry


 Opt     Sequence  Code  Type   Object      Library     Job        Time
             1     J     PR                             BL0566S1   10:50:41
             3     F     JM     INVPF       YOURLIB     BL0566S1   10:51:50
```

The first entry notes that the journal was created, and the second notes that the file INVPF was added to the journal.

6. Delete records from the file INVPF. Use Data File Utility (DFU) to delete some of the records in the file. An easy way to start DFU is with the UPDDTA command:

   UPDDTA INVPF

   Press the Page down key to advance to the first record and press F23 twice to delete it. Repeat this process five times, deleting the first five records. Press F3 twice to exit DFU.

7. View the journal entries (Figure 13.6), including the deleted records, using the following command:

   DSPJRN INVJRN

   Now our journal contains a copy of each deleted record. The F code records the file opens and closes; the R code records any changes to records. DL is delete. Use option 5, Display Entire Entry, to view the details. You will find that the journal contains the "image" of the record before it was deleted along with the time, date, user, program, and job that deleted it.

Figure 13.6
Display Journal
INVPF After
Deleting Five
Records

```
                            Display Journal Entries

 Journal  . . . . . . :    INVJRN          Library  . . . . . . :    YOURLIB

 Type options, press Enter.
   5=Display entire entry


 Opt     Sequence  Code  Type   Object      Library     Job        Time
             1     J     PR                             BL0566S1   11:22:31
             3     F     JM     INVPF       YOURLIB     BL0566S1   11:22:51
             4     F     OP     INVPF       YOURLIB     BL0566S1   11:25:15
             5     F     OP     INVPF       YOURLIB     BL0566S1   11:25:15
             7     R     DL     INVPF       YOURLIB     BL0566S1   11:25:34
             8     R     DL     INVPF       YOURLIB     BL0566S1   11:25:38
             9     R     DL     INVPF       YOURLIB     BL0566S1   11:25:40
            10     R     DL     INVPF       YOURLIB     BL0566S1   11:25:42
            16     R     DL     INVPF       YOURLIB     BL0566S1   11:25:57
            13     F     OP     INVPF       YOURLIB     BL0566S1   11:25:52
            14     F     OP     INVPF       YOURLIB     BL0566S1   11:25:52   +
 F3=Exit    F12=Cancel
```

Exercise 13.2, *Continued*

8. Recover the deleted records. To recover the five deleted records, we will back out the changes that were made to the file, which were recorded by the journal. The command for backing out the changes to a file is RMVJRNCHG (Remove Journal Changes).

   RMVJRNCHG JRN(INVJRN) FILE((INVPF))

   We've just asked the journal to remove the effects of all the entries that it had against INVPF, and the system responded with the following message: Remove failed. 5 entries removed from member INVPF. (Even though this message indicates that the remove request failed, it failed after five entries were removed because the remaining entries did not contain any file changes that could be removed. These entries indicated the start of journaling.) We can find out more details about the remove journal changes process by displaying our job log, using the command DSPJOBLOG. To see the detailed log, press F10, and to see previous messages, press Page up. One of the messages that you will find in your job log is

   Cannot perform operation beyond journal entry 3.

   Our command was supposed to back out the changes to the file INVPF from the very last change all the way back to entry #2. Our request to remove journal changes started with the most recent change, the journal entry with the highest number, and worked backward, removing each change until it removed journal entry 3. Five of the entries indicated changes to the data, and these were changed back to their previous values. (When the process reached journal entry 2, it stopped because the first and second entries were not removable — those entries indicated that this file would be journaled.)

   We could have been more explicit about which entries to remove by typing RMVJRNCHG and pressing F4 (Prompt). We could identify all the files from which to remove the entries — using the entry number range or the dates and times range. Because the removal works backward, the start would be the most recent time or the highest entry number and the end would be the earliest time or lowest entry number.

9. Check the file to see the effect of the RMVJRNCHG command. Use the command UPDDTA INVPF to verify that the records deleted in step 7 were actually restored.

   Use the DSPJRN command to see how the journal recorded the RMVJRNCHG command. You will see that it didn't remove the record of the deletions; rather, it added new records to the bottom that record the RMVJRNCHG process.

In our previous discussion and experiments, only a single physical file was journaled. The next experiment demonstrates that multiple files can be journaled to a single journal. Journaling more than one file to the same journal is an option when you use commitment control with multiple files as discussed later in this chapter.

Exercise 13.3 Further Experiments in Journaling

Purpose

To use journaling tools to remove specific changes to a database.

Instructions

Changes to the file INVPF will be made using the inventory maintenance program. Once these changes have been made, they will then be backed out using the RMVJRNCHG command. This project requires that the file INVPF is journaled.

1. Add the file ORDLNP to the journal INVJRN, recording *BOTH images.
2. Add two new records to INVPF.
3. Delete two records from INVPF.
4. Change two records from INVPF.
5. Use DSPJRN to determine the entry numbers that represent these changes.
6. Remove the last change by entry number.
7. View the file and confirm that the change has been removed.
8. Remove the range of changes that has not yet been removed.
9. View the file and confirm that the range has been removed.

Using your Order Line Maintenance program,

10. Add two new records to ORDLNP.
11. Delete two records from ORDLNP.
12. Change two records in ORDLNP.
13. Use DSPJRN command to display the journal INVJRN. Your are now viewing all changes to both files. Now exit the display and use the DSPJRN command again, but this time use prompting (by pressing F4) to display the journal INVJRN but only for file ORDLNP. Not only could you restrict the display to one or more files, but you could also restrict the display to a time/date range or entry number range, so you can find the specific entries that you're seeking.
14. Remove the last change by entry number.
15. View the file and confirm that the change has been removed.
16. Remove the range of changes that have not been removed.
17. View the file and confirm that the change has been removed.

Closing Words on Journaling

More than one file can be journaled to a single journal. Journals record all changes to the file. Journals can also record all opens and closes to the file. Journals can provide a way to back out one or a group of changes to one or more files. Journals can be used from the other direction by restoring an earlier backup and then using the command APPJRNCHG (Apply Journal Changes) up to the point at which a disaster occurred.

Exercise 13.4 Using Journaling to Reduce the Risk Inherent in Update Programs

Purpose
To demonstrate how to use journaling to reduce the risk inherent in updating data.

Instructions
You will analyze the changes to the data that occur under a number of different scenarios that use logic to post shipments to inventory and order detail.

Case 3 — All the files in Exercise 13.1 are journaled to the journal FAROUT. Both the before and after images are captured for all files. Our operator makes the same mistake that was made in Exercise 13.1, Case 2, and aborts the job before the third transaction is complete. The job name is POSTSHP.

1. Describe how you could remove the effects of the entire job POSTSHP. Take the image of the files at the time of the abort and "roll" them back until all the journal entries have been removed.

2. Starting with the files as they are at the completion of step 1, we run the shipment posting program again. What is the image of the files after it runs? How does it compare to the image after Exercise 13.1, Case 1?

Case 4 — As in Case 3, all files are journaled and the operator aborts the program.

1. Describe how you could determine what range of entries comprises the transaction that was aborted. Describe how to remove just these changes. Create an image of the file after these changes are removed.

2. Start with the file as it appears at the end of Case 3, step 2. Run the program to post shipments. How do the results of this run compare to the results from Case 1?

If you followed the path of bread crumbs properly, you are either a) at the witch's house, or b) at the same place that you reached in Exercise 13.1, Case 1. You found two ways to get there: by removing the entire process (Case 3) or by removing just the single corrupt transaction (Case 4).

In these exercises, both solutions yield the same results and with nearly the same amount of effort on the part of humans and machines. Commitment control provides both options — to roll back the entire job or just a single transaction. The best choice is primarily dependent on the nature of the application, as we will discuss.

Commitment Control

As you have seen in the preceding exercises, journaling contains the essence of the solution to improper or incomplete changes to a data file or a set of data files. However, to use it, you have had to discover that when the program aborts, you need to know the range of journal entries to remove and issue the commands to make the corrections. Until the journal entries are actually removed, the files are in error; and any processes that access these files can produce bad results. If any further changes occur to the affected records between the time of the aborted process and the attempt to remove the journal entries, those journal entries cannot be removed. The system compares the after image of the record to the current image of the record at the time the removal of the journal entry is attempted. This prevents the system from losing subsequent changes.

Commitment control adds to journaling in two ways:

1. It locks all records from the commitment boundary until either a commit or rollback request occurs. (Program abort is assumed to be a rollback.)

2. If a rollback is requested or the program aborts, commitment control automatically removes the journal entries back to the commitment boundary (defined in the next section).

Commitment Control Boundary

The commitment control boundary is the point at which the current commitment transaction begins. The first commitment transaction begins at the CL command STRCMTCTL (Start Commitment Control) and continues until the first commit, rollback, or program abort. Subsequently, the boundary's beginning is moved to the end of the last transaction — the last commit or rollback.

To provide the "all-or-nothing" option (all or no records are updated), the commit or rollback is done at the end of either the CL program or the RPG program.

In transaction-level commitment control, the commit operation will be placed just before the read of the first record of the next transaction. This commit will make the completed transaction permanent and move the commit boundary to the beginning of the new transaction. If a problem condition is detected that indicates that the transaction should not be carried out, a rollback is issued that backs out the changes and moves the boundary. Then the first record of the next transaction is read.

Commitment Control: Rules and Restriction

Commitment control will work only if the three following rules are observed:

- All files that are to be put under commitment control must be journaled and must have Record Image = *BOTH.
- The RPG update programs must be called by a CL program, which must issue the command to start commitment control before calling the RPG program. This must be a call, not a submit job, because the CL program that starts commitment control must be in the same job stream as the subsequent processing.
- The total number of record changes that can be contained within the commitment control boundary was limited to about 32,000 in OS/400 Version 2. Although that is not likely to be a problem for commitment on the single transaction level, it has proven to be a problem for the all-or-nothing option. In subsequent versions of OS/400, the commitment boundary has been changed to 2 billion record changes.

Commitment Control: CL Commands

To establish commitment control, the job stream must contain a CL program that issues the CL command STRCMTCTL (Start Commitment Control). The CL program must then call the RPG program, which contains special F-specs that identify the files that will be protected by commitment control. On completion of the RPG program, processing returns to the CL program, which issues a command to end commitment control. Commands to commit or roll back can be located at the RPG program level and/or in the CL program. Transaction level commitment, in which each transaction is committed or rolled back before the next transaction, requires a commit or rollback operation in the RPG program.

The CL commands to start, end, commit, and roll back will be described in this section. The RPG F-specs and operations for commitment control will be described thereafter.

Remember, the RPG update program must be called by a CL program that has already issued the command to start commitment control.

STRCMTCTL initiates the commitment control process. This command requires a value for the LCKLVL (Lock Level) parameter to define which records remain locked until they are committed or released with a rollback.

Without commitment control, records accessed from a file with update status will be locked until unlocked, updated, deleted, or released when the program accesses another record from the same file.

Commitment control must lock all of the records that are changed until the commit or rollback is issued to prevent other processes from changing or deleting these records before that program has ascertained that the change can be committed. The lock applies to records accessed from files designated as under commitment control in RPG F-specs. There are three different levels of lock:

- *ALL — All records that have been accessed are locked until the commit or rollback occurs even if they are not changed and would be unlocked if commitment control were not used.

- *CHG — All records that have been changed (updated, added, or deleted) are locked. Also the records that would be locked if commitment control were not used are locked (records which have been accessed but have not yet been released). Records can be released with the RPG UNLOK (Unlock) command, with the unlock value on the access specification, or by accessing another record from the file.

- *CS — All records that have been accessed are locked unless a record is released by accessing another record from the file without changing (updating or deleting) the record.

ENDCMTCTL (End Commitment Control) terminates commitment control. If you try to issue this command while records are still in limbo, an error occurs.

ROLLBACK (Roll Back) rolls back any records that have not been committed at the time the command is issued.

COMMIT (Commit the Pending Changes) commits the changes to any records that have not been committed at the time the command is issued.

The CL program shown in Figure 13.7 starts commitment control and calls the RPG program PGMRPG13A.

After the RPG program has completed, all uncommitted changes are rolled back and commitment control is ended.

```
/* Program PGMCLP11A   */
PGM
    STRCMTCTL *CS
    CALL PGMRPG11A
      /*Program will rollback */
      /*  uncommitted changes */
    ROLLBACK
    ENDCMTCTL
END:    ENDPGM
```

Figure 13.7
CL Program with Commitment Control

Commitment Control and RPG

Commitment control requires CL commands to start the commitment process described in the previous section of this chapter. Each file that will be protected by commitment control requires a continuation F-spec to declare that it will be protected by the commitment control process. Only files that are opened for update, output, or input with addition capabilities can be protected.

Two operation codes control the commitment process. The COMMIT (Commit Group) operation makes the current file changes permanent; the ROLBK (Roll Back) operation removes the current file changes.

F-Specs for Commitment Control

We identify the files to be protected by commitment control by adding a COMMIT Keyword to the F-spec line. Remember: Only files for update, output, or input with addition allowed can be under commitment control, and all files that are committed must be currently journaled with Image=*BOTH. The F-spec shown in Figure 13.8 places the file INVPF under commitment control.

Figure 13.8
F-Specs for a
File Under
Commitment Control

```
+....1....+....2....+....3....+....4....+....5....+....6....+....7....+....8

  FINVPF     UF   E          K DISK     Commit
```

The C-spec operation COMMIT will cause commitment control to commit the changed records, and the records are unlocked. The commitment boundary (the previous COMMIT or ROLBK) is restarted at this point. The changes are now permanent.

The C-spec operation ROLBK will cause commitment control to roll back records to the commitment boundary (the previous COMMIT or ROLBK). The changes are removed and the records are unlocked. The commitment boundary is restarted at this point.

Exercise 13.5 Commitment Control: Rollback at the Process Level

Purpose

To gain an understanding and appreciation of commitment control. This exercise will demonstrate how rollbacks can be implemented to control all of the changes in a process.

Instructions

The following sentences describe a situation that you will be asked to verify: An RPG program deletes all of the records of a file under commitment control but fails to issue either a commit or rollback command. The CL program that established commitment control and called the RPG program issues a rollback when the RPG program ends. The database file should be unchanged by the process.

continued

Exercise 13.5, *Continued*

1. Copy file INVPF to INVPF2 with the following command:

   CPYF INVPF YOURLIB/INVPF2 MBROPT(*REPLACE) CRTFILE(*YES)

2. Display the contents of the file with the following command:

   DSPPFM INVPF2

3. Enter and compile the CL program shown in Figure 13.7.

4. Enter and compile the RPG program shown in Figure 13.9. This program deletes all the records in INVPF, but it places INVPF under commitment control and doesn't contain a COMIT operation.

5. Start Journaling the new file with the following command:

Figure 13.9
Sample Program
PGMRPG13A

```
+....1....+....2....+....3....+....4....+....5....+....6....+....7....+....8

 FINVPF2    UF   E           K DISK      Commit

 C                    Read      INVPF2                            90
 C                    DoW       *IN90 = *OFF
 C                    Delete    INVPFR
 C                    Read      INVPF2                            90
 C                    EndDO
 C                    Eval      *INLR = *ON
 C                    Return
```

   STRJRNPF YOURLIB/INVPF2 JRN(INVJRN)

6. Call the CL program you created in step 3.

7. Display the contents of the file INVPF2 with the following command:

   DSPPFM INVPF2

   The file should be the same as it was at step 2.

Exercise 13.6 Commitment Control: Commit at the Process Level

Purpose

To gain an understanding of and appreciation for commitment control. This exercise will demonstrate how commitment control can be implemented to control all of the changes in a process.

Instructions

The following sentences describe a situation that you will be asked to verify: An RPG program under commitment control deletes all the records of a file. Just before it ends, the RPG program issues a commit operation. If the RPG program runs to completion, all of the records should be deleted. If it fails, none of the records will be deleted.

continued

Exercise 13.6, *Continued*

1. Modify program PGMRPG13A. Add a COMIT operation after the ENDDO. This is one way to commit at the all-or-nothing level. If this program fails, it doesn't reach the COMIT. And because the calling CL program has a rollback command immediately after the CALL to the RPG program, it will roll back any uncommitted records. Call the CL program you created in Exercise 13.5, step 3.
2. Display the records in file INVPF2 with the following command:

    DSPPFM INVPF2

    The member should not contain any records.

Placing Commit and Rollback

The commit and rollback commands could be placed in the CL program or the RPG program. In the RPG program, the COMMIT operation can be placed in the processing loop or at the end of processing. The ROLBK operation can be located in error-handling subroutines and called when aborting a partially executed transaction. This section provides guidelines on the placement of these commands.

All-or-Nothing Case 1 — Put a commit in the RPG program just before the Move *On to *INLR.

All-or-Nothing Case 2 — In this case, there is no commit/rollback in the RPG code. The CL code is modified as shown in Figure 13.10 so that the program will commit the changes unless the RPG program ends in error. If the program ends in error, the MONMSG (Monitor Message) command causes the program to skip down to the error: label and execute the ROLLBACK.

Figure 13.10
CL Program with a
Commit If the RPG
Program Ends
Normally and a
Rollback If It Ends
Abnormally

```
/* Simple CL program will roll back uncommitted changes */
PGM
            STRCMTCTL *CS
            CALL PGMRPG11A
            MONMSG CPF0000 RPG0000 MCH0000 EXEC( ERROR )
            COMMIT
            ENDCMTCTL
            GOTO END
ERROR:      ROLLBACK
            ENDCMTCTL
END:        ENDPGM
```

Commit at the Transaction Level — The commit should be placed in the code as soon as the transaction is complete, as shown in the screened line in Figure 13.11.

```
+....1....+....2....+....3....+....4....+....5....+....6....+....7....+....8

FINVPF2    UF   E            K DISK     Commit

C                    Read      INVPF2                              90
C                    DoW       *IN90 = *OFF
C                    Delete    INVPFR
C                    Commit
C                    Read      INVPF2                              90
C                    EndDO
C                    Eval      *INLR = *ON
C                    Return
```

Figure 13.11
RPG Program with
Transaction Level
Commitment

Rollback and *PSSR — If your program contains a *PSSR subroutine, the MONMSG and ROLLBACK commands in the CL program will not work; the *PSSR subroutine ensures that the RPG program will not abort. Therefore, the CL program won't skip to the ERROR label. Instead, the ROLBK operation must be included in the RPG *PSSR subroutine, as shown in the screened lines in Figure 13.12.

```
+....1....+....2....+....3....+....4....+....5....+....6....+....7....+....8

FINVPF2    UF   E            K DISK     Commit

C                    Read      INVPF2                              90
C                    DoW       *IN90 = *OFF
C                    Delete    INVPFR
C                    Commit
C                    Read      INVPF2                              90
C                    EndDO
C                    Eval      *INLR = *ON
C                    Return

C        *PSSR       BegSR
C                    ROLBK
C                    Eval      *INLR = *ON
C                    Return
C                    EndSR
```

Figure 13.12
RPG Program with
Rollback in Error
Handling Subroutine

Exercise 13.7 Adding Commitment Control to an Interactive Program

Purpose
To understand how to add commitment control to an interactive program.

Instructions
Add commitment control to the inventory maintenance program.

1. Modify your most recent inventory maintenance program to add transaction-level commitment control.
2. Create a CL program to start commitment control and call the RPG program.
3. Test the program.
4. Modify the program from step 1 so that it makes the changes to the file and shows the operator a window that displays the changes and asks for user approval. (If the user approves, the changes will be committed; if the user rejects, the changes will be rolled back.)

Review

1. For each of the following examples, describe why you would either back out all transactions and start the job over or back out only the corrupted transactions and start the job over.

   - The shipment posting program contains 2 million shipping records to post and aborts halfway through.
   - The home-shopping order entry system crashes.
   - Everyone in your company gets a 5 percent raise. You write a program to read each record, multiply the pay rate by 1.05, put the result in the pay rate field, and update the record. It crashes after updating about a million records.

2. Describe why commitment control is an important tool for RPG programmers.
3. What is the commitment control boundary and how does it restrict the effect of an RPG rollback operation or CL command?
4. A typical RPG program loops each time that a transaction is completed. Where should you locate the commit operation to

   a. establish transaction-level commitment
   b. establish program-level commitment

5. If a program has an error-handling subroutine *PSSR, would you expect to find a commitment control statement there? If so, which one? Why?
6. What are the CL commands required to support commitment control?

Chapter 14

Program-to-Program Communication and Data Queues

Chapter Overview

When you have completed Chapter 14, you will be able to

- define the types of program-to-program communication
- decide when each type of program-to-program communication is required
- describe data queues, a powerful AS/400 tool for program-to-program communication
- create programs using FIFO and LIFO data queues
- create programs using keyed data queues

Program-to-Program Communication

The first two sections of this chapter discuss, compare, and contrast the range of tools for program-to-program communication. The remainder of the chapter will explore the nature and applications of one of those tools: data queues. Unique to the AS/400, data queues comprise an extremely fast and powerful way to transmit data between programs.

Program-to-program communication techniques provide tools to address a range of system design challenges. Table 14.1 shows the basic uses for program-to-program communication.

Table 14.1
Uses for Program-to-Program Communication

Purpose	Timing	Issues
Program modularity	Synchronous	Simpler programs Reusable code
Subsequent processes	Asynchronous	Completion of a transaction lets a subsequent process proceed

Synchronous processing occurs when programs perform in a controlled sequence: Program A calls program B and waits for program B to finish before continuing. When program A calls program B, it can pass data to program B; when program B ends, it can pass back data to program A — one form of program-to-program communication.

Asynchronous processing occurs when two programs run independently. However, because one may still have to send requests for data or lists of completed transactions to the other program, some method of program-to-program communication is required.

Program-to-Program Communication Techniques

The program analyst or system designer on the AS/400 has four different program-to-program communication techniques available. These techniques vary in timing (synchronous, asynchronous, or both) and performance. Table 14.2 presents the various communication techniques.

Table 14.2
Communication Techniques

Technique	Timing	Comments
Passing data in call	Synchronous	Simple coding of synchronous processing
Data areas	Synchronous Asynchronous	Each data area can hold only one "record"
Trigger files	Asynchronous	File contains data or enough data to identify the records for subsequent processing
Data queues	Synchronous	Fastest transfer of data
	Asynchronous	Easy to make a program that waits for passed data

Program-to-Program Technique: Passing Data

RPG program A calls program B and passes parameters to it. Program A's processing is then suspended until program B is completed. The parameters "passed" or shared between the programs may include a value to indicate whether program B succeeded or failed. With this indicator or variable, program A can then continue processing based on the success or failure of program B. Synchronous processing is necessary when the primary processing must be delayed until the process in the called program has been completed.

RPG/400 offers two alternative forms of the CALL operation when parameters are passed or shared with the called program. Figure 14.1 shows a CALL operation followed by the parameter list.

Figure 14.1
Call to PROG14B with
Parameter List

```
+....1....+....2....+....3....+....4....+....5....+....6....+....7....+....8
C                      Call      'PROG12B'
C                      Parm                    Var1
C                      Parm                    Var2
C                      Parm                    Var3
```

Figure 14.2 shows the same CALL operation using a PLIST (a parameter list) that is defined in the program initialization subroutine. The PLIST presents a series of variables that will be passed to or shared with the called program.

```
+....1....+....2....+....3....+....4....+....5....+....6....+....7....+....8
C     PLST1         PLIST
C                   Parm                     Var1
C                   Parm                     Var2
C                   Parm                     Var3

C                   Call      'PROG14B'      PLST1
```

Figure 14.2
Call to PROG14B
with PLIST

Figure 14.3 shows a portion of a program that is called and receives (or more accurately shares) data. The called program identifies the internal field names of the shared fields in an *ENTRY PLIST that would be included in the called program in the initialization subroutine. The *ENTRY PLIST is a special plist that identifies the list of parameters shared with the calling program. A program can contain only one *ENTRY PLIST. This list should provide the same number of variables of the same types and sizes as the calling program passes.

```
+....1....+....2....+....3....+....4....+....5....+....6....+....7....+....8
C     Init          BegSR

C     *Entry        PLIST
C                   Parm                     Var1
C                   Parm                     Var2
C                   Parm                     Var3

C                   Call      'PROG14B'      PLST1
```

Figure 14.3
PROG14B Receives the
"Passed" or Shared
Variables with an
*ENTRY PLIST

Table 14.3 shows various outcomes of mismatching the passed parameters and the *Entry PLIST.

Table 14.3
Outcomes of Calling a Program and Passing Parameters

Calling Program: Program A	Called Program: Program B	Results
Passes parameters	*ENTRY PLIST matches passed parameters	Programs run as designed
Passes parameters	Does not have a *ENTRY PLIST or does not have as many entries in *ENTRY PLIST as are passed	Call fails
Passes parameters	Variables in *ENTRY PLIST are not of the same type or size	Program B runs but values passed to or from it may be corrupt and may cause logic or runtime errors
Does not pass parameters	Has *ENTRY PLIST	Call works but any attempt in Program B to use the variables in the *ENTRY PLIST will cause an error
Does not pass parameters	Does not have an *ENTRY PLIST	Programs run as designed

The parameter lists of the calling and called programs must contain the same number of variables with identical variable structures in the same sequence. The structure of any numeric variable that is passed by the calling program or received by the called program should be 15 digits wide with 5 decimal positions in both programs. Character fields should be the same width in both programs. The variable names do not have to be the same in the calling and called programs.

RPG does not actually pass the values of the variables to the called program; it passes the addresses of the variables. These locations are shared by both programs. If the called program changes the value of any variable in its PLIST, that value is placed in the shared location. When the called program ends, the calling program resumes but with the new value of the shared variable. For example, Prog14A places the value 'Hi Prog14B' in the variable VAR2 and then calls PROGB (Figure 14.1 and Figure 14.2). The *ENTRY PLIST for Prog 14B can use the variable X2, which is 'Hi Prog14B'. Before Prog 14B ends, it changes the value in variable X2 to 'Right back at you'. When ProgA resumes, the value in VAR2 is 'Right back at you'.

Program-to-Program Technique: Data Areas

A data area is an object of type *DTAARA. It can contain one numeric or character value. If the data area is created in a library other than QTEMP, it will continue to exist and retain the data stored in it until it is deleted. If the data area is created in QTEMP, it will exist only until the job ends because QTEMP is a unique library created for each job and deleted at job end. Each job also has a local data area created at the beginning of the job and accessible to all programs that run in the job stream.

Data areas can be used in two ways. In synchronous processing, the data area can be used much like a passed parameter to convey data to and from a program within the job stream. Unlike the use of parameters in which data must be actively passed from program to program to program, you can use a data area to share data with any program or programs in the job stream that access it.

Data areas are also useful for asynchronous processing in which a program stores a single piece of data for use at a later time — either by itself or by another program. For example, a data area is an excellent place to keep the last invoice number issued. Any program that needs to issue an invoice can lock the data area, pick up the last number from the data area, add 1 to it, write it back to the data area, and then unlock the data area. Any number of programs could "share" this data area. The data area used in asynchronous processing is likely to be created in a permanent library so it will be available to other jobs and later executions of the same job.

Program-to-Program Technique: Trigger Files

Data files that contain data or transaction requests to be processed (sometimes referred to as trigger files) can be used as a method of passing data from one program to another. This method is most common in asynchronous processing in which the first program doesn't wait for the completion of the second program. The second program may in fact be processing a record from the shared file that was created several cycles ago by the creating program. Any number of programs could place data in this file, and any number of programs could be reading the records and carrying on their component of the subsequent processing.

A good example of this might occur in a grocery store system. Processing may be broken down into two stages. Stage one includes only the processing required at the check-out counter. Stage two is a batch program run once a day that updates the inventories from the day's sales and transmits restocking orders. Stage one has to be fast; the customer and check-out clerk are waiting. For each item rung up in stage one, the stage-one program writes a record to the inventory change file. Later, the stage-two inventory-update/restocking program reads each record from the inventory change file, subtracts the sales from the inventory quantity, and reorders stock if the quantity falls below the reorder value. As the stage-two program processes, it may either remove each record or change the value in a field on each record to record that the processing has taken place.

Program-to-Program Technique: Data Queues

Data queues can be used for synchronous processing in which one program puts a request for processing into one data queue and then waits for a response provided by a second program, typically in a second data queue. Data queues also can be used for asynchronous processing in which a program puts a request for processing into a data queue and continues without waiting for a response.

Data queues are much faster than data files in program-to-program communication. Whereas data files are structured with fields, each entry in a data queue is only a single numeric value or character value. Structure over the data queue element will have to be created internally in any program. The fields to be sent to a data queue are all included in a single data structure along with a single character field that is the combined width of all the fields of the data structure. Once data is loaded into the subfields of the data structure, the field the width of the data structure is sent. The fields to be received from a data queue are all included in a single data structure along with a single character field that is the combined width of all the fields in the data structure. The element is received into the wide field of the data structure and then is structured and available through the subfields.

Data queues are less flexible than data files. Data file records can be viewed, added, changed, and deleted, using programs or utilities such as Data File Utility (DFU). Data queue elements can only be sent to and received from the queue.

Records are deleted from a data file by a unique step in the program that issues a delete. Elements in a data queue, however, are deleted from the queue automatically whenever they are received into a program. The one-step access and deletion is fast, but the risk of potentially losing an element when the receiving program has a logical or runtime error must be considered when you design a system.

Chapter 13 presented two powerful tools — journaling and commitment control — that can be used to protect or recover data from a data file. Neither of these tools applies to a data queue. Therefore, if a program, even one under commitment control, accesses an element in a data queue and subsequently aborts, that element is lost.

Data queues grow over time. Every element added takes space in the data queue. Receiving an element from a data queue removes the element, but does not reclaim the space. For example, if, over time, a data queue of 100-byte elements has been sent 50,000 elements, it occupies 5,000,000 bytes. Even if all elements have been received by the time the next element is sent to the data queue, the data queue will be enlarged to 5,000,100 bytes. To reset the queue's size, you must periodically delete and re-create the queue.

Using Data Queues

You can use data queues through a combination of CL commands and calls to IBM-supplied programs. This section introduces those commands and calls and demonstrates how to use them in RPG programs.

CRTDTAQ — The CRTDTAQ (Create Data Queue) command shown in Figure 14.4 is used to create a data queue. The data queue is an object and therefore has an object name and a library in which it is stored. The queue can be a standard queue (on the local AS/400) or a distributed data management queue (on a remote AS/400). Each element of the queue can be from 1 to 64,512 characters long. Each entry in the queue can be stored to disk before processing continues. Although this reduces the chance of lost data if the system crashes, it slows the performance of the data queue.

Figure 14.4
CRTDTAQ with
Additional
Parameters (F10)
and Keyed
Information

```
                              Create Data Queue (CRTDTAQ)

 Type choices, press Enter.

 Data queue . . . . . . . . . . . . . . . . .  _____    Name
    Library . . . . . . . . . . . . . . .     *CURLIB___    Name, *CURLIB
 TYPE . . . . . . . . . . . . . . . . . . .    *STD          *STD, *DDM
 Maximum entry length . . . . . . . . . .      _____    1-64512
 Force to auxiliary storage . . . . . . .      *No_          *NO, *YES
 Sequence . . . . . . . . . . . . . . . .      *KEYED        *FIFO, *LIFO, *KEYED
 Key Length . . . . . . . . . . . . . .        _____         1-256
 Include sender ID . . . . . . . . . . .       *NO_          *NO, *YES
 Text 'description'. . . . . . . . . . .        *BLANK_____

                              Additional Parameters

 Authority . . . . . . . . . . . . . . .       *LIBCRTAUT    NAME, *LIBCRTAUT, *CHANGE...
```

When you create a data queue, you must select the sequence that defines the order of retrieval of elements. Elements can be retrieved in first-in-first-out (FIFO) order, last-in-first-out (LIFO) order, or an order based on a key value.

A keyed data queue could contain data elements sent to the queue for a number of different programs. When each of those programs attempts to retrieve elements from the queue, the program would send the queue a key value and would receive only records that match that value.

Data is sent to the data queue by the IBM-supplied program QSNDDTAQ (Send to Data Queue). Because QSNDDTAQ is a program, it is called, and four required parameters must be passed to it:

- QNAME — The name of the queue.
- QLIB — The library containing the data queue or *LIBL or *CURLIB.
- FieldLen — The length of field that contains the value to send, which cannot exceed the data queue's element length. This field must be a packed-decimal field 5 digits wide with zero decimals.
- Field — The field that contains the value to send.

If you are using a keyed data queue, two additional parameters are required:

- Keylength — The length of the Keyvalue field, which cannot exceed the data queue's key field length. The field must be a packed-decimal field of 3 digits with zero decimals.
- Keyvalue — The actual key value.

Figure 14.5 shows a section of an RPG program that sends an element to the data queue DATQ1 in the job's library list (*LIBL). The value sent to the queue is stored in the variable SNDTOQ, and it is the value of the variable or data structure INVNUM. The value is 20 characters long.

```
+....1....+....2....+....3....+....4....+....5....+....6....+....7....+....8

  * Declare and Initialize fields for Send Data Queue Program Call.
D QName           S             10A    INZ('DATQ1')
D QLib            S             10A    INZ('*LIBL')
D SndToQ          S             20A
D Flen            S              5  0 INZ(20)

  *

C                     Eval      SndToQ = INVNUM
C                     Call      'QSndDtaQ'
C                     Parm                    QName
C                     Parm                    QLib
C                     Parm                    FLen
C                     Parm                    SndToQ
```

Figure 14.5
RPG Call to QSNDDTAQ
Without Key

Like Figure 14.5, Figure 14.6 sends an element to a data queue. Because queue DATAQ2 is keyed, two additional values are passed to program QSNDDTAQ. The key length is 5 characters and the key value is TYPE1. Later, to retrieve this element, the retrieval program will have to pass the same key value to the program to retrieve elements from the queue.

```
+....1....+....2....+....3....+....4....+....5....+....6....+....7....+....8

  * Declare and Initialize fields for Send Data Queue Program Call.
D QName           S             10A    INZ('DATQ2')
D QLib            S             10A    INZ('*LIBL')
D SndToQ          S             20A
D Flen            S              5  0 INZ(20)
D KeyVal          S              5A    INZ('TYPE1')
D KLen            S              3  0 INZ(5 )

  *

C                     Eval      SndToQ = INVNUM
C                     Call      'QSndDtaQ'
C                     Parm                    QName
C                     Parm                    QLib
C                     Parm                    FLen
C                     Parm                    SndToQ
C                     Parm                    KLen
C                     Parm                    KeyVal
```

Figure 14.6
RPG Call to
QSNDDTAQ with Key

Receiving data from the data queue is done with an IBM-supplied program called QRCVDTAQ, which requires the following five parameters:

- QNAME — The name of the data queue.
- QLIB — The library containing the data queue or *LIBL or *CURLIB.

- FieldLen — The length of the field that receives the value. This length cannot exceed the length of the data queue as defined in the CRTDTAQ command. This field must be packed decimal with a width of 5 digits and zero decimals.
- Field — The field to receive the value.
- Wait — The number of seconds to wait to receive an entry from the data queue. This field must be packed decimal, 5 digits wide, with zero decimals. The value of the Wait parameter controls how long the program waits for a data element to be returned from the data queue. (Caution: If the value of the Wait parameter is a negative number, the program will wait forever.)

If the value of the wait parameter is zero, the program will not wait. If no entry is available to be received, QRCVDTAQ will set the field length value to zero. Your program can tell that no elements were available to be received by checking the returning value of the field length.

If the wait parameter value is greater than zero, it represents the number of seconds that program can wait for element to be received. (Maximum value is 99999, which is about 28 hours.)

These additional parameters are required if the data queue is keyed:

- KeyRule — 2-byte character. Values are 'GT', 'LT', 'NE', 'EQ', 'GE', 'LE'. This is the test used to determine whether an element should be received. In the example, 'GT' would cause QRCVDTAQ to return the next element with a key value greater than the Request Key Value.
- RequestKeyLength — Length of Request key value field, which cannot exceed the length of the data queue's key field. This value must be a packed decimal with 3 digits and zero decimal positions.
- RequestKeyValue — Value used to test elements to determine whether they qualify for receipt; for example, if KeyRule is 'GT' and RequestKeyValue is 'AB', the next element with a KeyValue greater than 'AB' will be received.

If the parameters for the key are included, then the next two parameters must also be included — although they will be meaningless if you did not specify Include Sender ID in the CRTDTAQ command:

- SenderLength — Length of the field to receive sender data. It must be a packed-decimal field 3 digits wide with zero decimal positions. It can have a value of zero (no data will be returned) or a value from 8 to 44.
- Sender — The name of a character field to receive element sender data. If the SenderLength is not zero, then the sender data will contain at least the first two fields defined below. The actual amount of data received to Sender is determined by the value of SenderLength.
- 4 bytes — The length of returned data (packed decimal, 7 digits, zero decimal positions).
- 4 bytes — The length of all sender data available (packed decimal, 7 digits, zero decimal positions).
- 26 bytes — Character field with job name, user, job number.
- 10 bytes — Character field with name of sender's user profile.

Figure 14.7 shows the RPG code to receive from a data queue without key or sender information.

```
+....1....+....2....+....3....+....4....+....5....+....6....+....7....+....8
    * Declare and Initialize fields for Send Data Queue Program Call.
D QName          S             10A   INZ('DATQ1')
D QLib           S             10A   INZ('*LIBL')
D RcvFQ          S             20A
D Flen           S              5 0

    * Values for WaitQ are:   negative wait value - wait forever
    *                         zero wait value - do not wait
    *                         FLEN will be zero if no element
    *                         positive value  - wait that many seconds
    *                         (up to 99999)
D WaitQ          S              5 0 INZ(-5)

    *
C                   Call      'QRcvDtaQ'
C                   Parm                    Qname
C                   Parm                    QLib
C                   Parm                    FLen
C                   Parm                    RcvFQ
C                   Parm                    WaitQ

C                   If        FLen > *zero
C                   Eval      INVNUM = RcvFQ
C                   Else
C                   Exsr      NoElem
C                   EndIf
```

Figure 14.7
RPG Call to QRCVDTAQ
without Key

Figure 14.8 is an example of the code that retrieves entries with the key 'TYPE1' from the data queue. The sender information is captured in SNDVAL, and the structure SNDR provides sender job name, sender user, and sender job number.

```
+....1....+....2....+....3....+....4....+....5....+....6....+....7....+....8
    * Declare and Initialize fields for Send Data Queue Program Call.
D QName          S             10A   INZ('DATQ1')
D QLib           S             10A   INZ('*LIBL')
D RcvFQ          S             20A
D Flen           S              5 0
D WaitQ          S              5 0 INZ(-5)
D KRule          S              2   INZ('EQ')
D KLen           S              3 0 INZ(5)
D KeyVal         S              5A  INZ('TYPE1')
D SdrLen         S              3 0 INZ(44)

    *   Queue Entry Sender Data.
DSdrVal          DS
D LenRtv                        4P 0
D LenAvl                        4P 0
D SJobName                     10A
D SUser                        10A
D SJobNum                       6A
D SusrPrf                      10A

    *
C                   Call      'QRcvDtaQ'
C                   Parm                    QName
C                   Parm                    QLib
C                   Parm                    FLen
C                   Parm                    RcvFQ
```

Figure 14.8
RPG Call to QRCVDTAQ
with Key and Sender
Information

continued

Figure 14.8
Continued

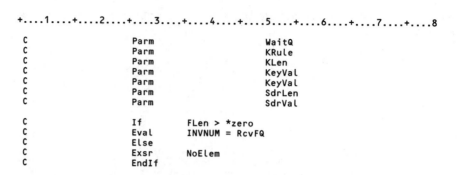

```
+....1....+....2....+....3....+....4....+....5....+....6....+....7....+....8
C                        Parm                      WaitQ
C                        Parm                      KRule
C                        Parm                      KLen
C                        Parm                      KeyVal
C                        Parm                      KeyVal
C                        Parm                      SdrLen
C                        Parm                      SdrVal

C                        If         FLen > *zero
C                        Eval       INVNUM = RcvFQ
C                        Else
C                        Exsr       NoElem
C                        EndIf
```

Program QCLRDTAQ clears the data queue. But remember: it doesn't reclaim the space. To reclaim the space, you will have to delete the data queue and recreate it. When QCLRDTAQ is called, it must be passed the Queue Name and Library Name (or *LIBL or *CURLIB).

The command DLTDTAQ (Delete Data Queue) deletes the data queue.

Exercise 14.1 Data Queue Exercise Without Key

Purpose
To develop a further understanding of passing values using data queues.

Instructions
Create data queue DQ1, send elements to the data queue, and retrieve elements from the data queue.

1. Create a data queue named DQ1, which is 60 bytes wide, unkeyed, and FIFO.

2. Copy and modify one of your interactive programs that updates the inventory file. Modify the program so that every time it adds a record to the file, it will send a copy of that record to the data queue. You cannot actually send a record to the data queue (only a field or data structure). Therefore, you will need to create a structure that is identical to your file structure. The easiest way to create a data structure identical to an externally defined file is to use an externally defined data structure. This is done using a D-spec for an externally defined data structure, as shown in Figure 14.9. This structure, called SNDVAR in Figure 14.9, adopts the structure as defined in file INVPF. If your program moves this data structure to a field of the correct length, your program can then pass that field to the program and send that field the data queue.

Figure 14.9
Defining an Externally
Defined Data Structure
Identical to the Record
Structure of File INVPF

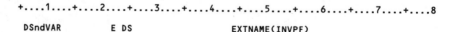

```
+....1....+....2....+....3....+....4....+....5....+....6....+....7....+....8
DSndVAR         E DS                   EXTNAME(INVPF)
```

3. Use your program to add records to the file. Each time you add a record, your program should send copies of each record to the data queue.

continued

Exercise 14.1, *Continued*

4. Write a second program to receive each value from the data queue and print out each entry. This program will read each entry from the data queue. Transfer the entry to a data structure as defined in Figure 14.9 and print the field data. The request to receive from the data queue will have a zero wait condition. When there are no more entries, the program will end. Remember, every time that you run this program, it will remove all entries from the data queue. If you want to run this program again, you will have to run the maintenance program that you created in step 2 to send new entries to the data queue.

Exercise 14.2 Data Queue Exercise with Key

Purpose
To develop a further understanding of passing values using data queues with keys.

Instructions
Create data queue DQ2, send elements to the data queue, and retrieve elements from the data queue.

1. Create a new data queue, DQ2, which includes a 1-byte key and sender information.
2. Copy and modify the program created in Exercise 14.1, step 2, to send records to DQ2 whenever a record is added, deleted, or changed. When a record is sent to the queue, the action taken should be keyed with A, D, or C.
3. Run your program and add, delete, and change inventory data.
4. Copy and modify your program from Exercise 14.1, step 4, so that it will loop three times. The first loop will receive entries keyed with a 'D' and write a report of all deleted records. The second will write a report of all added records. The third will write a report of all changed records.
5. Copy and modify your program from step 4. Change it to a single loop that retrieves only added entries. Change the wait value to a negative number, which will make it wait forever. Do not run the program until you read step 6.
6. Do not call the program that you created in step 5. Because it will run forever, it will lock up your terminal session. Instead, submit the Receiver program to run in batch with the SBMJOB (Submit Job) command.

   SBMJOB CMD(CALL yourpgmnm) JOB(YourLastName)

   Check to make sure that the job is running using the command

   DSPJOB YourLastName

7. Now add about 75 records to the inventory file using your modified inventory maintence program from step 2.
8. Check on your program with the DSPJOB option. It should still be active. Check option 14, Display Open Files, and select the option to display I/O details (either F10 or F11). Note how many records have been written to your output file. Press Enter and select option 4, Work with Spool Files. If your program is on the second page, you will be able to view the first page. If not, go back and add more inventory items and try again.
9. To end the job, issue the command

   WRKSBMJOB

Move to your batch job and end it by pressing 4 (F4) *IMMED. Make sure that it ends. (You may have to press F5 to refresh the screen to make sure that the job has ended.)

Review

1. Describe how you could make synchronous processing occur between two programs using two data queues.
2. Describe how you could make synchronous processing occur between two programs using a single keyed data queue.
3. Describe the dangers of using data queues. In what ways are data files safer?
4. How can you "impose" a structure on a single element of a data queue?
5. Why might a daily job start by deleting a data queue and then re-creating it?

Appendix A

A Matter of Style

Standards and Style

An organization's IS department establishes its own standards. When you join a programming team, they will give you a copy of a standards document. That document will probably

- Identify test and production libraries
- Describe program- and object-naming conventions

It may also identify

- Standard subroutines
- Variable-naming conventions
- Commands to use or avoid
- General programming methodology
- Standard program headers

You will want to study the standards and use them.

But beyond these standards, much about how your programs work is your decision. Where standards end, style takes over. Each individual must develop his or her own style. Style doesn't necessarily make a program better, but it can clearly make your work appear and be more professional. This appendix contains my opinions on some key matters of style, developed over years of working with many organizations.

Every program that you design, develop, or maintain reflects your skill and methodology. If you're in a rush or sloppy, those qualities will be reflected in your code — its appearance, performance, and maintainability. You should be proud of every line that you code and of the mark that your style leaves on every program.

Three areas where style can make a difference are program headings, subroutines, and program modifications.

Program Headings

Programs, data files, and other objects should be clearly identified with an introductory or heading section. This heading section comprises comments that could contain some or all of the following:

- Who wrote the program and when
- Why it was written
- What it does
- A short narrative that describes the program
- Pseudocode for the program
- A list of all files and how they are used
- A list of all variable names and how they are used

- A list of all indicators and how they are used
- A list of all modifications to the program, with the following information for each:
  - Who made a modification
  - When a modification was made
  - Why a modification was made
  - What was modified
  - The modification "mark" (if used) that identifies modified lines

That's a lot of information to include in every program. You will want to save time and keep the headings of all programs similar by laying out a heading once and then copying it into every program. An example of a program heading is shown in Figure A.1. Similar headings should be used for CL programs, physical and logical files, and any other source developed. The cost of these extra lines is that the compiler runs for an extra few fractions of a second and the source code takes a little more space on disk. The compiler does not transfer any of the comments to the object code, so the actual program is not affected by the number of comments included in the source code.

Figure A.1

Sample RPG Program Heading

```
******************************************************************************
*     Jefferson College
*     PROGRAMMER:              - Professor Levinson
*     DATE:                    - 12/15/99
*     APPLICATION NAME:        - Inventory System
*     PROGRAM NAME:            - INVRØ1
*
*     DESCRIPTION  - 1. Clears Subfile   2. Loads Subfile  3. Displays Footer
*                    4. Exercises the Screen Display with the Subfile
******************************************************************************
*  L O G   O F   M O D I F I C A T I O N S
*
*  DATE          PGMR          DESCRIPTION
* ---------------------------------------------------------------------------
*  /  /
******************************************************************************
*  F U N C T I O N   O F   I N D I C A T O R S
*  IND              FUNCTION
* ---------------------------------------------------------------------------
*  Ø3               USED TO EXIT DISPLAY
*  5Ø               USED TO DISPLAY/CLEAR SUBFILE
*  9Ø               EOF FLAG FOR INVPF
*  LR               SET ON LAST RECORD
******************************************************************************
*  S U B R O U T I N E   I N D E X
******************************************************************************
*  INIT          - INITIALIZATION
*  LOAD          - CLEAR AND ACTIVATE SUBFILE DSPØ1
*  DISP          - DISPLAY SUBFILE
******************************************************************************
```

The header section becomes especially valuable when the program needs to be maintained. For example, the code may be very complex, and the pseudocode is crucial because it gives a clear picture of how the parts of the program fit together. The most recent modifications may point to the cause of the newest bug.

Subroutines

The basic organization of a program into subroutines may be specified by your company's standards. However, you will probably have some discretion about creating additional subroutines. Opinions vary about the number of subroutines that should be used in RPG/400 programs. Here are three opinions with rationales:

- None — RPG runs best with straight-line code. Every call to a subroutine wastes processing time.
- Few — RPG runs best with straight-line code. Every call to a subroutine wastes processing time.
- However many the program needs — Create one subroutine for each repeated task.

And the right answer is — one for each identifiable, repeated task. At least that's my opinion. Code that is easy to write, debug, understand, and modify will generally save more in programmer costs than will be saved in other ways by designing faster programs. Subroutines are the result of good modular design. Good code should, in fact, contain many short subroutines — because, as a rule of thumb, a subroutine should not be longer than 20 lines. If you cannot see an entire subroutine on the screen, you may overlook some important feature when you do the initial coding and debugging, when you perform program maintenance, or when you modify the program. Subroutines should always place the next level of nesting in a subordinate, or "child," subroutine.

Create as many subroutines as are necessary so that no subroutine contains nested code. Instead, subroutines should always place the next level of nesting in subordinate subroutines. With this methodology, each subroutine will do a clear and simple task.

I use modular design techniques and coding, which make more sense today than ever before. Modular design reduces time spent designing, coding, testing, and debugging. When you use modular design techniques, you create subroutines that are likely to be reusable in future programs. And with these techniques, you prepare your code to take advantage of the move to RPG IV. In particular, RPG IV lets your program efficiently call other programs and procedures. In RPG/400, the same task may be coded into hundreds of programs or included in a copy book that must be copied into hundreds of programs. In RPG IV, only one copy of the code to perform a task is necessary; it can be called from all other RPG programs.

The exact number of subroutines is dependent on the number of clear tasks or modules. However, anytime a module becomes complicated, it makes sense to divide its tasks further.

> **Note:** Complicated code, including code with multiple levels of nesting, is difficult to read and comprehend. Such code will also be hard to debug, maintain, and modify. Therefore, anytime a module becomes complicated, it makes sense to divide its tasks further, moving nested code into subroutines that are called by the controlling or "parent" subroutine.

Subroutine Sequence

Subroutine sequencing may be specified in your organization's standards. If it is not, it becomes a matter of style. Among the options for ordering your subroutine are

- using the sequence in which the subroutines are processed
- placing the subroutines that are used the most at the beginning and those used the least at the end of the source code (This puts the initialization, end of job, and error handling at the end of a program.)
- putting the subroutines in order by relationship
- putting the subroutines in alphabetical order

The performance impact of subroutine order is usually too small to measure. And by using the "find" capability in the editor, it is always easy to find a subroutine — wherever it's located. However, when I'm coding, I attempt to place subroutines in the sequence in which they are processed. The reason is this: if Subroutine A, which is located near the beginning of a large program, calls Subroutine B, which is located near the end of the program, system performance can be affected. The system might have to swap the page containing Subroutine B into memory and, when Subroutine B ends, swap the page containing Subroutine A back into memory if it has been swapped out. Swapping does slow a program and — if it occurs frequently — lead to a measurable drop in performance. If the two subroutines were in the same logical page, swapping would not occur. And in theory, the chances that the two would be in the same page are greater if they are near each other in the source code.

Subroutine Headings

Subroutines should be clearly identified with a subroutine heading that is easily visible when you read the subroutine on the screen or in printed form. It should contain the name of the subroutine (and because the subroutine name is only six characters long, the heading should also include a meaningful name). Some standards require that the subroutine heading include

- the pseudocode for the subroutine
- the subroutines that call this subroutine
- the subroutines called by this subroutine

Figure A.2 presents a sample subroutine heading. The source shown includes a /EJECT, a compiler directive to start a new page in the listing at that point. The use of /EJECT before each subroutine creates compiler listings that are easy to read.

Figure A.2
Sample Subroutine
Heading

```
    +....1....+....2....+....3....+....4....+....5....+....6....+....7....+....8

    /EJECT
    ****************************************************************
    **   Subroutine Load - Loads 8 records into the inventory       **
    **                     subfile INVSF from the datafile INVPF.   **
    **                                                              **
    **      Called by:  MainLine, Respnd                           **
    **      Calls:      None                                       **
    ****************************************************************
    C     Load          BegSR
```

Modifications

Programs are modified for many reasons:

- to debug them
- to respond to specification changes
- to respond to system changes

Whenever a program is changed, the change should be recorded. The program heading should indicate who made the change, when, why, and what the change is. Although modification notes are often short, they can be invaluable in hunting down problems or when subsequent changes are needed.

Many organizations use modification marks (mod marks) to record the exact changes that are made. When using mod marks, lines are not deleted or changed but rather converted to comments by adding an * in column 7. In the case of an addition or change, a new line is then inserted. The modified lines are "marked" in columns 2 through 6 with the mod mark beginning with the letter D for the deleted line or A for the added line. To view columns 2 through 6 press F19 (Shift left) while in SEU. An example of a program modification is shown in Figure A.3. In this example, you can see that mod mark 101 changed a calculation from an addition to a division.

```
FMT *    ..... *..1....+....2....+....3....+....4....+....5....+....6....+....7....+....8
0001.01
0002.01         **************************************
0002.02         **   Demonstration Routine          **
0002.03         **   Shows how mod marks can be used. **
0002.04         **************************************
0002.08    C       Demo        BegSR
0002.09
0003.00 D101 C*              Eval      RstFld = Fld1 + Fld2
0004.00 A101 C               Eval      RstFld = Fld1 / Fld2
0005.00
0006.00    C                 EndSR
```

Figure A.3
Code with Modification
Mark 101

In Figure A.4, you see that the division was replaced by multiplication, using the mod mark 102. Unfortunately, when a second modification occurs to the same line, the mod mark will tell the number of the last change but mask the origin of the line. In this case, it would be impossible to tell that the division was added in modification 101.

```
FMT *    ..... *..1....+....2....+....3....+....4....+....5....+....6....+....7....+....8
0001.01
0002.01         **************************************
0002.02         **   Demonstration Routine          **
0002.03         **   Shows how mod marks can be used. **
0002.04         **************************************
0002.08    C       Demo        BegSR
0002.09
0003.00 D101 C*              Eval      RstFld = Fld1 + Fld2
0004.00 D102 C*              Eval      RstFld = Fld1 / Fld2
0004.01 D102 C*              Eval      RstFld = Fld1 * Fld2
0005.00
0006.00    C                 EndSR
```

Figure A.4
Code with Modification
Mark 102

Depending on the organization's standards, the modification number may be a number assigned to the request for program modification, a project number, or a number kept in a file that contains a record of all modifications.

As was stated at the beginning of this appendix, where standards end, style takes over. Style alone can't correct an incorrect program, but it may make it easier to find and fix an error. Style can't make a bad design better, but it may make its flaws obvious sooner. Style is worth "points" when it takes you beyond the minimal standards. Other programmers will see that you know clear and well-documented code is a pleasure to work on.

Appendix B

Testing and Debugging Programs

Testing and debugging programs is an essential element of programming. This appendix covers

- fast code vs. good code
- syntax, runtime, and logic errors
- resolving errors (finding the right suspects)
- debugging techniques: temporary print output lines, the DISPLAY operation, and the DUMP operation

Testing and Debugging: Part of the Job!

The old joke runs something like this: As the plane took off, a voice came over the intercom, announcing, "This airplane is totally computerized. Nothing can go wrong … go wrong … go wrong …"

In fact, things do go wrong. Your job, your challenge, and I hope your entertainment will be in testing to prevent errors and when they do occur, finding what's gone wrong and making it right. This appendix is devoted to helping you do that.

Fast Code vs. Good Code: The Importance of Testing

You probably would like to be a great programmer and to get the job rewards for being one — the raises and promotions you deserve. Although many programmers share these goals, there are differences in the way they try to achieve them. Some become "hackers" who turn out "fast and dirty" code that is often error prone and hard to maintain. They take pride in speed and cleverness. Other programmers produce fewer lines of code per day but also fewer errors. Their code is usually cleaner and easier to maintain — often because they take time to test their programs extensively.

There are times when speed is everything — usually in maintenance programming, when an essential production program is down and is needed immediately. However, I would prefer to manage a team of careful rather than fast programmers.

Careful programmers design extensive tests for any program, even a program to which they are making only minor changes. Testing procedures must run a program through all of its paces. The testing must work the program functions in all possible sequences. These tests are necessary to find instances in which one function may cause another function to perform improperly. A batch program can be run through a range of functions by providing it with enough variations in the data to exercise all functions of the program. Then, by providing the data records in all possible sequences, the effect of sequence can also be detected. Interactive programs generally require extensive testing using all the functions and variations of activities available to the user. In the modified program, this testing checks for unexpected "side-effects" of the changes. A program must run properly through these tests and produce the correct results every time. The tester must determine what the correct results should be and check each carefully. If an additional modification to a program results from the testing, the entire testing regimen should be repeated.

Many large IS shops have a quality control department that tests all code. Your goal is to become so dependable that the quality control department considers your code exemplary.

If the organization doesn't have an IS quality control department, users become the final step in quality control. If your users become frustrated by program errors, your organization will be impaired — and eventually your career may be in jeopardy.

Syntax, Logic, and Runtime Errors

There are three basic types of errors:

Syntax errors — Syntax errors are grammar errors — errors in your use of the programming language. They are easy to detect because the compiler finds them for you. Fix them, and your program will compile and, assuming there are no other errors, will be nearly perfect.

Logic errors — Logic errors are errors in program design. Because they are the hardest kind of error to detect, they are usually the hardest to correct. Logic errors do not create compiler errors nor do they cause the program to end abnormally (abend). On some or all conditions, logic errors simply produce the wrong results. The occurrence of an extremely unlikely situation or event could cause the wrong result. For example, when the first 10.0 was awarded in an Olympic gymnastics, the board showed 0.0. Because the score had not been anticipated, the scoreboard hardware and software had not been designed and tested to show it.

To detect logic errors, you must test every program extensively. The tests must give the program a thorough "workout" with a complete range of data and conditions. As a programmer, you will be expected to design, carry out, and evaluate tests. And keep in mind that programs do not pass tests with a C — any performance short of perfect is failure.

Runtime errors — Runtime errors are actually a kind of logic error that prevents your program from completing normally. Runtime errors occur when your program compiles and runs but at some point aborts. Whether the program aborts once in a thousand or once in a million records, the error is unacceptable. The program may abort for many reasons. It may have tried to divide a number by zero, access an array out of range, write a subfile with no records, or read a record that was locked. Fortunately, when a program aborts, a great deal of information is available to help you discover the error so you can correct it.

Among the tools that can help you analyze a runtime error are the job log, the error display, and the program dump.

- **Job log** — Job logs are saved as spooled files if the job ended abnormally and had a level of message logging greater than 0. Job logs will also be saved as a spooled file if the job ends normally, has a job level of message logging greater than 0, and the message logging text is not equal to *NOTEXT. All jobs that are active have job logs.

    If a program runs interactively, then messages from that process are included in the user's current job log. While the user is still logged on, these messages can be investigated by first finding the job with the command WRKUSRJOB (Work with User Job). If there are multiple jobs, the correct job must then be selected. You then use option 10, Display Job Log, to display the current job log. The most recent command or message is displayed. To see earlier commands or messages, press the F10 key and then press the Page up key. To see more information about any message or command in an active job log, point to the message or command and press F1. You can also reach the Work with Job menu if you know the job's name, using the WRKJOB command. If the job has the logging of CL commands value set to *YES, then the job log will contain all of the CL commands issued as well as the messages that were logged.

- Error messages — Depending on the message type, severity, and your job description, the system will convey error messages differently. It may display them, for example, on your screen or even interrupt your processing with a message screen requiring a response. In these cases, you can learn more about the message by pointing to it and pressing F1. In other cases, the messages will be sent to your session's message queue, with the command DSPMSG (Display Message). Finally, the message may be sent to the system operator (message queue QSYSOPR), and you can display these messages with the command DSPMSG QSYSOPR. If an error has occurred, the system will have sent a message somewhere, and you may learn what went wrong when you find the message. Remember, these messages were probably logged onto a job log.

- Dump — The error message may let you respond with a D to request a dump, a spooled file that you can view or print. The RPG- or CL-formatted dump contains a detailed picture of what the program was doing at the time of the error, the error message itself, and the values of every variable in the system. (Later, we will discuss how to get dumps of programs even when the system doesn't invite you to do so.)

Resolving Errors: The Right Suspects

Resolving runtime and logic errors is a little like solving a murder mystery. You can see the final results of the program: the reports, database changes, and screen displays. From these results and a knowledge of the program, you must deduce possible causes of the outcomes that occurred. The sequence of events by which you should collect and analyze errors is outlined in the three steps below.

1. You should perform runtime program tests during development, modification, and whenever you suspect a runtime error. During these tests, you should keep a log of the data or screen interactions and the results. Obviously, the conditions that lead to errors are of special interest, but the conditions under which the program performs correctly are also important.

   As an example, if the payroll program produces the wrong values for gross pay for hourly employees who work overtime but the correct gross pay for all other employees, then we would suspect that the problem is in the code that detects and computes gross pay for hourly employees working overtime. We could focus our attention first on that area of the code.

   Some of the errors that you detect may be the result of other errors. In the previous example, one would assume that an error in gross pay would result in subsequent errors in withholding and net pay. This does not, however, mean that the error causing the the wrong value for gross pay is the only error affecting the values of the withholding and net pay. When multiple errors are affecting the results, you may have to fix the most obvious, retest, reanalyze, fix the next error, and repeat the process until the results are correct.

2. For each error, identify the conditions under which it occurs. The conditions can be determined from the data processed that led to the error or the user interaction that led to the error. Detecting the conditions may require the use of display operations, program dumps, or a debugger (all discussed later in this appendix). Here is a list of typical key factors that you will need to analyze the error. However, in a specific situation, you will have to determine the best list of factors based on your program and the errors that occur.

- Does the error occur for every detailed record?
- Does the error occur only for records with a specific value or code?
- Does the error occur for every summary field at a specific level break?

3. Go back to your design armed with this list. Where did the records that failed fail? What conditions or what inherent qualities make the records that passed different from those that failed? All the places, actions, and differences in records are suspects.

If you pick the right suspect, you can now find the piece of code in which you think the error occurs. You now know what should be happening at that point. Do a walk-through of the code. A walk-through is a mental exercise in which you trace the program steps that will be executed and the values that will be computed or changed within the entire program or a specific part that is of immediate interest. Take a record that fails, and write down what happens at each step within the suspect segment of code. Keep a record of the values of each variable as each statement is processed. When you analyze IF statements, it is necessary to determine what code is actually executed and follow the effects of that code on the variables and on subsequent processing. Pretend that you are the data going through the program maze. Where do you go, and what happens to you along the way?

If you find the problem, fix it and test again.

If your analysis doesn't locate the problem, then you will need to use more sophisticated debugging tools that will help you determine the sequence of operations that is actually performed by the program and the values of variables as the program executes. These tools are described in the remainder of this appendix. They will provide results that can be compared with the sequence and variable values that you predicted as you did your walk-through of the code. Where the tools show that something happened that you didn't predict, you will need to return to the code and determine why the sequence or values aren't what you expected and whether the different sequence or values are, in fact, causing the error.

Using Temporary Print Output Lines

The simplest technique that is available, a technique that can be used with virtually every programming language, is to add temporary code to print intermediate results. You add WRITE (Write) or EXFMT (Execute Format) operations at critical locations in the program — points at which you've determined you should test to verify the values that you predicted manually would be warranted. In RPG, it's also necessary to add the appropriate O-specs for the EXFMT operations or the appropriate O-specs in the print file for the WRITE operations. The critical points at which these temporary operations are added are chosen to determine both values of critical variables and the sequence of statements actually performed when the program is processing a record or interaction that produces the wrong results. The output of these temporary print operations should indicate the route that the program takes by printing the subroutine name or the sequence number of the output operations. Figures B.1 and B.2 show how these temporary operations can be added. Figure B.1 contains some suspect code, and Figure B.2 shows the additional operations and the O-specs that would be added to report the variable values and the statement number, which can be used to trace the processing sequence.

```
FMT *+       ....1....+....2....+....3....+....4....+....5....+....6....+....7....+....8
0001.01
0002.00    C              Eval      Fld3 = Fld1 * Fld2
0003.00    C              Eval      Fld4 = Fld1 + Fld3
```

Figure B.1
Suspect Code

If the values of intermediate variables are important to debugging the program, locate temporary output operations in the locations where the values of these variables are critical to the final results and print the variables along with the subroutine name or sequence number, as shown in the shaded lines of Figure B.2.

```
FMT * +      ....1....+....2....+....3....+....4....+....5....+....6....+....7....+....8
0001.01
0002.00    C              Eval      Fld3 = Fld1 * Fld2
0003.00    C              Eval      Fld4 = Fld1 + Fld3
0003.01 Temp C            MoveL     '0003.01'        SeqNo          8
0003.02 Temp C            EXCEPT    Temp1
0004.00

0100.00
0101.00 Temp OQPRINT  E             Temp1           02 02
0102.00 Temp O                      SeqNo                  15
0103.00 Temp O                      Fld1            1      25
0104.00 Temp O                      Fld2            1      35
0105.00 Temp O                      Fld3            1      45
0106.00 Temp O                      Fld4            1      55
```

Figure B.2
Suspect Code with Temporary Output

When you are working with large data sets, this debugging technique is better than most others because you can run the program and then analyze the data at your leisure, comparing the intermediate results produced when records that lead to errors are processed and records that lead to the correct values are processed.

Using the DSPLY (Display) Operation

Another tool you can use to debug either interactive or interactively called jobs is the DSPLY operation, which can display a character variable or constant value. Batch jobs are submitted with the CL command SBMJOB (Submit Job) and cannot be debugged with this tool. The DSPLY operation can be used to debug code in a way similar to adding temporary print operations. As shown in Figure B.3, DSPLY operations are added temporarily to assist with debugging. The DSPLY operation uses Factor 1 for either a constant, such as the statement number '000401', or a variable name. When the program reaches a DSPLY operation, it displays the value and waits for the variable identified in the display operation, waits until the user presses the Enter key, and then continues processing. The DSPLY operation is good for tracing the flow of a program, as well as for tracing the intermediate results created during processing.

Figure B.3

Suspect Code with
DSPLY Operations

```
FMT *+.      ....1....+....2....+....3....+....4....+....5....+....6....+....7....+....8
0001.01
0002.00      C                      Eval      Fld3 = Fld1 * Fld2
0003.00      C                      Eval      Fld4 = Fld1 + Fld3
0004.00 Temp C     '0003.01'        Dsply
0005.00 Temp C     Fld1             Dsply
0006.00 Temp C     Fld2             Dsply
0007.00 Temp C     Fld3             Dsply
0008.00 Temp C     Fld4             Dsply                              1      55
```

DSPLY is a quick and easy-to-use debugging tool. Every time the program encounters a DSPLY operation, it stops and displays the value. This tool is best suited to displaying a few data elements for a few records; it becomes cumbersome and slow for large data sets.

Using the DUMP Operation

If you want to know everything about a program at one point or at a few points during program execution, use the DUMP operation. The DUMP operation offers abundant information, including the values of every variable, the last processes performed on every file, and the outcome of those operations. Nothing matches a dump for its useful wealth of data; just as with murder mysteries, among the many, the guilty party may be the one least suspected.

To trigger a dump, add a C-spec with the DUMP operation at the point at which you want the dump to occur. To use the DUMP operation, your program must begin with an H-specification with the keyword DEBUG(*YES). Caution: if you put the DUMP in a section of the code that is exercised repeatedly, you get a dump every time the command is executed.

Using the Interactive Debugger

The AS/400 provides more advanced tools for debugging RPGLE programs. The DEBUG tool is started with the command STRDBG. To get the best view of your source code while debugging, prompt the compiler when you create a module (option **14** or **15** from WRKMBRPDM or the CL Commands CRTBNDRPG or CRTRPGMOD). To prompt these commands type **14**, **15**, or the CL command and press F4 and F10 for additional parameters. Set the parameter OPTION (compiler options) to *SHOWCPY and *EXPDDS. These options cause the compiler listing to include /COPY books and the details of the data structures of the physical, logical, printer, and display files. Viewing all the code, including that in copy books and the data structures of files, can be helpful during debugging. Set the parameter DBGVIEW (Debug View) to LIST to use the listing created for the compiler. You'll also want to refer to this listing because statement numbers during debugging are based on the compiler statement numbers shown in the listing, not on the source statement numbers.

Note: Remember, to use the source debugger, create your programs or modules using the following parameters:

- Compiler Options: *SHOWCPY, *EXPDDS

- Debug View: *LIST

/COPY

The /COPY compiler directive causes the compiler to load source code from another member before compiling. /COPY is typically used for commonly used routines, procedures, D-specs, and F-specs. It reduces the maintenance burden by requiring changes to only one set of code.

The format of the /COPY directive is

/COPY libraryname/filename,membername

with /COPY beginning in column 7. If the file name is not specified, QRP-GLESRC is assumed. If the library name is not specified, each file in the library list is searched until a member with the member name is found. The entire code in the member name is put into the location where the /COPY directive is entered. This means that each copy member (often referred to as a copy book) should contain only code which can be put into a specific area of a module.

For example, if you want a procedure and its prototype to be available in copy books, you put the D-specs of the prototype and the procedure in separate members. If you wanted to include the prototype in any member, you would include the/COPY directive for the prototype in the D-spec area of the module and the /COPY directive for the procedure at the end of the C-specs.

To start the debugger, type STRDBG at any command line. The screen shown in Figure B.4 appears. Identify the program or programs to debug (in this example INV016E). If you set *YES as the value for the field update production files, the program actually adds, deletes, or changes data in libraries of type production. When the value is set to *NO, the program does not run if it would alter data in production libraries.

Figure B.4
Start Debug Screen

```
                              Start Debug (STRDBG)

 Type choices, press Enter.

 Program  . . . . . . . . . . . . . >  INV016E         Name, *NONE
   Library . . . . . . . . . .          *LIBL          Name, *LIBL, *CURLIB
                 + for more values
                                        *LIBL
 Default program  . . . . . . . .       *PGM           Name, *PGM, *NONE
 Maximum trace statements . . . . >     200            Number
 Trace full . . . . . . . . . . .       *STOPTRC       *STOPTRC, *WRAP
 Update production files  . . . . >     YES            *NO, *YES
 OPM source level debug . . . . .       *NO            *NO, *YES




                                                                     Bottom
 F3=Exit    F4=Prompt    F5=Refresh    F10=Additional parameters   F12=Cancel
 F13=How to use this display          F24=More keys
```

Ending Debug

Enter the ENDDBG command at a command line to end the source debugger. If you attempt to start the source debugger while it is still active, you receive the message

> Command STRDBG not valid in this mode

If you receive this message, issue the command ENDDBG and you should be able to restart the debugger.

Returning to Main Debug Screen

When you want to return to the main debug screen (Figure B.5), issue the CL command **DSPMODSRC** (Display Module Source).

Figure B.5
Display Module Source

```
                            Display Module Source
 Program:  INV016E        Library:   A300C1_BOK     Module:   INV016E
      1          *....1....+....2....+....3....+....4....+....5....+....6....+....7
      2          *Jefferson College   Professor Levinson     12/21/99
      3          *APPLICATION NAME     - Inventory System
      4          *PROGRAM NAME         - INV016E
      5          *DESCRIPTION  -        SELECTION on main SCREEN
      6          *
      7          *
      8          *
      9          *
     10          **************************************************************
     11          *  L O G    O F    M O D I F I C A T I O N S
     12          *
     13          *  DATE     PGMR     DESCRIPTION
     14          * ------------------------------------------------------------
     15          *   /  /
                                                                     More...
 Debug . . . _____

 F3=End program    F6=Add/Clear breakpoint   F10=Step    F11=Display variable
 F12=Resume        F17=Watch variable    F18=Work with watch    F24=More keys
 Additional Function keys (seen by pressing F24)
 F5=Refresh          F9=Retrieve    F14=Work with module list    F15=Select view
 F16=Repeat find    F21=Command entry    F22=Step into         F24=More keys
 F13=Work with module breakpoints   F19=Left    F20=Right    F23=Display output
```

Finding Code

To find code, type **Find** on the Debug command line followed by the text desired. To find subsequent entries of the same text string press F16. If the string to be found has spaces in it, enclose it in quotation marks. For example, to find the word LOAD, type

Find Load

To find RRR = 0, type

Find 'RRN = 0'

To review or recall previous debug commands, press enter, point to the command in the command list, and press F9 (Retrieve Command). To return to the Code screen press Enter.

Setting Breakpoints

Program processing is suspended when it encounters a breakpoint. Variable values can be investigated and changed if you wish, and the program can be continued from that point either in run or single-step mode. To set a breakpoint, move to the line and press F6 (Add/Clear breakpoint). The statement "number of lines with breaks set" is shown in a different color. To remove a breakpoint, move to the line and press F6 again. Set breakpoints at strategic points in your program.

Starting the Program

After appropriate breakpoints are set, press F21 and call your program. The program runs normally until a breakpoint is encountered.

Finding the Value of Any Variable

To view the value of a field, point to any variable in the displayed source listing and press F11. Alternatively, type **EVAL** followed by the field name. Either method displays the value at the bottom of the screen.

Changing the Value of Any Variable

The Debug EVAL command changes the value of any variable. Examples of this command include

```
EVAL *IN50 = '0'
EVAL *IN50 = '1'
EVAL D1PN = 'A310'
EVAL D1QOH = 654
```

Continuing the Program

Press F12 (Resume) to continue the program. The program continues until it reaches the next break, the value of a variable which is being watched changes, or the program ends. Watch is described later in this appendix in the section titled "Watch Field Values."

Step

You can step through the program or a section of the program one statement at a time by pressing F10.

To step further, type **STEP** followed by the number of statements that should be processed. For example, Step 30 processes the next 30 statements. Processing is interrupted by a break or watch.

Exercise B.1 Using the Source Debugger

Purpose

To learn how to use the debugger.

Instructions

1. Start the debugger on one of your interactive programs by issuing the CL command

STRDBG PGM(INV016E) MAXTRC(2000) UPDPROD(*YES)

2. Set a breakpoint at the first operation in the Load subroutine.
3. Press F21 and issue the command **CALL INV016E** to start your program.
4. Run the program until it reaches the breakpoint.
5. Use F11 to evaluate the values of various variables.
6. Step through the subroutine one step at a time by pressing F10. Check the values of the statements that are complete.
7. Step through 50 statements by typing **STEP 50**.
8. Press F12 to continue the program.
9. Exit the debugger (F3).
10. Type **ENDDBG** to end the debug session.

Conditional Breakpoints

To define a break that occurs only under special conditions on a specific statement, use the DEBUG command "Break xxx when expression." For example,

Break 94 when RRN = 0
Break 256 when *IN90 = '1'
Break 1525 when CNTY = 'CAN'

The use of such a conditional statement lets you run the program until it reaches the specific conditions that you suspect are causing a problem. There might be hundreds or thousands of records that process properly but every record with CNTY = 'CAN' processes incorrectly. You can set the program to break at a specific line when this condition occurs and then evaluate the values or variables and step or trace the results.

Watch Field Value

Debug breaks whenever the value of a watched field changes. To set a watch, type **WATCH** followed by the field name, or point to a variable and press F17. F18 provides a Work with Watch screen, shows a list of watched variables, and lets you remove any variables from the list. Watching field values lets you keep tabs on specific fields that you suspect are given erroneous values.

Exercise B.2 Using the Source Debugger with Conditional Breaks and Watch Variables

Purpose

To learn how to use the source debugger with conditional breaks and watch variables.

Instructions

1. Start the debugger on one of your interactive programs by issuing the CL command
   STRDBG PGM(INV016E) MAXTRC(2000) UPDPROD(*YES)

2. Set a conditional breakpoint to stop in the LOAD subroutine when INPN is equal to the value of the third record in the file INVPF.

3. To start your program, press F21 and issue the CALL INV016E command.

4. Run the program until it reaches the breakpoint.

5. Use F11 to evaluate the values of various variables.

6. Add a watch on variable D1PN. Point at D1PN and press F17.

7. Step through 100 statements by typing **STEP 100**. You should see the program break as soon as the value of D1PN changes.

8. Exit the debugger (F3).

9. Type **ENDDBG** to end the debug session.

Using Indented Listings

The compiler can provide an indented listing, which is especially valuable when you are searching for missing END statements or when you are attempting to make sense out of complicated nested code. The indented listing indents each level of nesting by two characters and puts a character of your choosing (usually a vertical line) in the first position to indicate the level of nesting of the code. As shown in Figure B.5, the VARI IFGT VAR2 is itself nested one level, and that operation controls the lines that follow, which are nested two levels. It is easy to follow the vertical bars down to the ENDIF operation and to see which operations are nested within the specific structure.

Figure B.6

Example of
Indented Listing

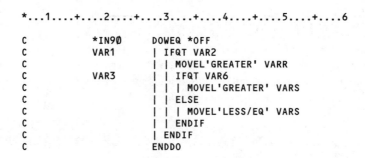

```
*...1....+....2....+....3....+....4....+....5....+....6
C           *IN90       DOWEQ *OFF
C           VAR1        | IFQT VAR2
C                       | | MOVEL'GREATER' VARR
C           VAR3        | | IFQT VAR6
C                       | | | MOVEL'GREATER' VARS
C                       | | ELSE
C                       | | | MOVEL'LESS/EQ' VARS
C                       | | ENDIF
C                       | ENDIF
C                       ENDDO
```

To request an indented listing from the WRKMBRPDM (Work with Members in PDM) screen,

1. select 14 (compile) but don't press Enter,

2. press F4 (Prompt),

3. press use F10 (Additional Values),

4. press Page down to move to the Source Listing Indentation, and

5. type a quote, a vertical line, a space, and a quote ('| ').

Summary

Tracking down errors is a challenging task. If you've written a piece of code, it is difficult to believe in and/or find errors in the code. It is often easier for others to find the errors in your code (and for you to find the errors in theirs). Therefore, it often saves time to have someone else help you find code errors.

Getting familiar with techniques and tools introduced in this appendix will prove beneficial to your career. Many graduates find that their first assignments involve program maintenance. They are often asked to track down errors in complex code. This is not the simplest job in the department — just one that often no one wants or has time for. With the debugging techniques described in this appendix, you can succeed with these tough assignments.

Appendix C

Using Screen Design Aid (SDA)

One of the tools many AS/400 shops use to create a simple display is Screen Design Aid (SDA). This appendix covers the following elements of screen design using SDA:

- Creating a simple display
- Testing the display
- Editing the display
- Creating a window
- Creating a subfile record
- Creating a subfile control record
- Testing the subfile

What Is SDA?

SDA is a powerful tool that IBM provides with the AS/400. It is a screen painter, a screen editor, and a screen tester. It reads and writes display-file members and submits the compiles of the screen files. (It is also a menu builder, a feature not covered in this text.) SDA offers an easy way to develop and test screens for use with RPG, Cobol, and CL.

Some organizations do not use SDA because it does not add modification marks to changes in the display files. When you delete or change a field in SDA, SDA deletes or changes the line but doesn't keep any note of the old value. Even if you're in an organization that doesn't encourage the use of SDA for modification of screen designs, however, you will still find SDA useful to view and test screens.

Creating a Simple Display

SDA can be used to create simple display formats, window formats, and subfile formats. This section will demonstrate how to create the simple screen format shown in Figure C.1.

```
A300C1            COMPUTERS ARE US INV SYS            09/21/99
                  WORK WITH INVENTORY LIST

   Locate Part Number:_____



 ================================================================
 * F3=Exit Subsystem
```

Figure C.1
Simple Input Screen

Type STRSDA (Start Screen Design Aid) to bring up the initial SDA screen (Figure C.2).

Figure C.2
Start SDA Screen

```
                         AS/400 Screen Design Aid (SDA)

Select one of the following:

        1. Design screens
        2. Design menus
        3. Test display files


Selection or command
===>

F1=Help    F3=Exit    F4=Prompt    F9=Retrieve    F12=Cancel
                                        (C) COPYRIGHT IBM CORP. 1981, 1995
```

To design screens, select option 1. SDA displays the Design Screens screen shown in Figure C.3. This display is used to specify the name of the display-file member, the source file, and the library in which the display-file member will be stored.

Figure C.3
Design Screens
Screen

```
                              Design Screens
Type choices, press Enter.

    Source file . . . . . . . .   QDDSSRC     Name, F4 for list

      Library . . . . . . . . .    PHILSLIB   Name, *LIBL, *CURLIB

    Member  . . . . . . . . . .   APPENDIXC1  Name, F4 for list




    F3=Exit      F4=Prompt      F12=Cancel
```

Fill in the name of the file in which you want the source member to be stored, the library where that file is located, and the name of the screen member. If the screen exists, it will be brought into SDA for editing. If it doesn't exist, you will be starting a new member. Either way, the next screen to appear is the Work with Display Records screen (shown in Figure C.4). If the DDS previously existed, the list would contain the record names and types.

```
                      Work with Display Records

     File . . . . . . :    APPENDIXC           Member . . . . . . :    APPENDIXC1
       Library . . . . :     A300C1_BOK        Source type  . . . :    DSPF

     Type options, press Enter.
       1=Add              2=Edit comments       3=Copy            4=Delete
       7=Rename           8=Select keywords    12=Design image

     Opt  Order   Record        Type       Related Subfile    Date        DDS Error


          (No records in file)



                                                                      Bottom
     F3=Exit                    F12=Cancel       F14=File-level keywords
     F15=File-level comments    F17=Subset       F24=More keys
```

Figure C.4
Work with Display
Records Screen

File-Level Comments

Before creating the format, we will create file-level comments with function key F15.
These comments will be placed in the member before the first record.

Press F15 and enter the following comments:

```
+....1....+....2....+....3....+....4....+....5....+....6....+....7....+....8

A*****************************************************************
A*  APPENDIX C SCREEN 1     YOURNAME         DATE
A*****************************************************************
```

The editor works much the same way SEU works. Press F3 to exit and save your
comments.

File-Level Keywords

File-level keywords can be added or modified by pressing function key F14. SDA will
put all file-level keywords before the first record. File-level keywords are in effect for
all formats in the display file. When you press F14, SDA displays the Select File Keywords screen shown in Figure C.5. For this demonstration, we will add the file-level
keywords CF03(03) and Print.

To add or edit an indicator keyword, type Y beside Indicator keywords on the
Select File Keywords screen and press Enter. SDA will now display the Define Indicator Keywords screen shown in Figure C.6.

Figure C.5
Select File
Keywords Screen

```
                              Select File Keywords

     Member . . . :   APPENDIXC1

     Type choices, press Enter.

        General keywords
        Indicator keywords. . . . . . . .  Y
        Print keywords. . . . . . . . . .  _
        Help keywords . . . . . . . . . .  _
        Display sizes . . . . . . . . . .  _
        Alternate keywords  . . . . . . .  _
        DBCS conversion . . . . . . . . .  _
        Window Borders  . . . . . . . . .  _
        Menu-bar keywords . . . . . . . .  _




     F3=Exit    F4=Display Selected Keywords    F12=Cancel
```

Figure C.6
Define Indicator
Keywords Screen
with Command
Function 03
Defined

```
                            Define Indicator Keywords

     Member . . . :   APPENDIXC1

     Type keywords and parameters, press Enter.
        Conditioned keywords:        CFnn CAnn CLEAR PAGEDOWN/ROLLUP PAGEUP/ROLLDOWN
                                     HOME HELP HLPRTN
        Unconditioned keywords:      INDTXT VLDCMDKEY

     Keyword    Indicators/+ Resp Text
      CF03      __ __ __     03   F3=Exit




                                                                        Bottom
     F3=Exit    F12=Cancel
```

As shown in Figure C.6, you fill out the definition for command function 03 (CF03). The keyword to be defined is entered into the keyword column. The three indicators columns hold the conditioning indicators. They appear to the right of the A-spec and control when a keyword is active. Because we want CF03 active all the time, we will leave these blank. The RESP indicator, the indicator that the keyword turns on, should be 03. Finally, we can provide comments such as F3=Exit. Use the Enter key to exit this screen and save the changes (F3 exits without saving the changes). SDA will take this data and create the file-level keyword CF03.

```
+....1....+....2....+....3....+....4....+....5....+....6....+....7....+....8
A                                        CF03(03 'F3=Exit')
```

To add or edit a print keyword, type Y beside Print keywords on the File Keywords screen and press Enter. SDA will now display the Define Print Keywords screen (Figure C.7). The print keyword lets the user use the Print or PrtScr keys to print a screen to a spool file.

```
                        Define Print Keywords

Member . . . :   APPENDIXC1

Type choices, press Enter.
                                         Keyword
   Enable keyword . . . . . . . . . .    PRINT     Y             Y=Yes
      Indicators . . . . . . . . . . .

   Program handles print:
      Response indicator . . . . . . .                          01-99
      Text . . . . . . . . . . . . . .


System handles print:
   Print file . . . . . . . . . . .                             Name, *PGM
      Library  . . . . . . . . . . .                            Name,
                                                                  *LIBL, *CURLIB

   Leave print file open until
      display file is closed . . . .    OPENPRT                 Y=Yes


F3=Exit    F12=Cancel
```

Figure C.7

Define Print Keywords Screen with Enable Keyword Selected

To add the file-level keyword Print, type Y in the Enable Keyword field and then press Enter (not F3, which fails to record the change). Press F3 to exit the Select File Keywords field and select 1 to save and exit the File Keywords screen.

Adding a Record

To add a record format to the display file, type a 1 in the options column of the Work with Display Records screen. SDA displays the Add New Record screen (Figure C.8).

```
                        Add New Record

File . . . . . . . :   APPENDIXC        Member . . . . . . :   APPENDIXC1
   Library . . . . :   A300C1_BOK       Source type  . . . :   DSPF

Type choices, press Enter.

   New record  . . . . . . . . . . . . . . . .   TESTREC1     Name

   Type  . . . . . . . . . . . . . . . . . . .   RECORD       RECORD, USRDFN
                                                              SFL,    SFLMSG
                                                              WINDOW, WDWSFL
                                                              PULDWN, PDNSFL
                                                              MNUBAR




F3=Exit     F5=Refresh      F12=Cancel
```

Figure C.8

Add New Record Screen

On the Add New Record screen, enter the name of the record format. Notice that the second field on that screen is used to define the type of record entered. A simple screen such as the screen that we are developing is of type RECORD.

When you press Enter, you will see the blank screen where you will paint your record. To add the user ID, move to the position row 2, column 10. The cursor position is displayed in the lower left corner of the screen (row 2, column 10 would be shown as 02-10). Type *USER and press Enter. The *USER should be replaced with 10 Us to represent the user ID's 10-character length.

Move to the position row 2, column 28 (02-28) and type **COMPUTERS ARE US INV SYS** and press Enter. Then press F20, which highlights blocks of text. Notice that it breaks this string into four separate strings at the blank spaces. We will find it more practical to keep this string together. Had we included single quotes before and after the string, it would have been treated as a single block. (It's not too late. Just type a single quote before and after the string and press Enter. The entire length of the string is now highlighted, indicating that it's a single string.)

Move to the position row 2, column 56 (02-56) and type *DATE, which inserts the keyword and format for the system date. These fields aren't very well centered, but you can move fields left one character for each < you type before the field. To move fields to the right, type the number of > symbols that represent the number of characters you want to move the field.

Place the cursor beneath C in "Computers," and then move it one space to the left. Type **WORK WITH INVENTORY LIST** at 03-20. Move to 07-13 and type **Locate Part Number:**.

Move one space after the colon (:) and type +I(11) to define an input field 11 characters long. Alpha fields use I (Input), O (Output), and B (Both). Numeric fields use 3 for Input, 6 for Output, and 9 for Both. The system has named the field FLD01 and would name the next field FLD02. To give the field a more meaningful name, press F4 and type over FLD01 the new name **SELPN**.

We would like to do to more with SELPN, and there are two ways to get to the field-level keywords for this field. On the Work with Fields screen, type a 1 next to the field that you want to work with; from the screen painter, type an asterisk (*) immediately in front of the field that you want to work with and Select Field Keywords appears.

I suspect that you can work out the COLOR keyword for yourself.

The Define Database Reference screen (Figure C.9, page 245) will let you change the structural definition of SELPN to be just like field INPN. This ensures that subsequent changes in the physical-file structure will automatically be incorporated into the display-file structure with a recompile of the DSPF.

The original screen (Figure C.1) has a double line near the bottom, which has been created by typing a series of equals signs ('='). Remember to put single quotes around the line, as follows:

'=='

and below the line add the text **F3 = Exit Subsystem**.

To change the color of text, you treat it just like a field. An * just before the text will bring you to the screen where you can select colors.

```
                  Define Database Reference

   Field . . . . . :   SELPN            Usage . . :   I
   Length  . . . . :   11               Row . . . :   7      Column . . . :   35

   Type choices, press Enter.
                                       Keyword
       Reference field  . . . . . . . .   REFFLD      Y          Y=Yes
       Reference current DDS source . .   *SRC                   Y=Yes
       Field (if different) . . . . . .               INPN       Name
       Database file . . . . . . . . .                INVPF      Name
         Library . . . . . . . . . . .                *Libl      Name, *LIBL, *CURLIB
         Record . . . . . . . . . . . .                          Name
       Override existing field definition:
         New field length . . . . . . .                          +nnnn, −nnnn, nnnn
         New decimal positions  . . . .                          +n, −n, nn
         New keyboard shift . . . . . .                          N A X W I D M
                                                                 J O E G

       Ignore previously specified:
         Validity check . . . . . . . .   DLTCHK                 Y=Yes
         Editing  . . . . . . . . . . .   DLTEDT                 Y=Yes

   F3=Exit    F12=Cancel
```

Figure C.9

Define Database
Reference Screen

You can "cut and paste" data from the screen by marking a rectangular block with a hyphen at the beginning and end (upper left and lower right) and then putting an equals sign at the position to which you want the upper left corner of the block moved.

You can delete a rectangular block by marking the upper left and lower right with double hyphens.

F1 provides additional Help.

You can exit your design screen by pressing F3 and selecting 1 to save the design. You can exit the Work with Display Records screen by pressing F3.

Check over the Create Display File screen; you will want to be sure it has identified the correct library in which to create the display file. The Library field is in the middle of the screen. The upper section of the display-file screen defines where the source member is to be stored. The middle and the bottom of the display-file screen control the creation of the display-file object, including the object name and library.

Exercise C.1 Using SDA to Create a Simple Screen

Purpose
To demonstrate using SDA to create a simple format, edit the format, and compile the display file.

Instructions
Create the display file SDAC1. It should have a single record that is similar to the simple screen shown in Figure C.1.

1. Create the input screen to locate part number using SDA as described in the previous sections of this appendix.

Testing Screen Designs

The display file must be successfully compiled before it can be tested. Press F3 to Exit as far as the initial SDA screen and select option 3, Test display files. SDA will assume that you want to test the most recently designed screen. Enter the Record name or Press F4 and select the record name to be tested and press Enter.

The testing process has the following three steps:

1. We can prepare values for fields and indicators that are output from the program to the screen. In our current record, no fields are Output or Both, and our only indicator, 03, is used as an output from the screen. Therefore, the first step is blank except for the text "No output fields for this record." Press Enter.

2. This step displays our record as it will appear to the user. With our file and record rules, we could

   - Press Enter.
   - Press F3.
   - Type a Part Number and press Enter.
   - Type a Part Number and press F3.

Try any of these and you will see that after pressing Enter or F3, the test system will advance to step 3.

   3. This step displays the results that would be returned to your program.

You can then press Enter to wrap around and repeat the test. Try all four possibilities. How would the results be different if the F3 definition were CA03 instead of CF03?

Exit the test with F3 and go back to the design phase. Use F14 to change indicator 03 from CF to CA and return and test out your assumption. Which options produce different results? How are they different?

Adding a Window

Return to the Work With Display Records screen by exiting the test environment and selecting 1 to go into the design environment. SDA will assume that you want to continue working with the same member that you were most recently editing. This time we want to add a new format, window1, the window shown in Figure C.10.

Figure C.10
WINDOW1
Window

```
 _____
/                                                         \
|          CHANGE Inventory Values                        |
|                                                         |
|    Part Number: A124                                    |
|    Description: COMPUTER PENT                           |
|    Quantity on Hand:    215                             |
|    Unit Cost:      2100.16                              |
|    Warehouse Stored In:   FTW                           |
|    Warehouse Location:    219                           |
|                                                         |
|    F12 = Cancel                                         |
_____/
```

Also, unlike our window in Chapter 2, we would like to use the actual fields from the data file. This would simplify the RPG code because this window will display whatever record is current from the data file. If you change the data on the window, all your program would have to do is an UPDATE. This saves several

MOVE operations, but it also means that we get to experiment with picking fields directly from the file and placing them in the window.

The following steps are used to create a window:

1. On the Work with Display Records screen, select 1 to add a new record format.
2. On the Add New Records screen, enter the record name, WINDOW1, of the type, WINDOW.
3. Select General Keywords.
4. Use a Y to choose the Select parameters entry immediately below the Window parameters line.
5. Change the value of the Actual Line so that the window begins on 4.
6. Change the value of the Actual Position (the Column) to 5.
7. Change the value of the Window Lines to 12.
8. Change the value of the Window Position (Number of Columns in the window) to 60.
9. Press Enter twice to return to Select Windows Keywords.
10. Select Record Keywords. Add CA12(12) as an indicator keyword.
11. Press Enter until you return to the Work With Display Records screen.

WINDOW1 now exists but is blank. Select 12 to design WINDOW1.

The window border is displayed on the design screen. Type your text in the window. Remember to use single quotes before and after strings and recall that F20 will show you the text in reverse video.

Now we're ready to add the database fields to the screen.

Press F10 to Select Database Files. The screen shown in Figure C.11 will be displayed. This screen lets you make the fields of one or more databases available for your design. Option 2 will make all of the fields of the database available for use in your screen design. These fields will be Input only. Options 3 and 4 also make all of the fields available but with usage levels of Output and Both, respectively. Use option 4 to select all fields as Both.

```
                        Select Database Files

   Type options and names, press Enter.
      1=Display database field list
      2=Select all fields for input (I)
      3=Select all fields for output (O)
      4=Select all fields for both (B) input and output

   Option    Database File   Library     Record
      4       INVPF          *LIBL       INVPFR




   F3=Exit     F4=Prompt      F12=Cancel
```

Figure C.11
Select Database Files Screen

Press Enter twice to return to the design screen. Now the field names appear at the bottom of the screen with a reference number. For example, 1: INPN indicates that the field INPN will be treated as field number 1. Go to where you want a field to be positioned and type **&RefNum.** Notice that the remaining fields' reference numbers will be renumbered immediately. So, if you were to place the field INPN with the command&1, the field INDESC would then have the reference number of 1. Locate the rest of the fields. You can place one or more fields on the display at a time by entering **&RefNum** on the screen wherever you want to add the field(s).

The Unit Cost field would look good with the edit code of J. Place your cursor immediately in front of that field and type an asterisk (*). Select Editing Keywords and type a **J** for the edit code.

Put the edit code of J on the Quantity on Hand field.

Exercise C.2 Using SDA to Create a Window

Purpose
To use SDA to create a window and to use a field reference file.

Instructions
Modify display file SDAC1. Add a window record format, WINDOW1, as shown in Figure C.10.

1. Modify the input screen of the window format WINDOW1 as shown in Figure C.10.

Creating a Subfile Record and a Subfile Control Record Using SDA

To demonstrate the design and creation of a subfile record format and its control record, we will step through the creation of the subfile record and subfile control record shown in Figure C.12.

Figure C.12
Computers Are US
Inventory List Screen

```
USERID                      COMPUTERS ARE US INV SYS              12/18/99
                            WORK WITH INVENTORY LISTS

PART NUMBER  DESCRIPTION                      QNTY      COST     EXTENDED

A123         Computer x486                      21  1,301.15   27,324.15
A124         Computer Pent                     215  2,100.16  451,534.40
A125         Printer - Laser                    81    974.21   78,911.01
A213         Printer - Ink Jet                  15    457.15    6,857.25
A214         Printer - Dot Matrix               21    251.14    5,273.94
A215         Scanner - Hand                     15    127.19    1,907.85
A216         Scanner - Flat Bed                  5    421.15    2,105.75
A319         CD-ROM                              6    115.96      695.76

==============================================================================
F3=Exit Subsystem
```

To create a subfile record and subfile control record in SDA,

1. Select option 1 (create record) from the SDA Work with Display Records screen.
2. Enter the record name and the type SFL on the Add New Record screen (Figure C.13).

```
                       Add New Record

File . . . . . . :   QDDSSRC           Member . . . . . . :   SDADEMO1
  Library . . . . :    A300C1_TMP      Source type . . . :    DSPF

Type choices, press Enter.

  New record . . . . . . . . . . . . . . . SFL1       Name

  Type . . . . . . . . . . . . . . . . . . SFL        RECORD, USRDFN
                                                        SFL,    SFLMSG
                                                      WINDOW, WDWSFL
                                                      PULDWN, PDNSFL
                                                      MNUBAR




F3=Exit     F5=Refresh     F12=Cancel
```

Figure C.13
Add New Record
Screen

SDA will redisplay the Add New Record screen with an additional line for the name of the subfile control record (Figure C.14).

```
                       Add New Record

File . . . . . . :   QDDSSRC           Member . . . . . . :   SDADEMO1
  Library . . . . :    A300C1_TMP      Source type . . . :    DSPF

Type choices, press Enter.

  New record . . . . . . . . . . . . . . . SFL1       Name

  Type . . . . . . . . . . . . . . . . . . SFL        RECORD, USRDFN
                                                        SFL,    SFLMSG
                                                      WINDOW, WDWSFL
                                                      PULDWN, PDNSFL
                                                      MNUBAR




  Subfile control record . . . . . . . . SFLCTL1

F3=Exit     F5=Refresh     F12=Cancel
```

Figure C.14
Second View of
Add New Record
Screen with
Subfile Control
Record

3. Enter the name of the control record.

SDA will display the Select Subfile Keywords screen (Figure C.15). At the moment we don't need these options.

Figure C.15

Select Subfile
Keywords Screen

```
                          Select Subfile Keywords

    Subfile record . . . . . . . :   SFL1

    Type choices, press Enter

                                           Y=Yes
       General keywords  . . . . . . . . _
       Indicator keywords  . . . . . . . _


    TEXT keyword . . . . . . . . . . . . _




    F3=Exit    F4=Display Selected Keywords
```

4. Press Enter to advance to the next screen.

Figure C.16

Select Subfile
Control
Keywords
Screen

```
                          Select Subfile Control Keywords

    Subfile control record . . . . . . . . . :   SFLCTL1

    Type choices, press Enter.


    General keywords . . . . . . . . . . _
       Subfile display layout  . . . . . _
       Subfile messages  . . . . . . . . _

       Select record keywords  . . . . . _

       TEXT keyword  . . . . . . . . . . _




    F3=Exit    F4=Display Selected Keywords    F12=Cancel
```

SDA will display the Select Subfile Control Keywords screen (Figure C.16).

5. Type **Y** in the field for General Keywords on the Select Subfile Control Keywords screen. SDA will display the Define General Keywords screen (Figure C.17).

```
                    Define General Keywords

Subfile control record . . . . . . . . . :   SFLCTL1

Type choices, press Enter.            Keyword
   Related subfile record . . . . . . .  SFLCTL    SFL1_____   Name
   Subfile cursor relative record . . .  SFLCSRRRN _____    Name
   Subfile mode . . . . . . . . . . . .  SFLMODE   _____    Name


Y=Yes        Indicators/+
   Display subfile records . . . . . .   SFLDSP      Y         50
   Display control record . . . . . . .  SFLDSPCTL   Y         50
   Initialize subfile fields . . . . .   SFLINZ      _
   Delete subfile area . . . . . . . .   SFLDLT      _
   Clear subfile records . . . . . . .   SFLCLR                N50
   Indicate more records . . . . . . .   SFLEND                90
     SFLEND parameter  . . . . . . . .   *MORE       Y
     SFLEND parameter  . . . . . . . .   *SCRBAR     _         *MORE ...
   Record not active . . . . . . . . .   SFLRNA      _
                                                               More...

F3=Exit    F12=Cancel

                                      Keyword   CFnn/CAnn   Indicators/+
   Subfile initially truncated . . . .  SFLDROP
   Subfile initially folded . . . . .   SFLFOLD
   Use instead of Enter key . . . . .   SFLENTER
```

Figure C.17
Define General
Keywords Screen

As shown in Figure C.17, the Define General Keywords screen can be used to add the SFLCSRRN, SFLMODE, SFLDSP, SFLDSPCTL, SFLCLR, SFLEND, SFLDROP, and SFLFOLD keywords, which were introduced in Chapters 1 through 6 of this text. Only a few of these keywords will be needed at this time.

6. Enter the field names and indicators as shown in Figure C.17.

Exit the Define General Keywords screen, returning to the Select Subfile Control Keywords screen (Figure C.16).

7. Type a **Y** in the field for the Subfile display layout screen. SDA will display the Define Display Layout screen (Figure C.18).

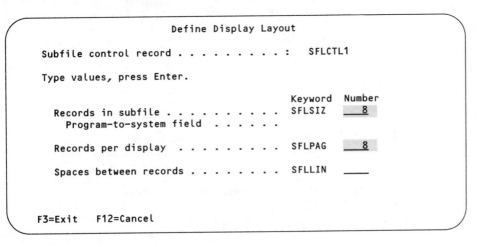

```
                  Define Display Layout

Subfile control record . . . . . . . . . :    SFLCTL1

Type values, press Enter.

                                    Keyword   Number
   Records in subfile . . . . . . . . .  SFLSIZ      8
      Program-to-system field . . . . .  .

   Records per display . . . . . . . .   SFLPAG      8

   Spaces between records . . . . . . .  SFLLIN    ____


F3=Exit    F12=Cancel
```

Figure C.18
Define Display
Layout Screen

8. Enter the correct values for the SFLSIZ and SFLPAG fields as described in Chapter 3.
9. Exit by pressing F3 until you reach the Work with Display Records screen, Figure C.19.

Figure C.19
Work with Display Records Screen with SFL1 and SFLCTL1 Records

```
                           Work with Display Records
File . . . . . . . :   QDDSSRC               Member . . . . . . :   SDADEM01
   Library . . . . :      A300C1_TMP         Source type  . . . :   DSPF

Type options, press Enter.
  1=Add                  2=Edit comments          3=Copy          4=Delete
  7=Rename               8=Select keywords       12=Design image

Opt  Order     Record          Type      Related Subfile   Date        DDS Error

        10     SFL1            SFL                          10/13/98
        20     SFLCTL1         SFLCTL    SFL1               10/13/98




                                                                       Bottom
F3=Exit                        F12=Cancel        F14=File-level keywords
F15=File-level comments        F17=Subset        F24=More keys
Record SFL1 added to member SDADEM01.                                       +
```

10. Use Option 12 to work with the record SFLCTL1. SDA will display the paint screen for the control record for editing, and it will also display the subfile record (currently blank) to make alignment of the heading columns easy.
11. Fill in the heading information for the control record as shown in Figure C.20.

Figure C.20
Adding Text, User ID, and Date to the Control Record

```
*USER                    'COMPUTERS ARE US INV SYS'                    *DATE
                         'WORK WITH INVENTORY LISTS'

'PART NUMBER'   'DESCRIPTION'                     'QNTY'    'COST'    'EXTENDED'






Work screen for SFLCTL1. SFL1 displayed as additional record.
```

12. Press Enter to have SDA evaluate your entries and substitute the fields, such as user ID, or the *USER request.
13. Exit and save the changes to the record.

14. Select work with the record SFL1.

When you are working with the subfile record, SDA displays the headings on control record while you enter and edit the subfile record, which makes it easy to align the columns (Figure C.21).

```
 ┌──────────────────────────────────────────────────────────────────────────
 │  UUUUUUUUUU            COMPUTERS ARE US INV SYS              DD/DD/DD
 │                        WORK WITH INVENTORY LISTS
 │
 │  PART NUMBER      DESCRIPTION              QNTY      COST      EXTENDED
 │
 │  +0(11)           +0(25)                  +6(7,0)   +6(9,2)   +6(9,2)
 │
 │
 │
 │
 │
 │
 │  Work screen for SFL1. SFLCTL1 displayed as additional record.
 └──────────────────────────────────────────────────────────────────────────
```

Figure C.21
Work with the Subfile Record SFL1 Screen

15. Enter the Output field types and sizes as shown in Figure C.21 and press Enter. SDA evaluates your request, and because it's a subfile with eight records, shows the layout of the eight records as shown in Figure C.22.

```
 ┌──────────────────────────────────────────────────────────────────────────
 │  UUUUUUUUUU            COMPUTERS ARE US INV SYS              DD/DD/DD
 │                        WORK WITH INVENTORY LISTS
 │
 │  PART NUMBER      DESCRIPTION              QNTY      COST      EXTENDED
 │  00000000000  00000000000000000000000000  6666666  666666666  666666666
 │  00000000000  00000000000000000000000000  6666666  666666666  666666666
 │  00000000000  00000000000000000000000000  6666666  666666666  666666666
 │  00000000000  00000000000000000000000000  6666666  666666666  666666666
 │  00000000000  00000000000000000000000000  6666666  666666666  666666666
 │  00000000000  00000000000000000000000000  6666666  666666666  666666666
 │  00000000000  00000000000000000000000000  6666666  666666666  666666666
 │  00000000000  00000000000000000000000000  6666666  666666666  666666666
 │
 │  Work screen for SFL1. SFLCTL1 displayed as additional record.
 └──────────────────────────────────────────────────────────────────────────
```

Figure C.22
Work Screen for SFL1 with Layout for Eight Records

To adjust the alignment of subfile fields, use the < or > to the left or right of the fields. To adjust the alignment of the headings, you must exit the Work screen for the subfile record and work with the subfile control record. Then use < or > to adjust the headings to the left or right.

While in the Work with Subfile screen, you can rename the fields by pressing F4. You can change the edit codes, colors, and other features by typing an asterisk (*) immediately in front of the field to be changed.

Exercise C.3 Creating a Subfile Using SDA

Purpose
To demonstrate your capability to use SDA to create, edit, and test a subfile.

Instructions
Create the subfile shown in Figure C.12.

1. Follow the suggestions in the section on creating subfiles using SDA to create the subfile shown in Figure C.12.

2. Exit, save, and compile the display file. Enter the test mode and select to test the record SFLCTL1. Set indicator 50 on and indicator 90 off. Try the record with indicator 90 on. Try it with indicator 50 off.

Exiting, Compiling, and Saving the Design

Figure C.23 shows the Create Display File screen. Whenever you have made changes to the display, you will encounter the Save DDS — Create Display File screen as you exit the Work with Display Records screen.

The first section of this screen is used to determine whether and where the source is to be saved, as well as its name. The next section defines whether a display file is to be created, its name, and its library.

Figure C.23
Save DDS - Create
Display File Screen

```
                        Save DDS - Create Display File

     Type choices, press Enter.

         Save DDS source  . . . . . . . . . . . .    Y            Y=Yes
            Source file  . . . . . . . . . . . .     QDDSSRC      F4 for list
               Library  . . . . . . . . . . . . .    A300C1_TMP   Name, *LIBL
            Member . . . . . . . . . . . . . . .     SDADEMO1     F4 for list
            Text . . . . . . . . . . . . . . . .

         Create display file  . . . . . . . . . .    Y            Y=Yes
            Prompt for parameters  . . . . . . . .                Y=Yes
            Display file . . . . . . . . . . . .     SDADEMO1     F4 for list
               Library  . . . . . . . . . . . . .    RDTSRC       Name, *CURLIB
            Replace existing file  . . . . . . . .                Y=Yes

         Submit create job in batch . . . . . . .    Y            Y=Yes

         Specify additional
            save or create options . . . . . . . .                Y=Yes

     F3=Exit    F4=Prompt    F12=Cancel
     Member SDADEMO1 already exists. Press Enter to replace.
```

Index

New AS/400 Books in the 29th Street Press Library

THE AS/400 EXPERT: READY-TO-RUN RPG/400 TECHNIQUES

By Julian Monypenny and Roger Pence

As the first book in The AS/400 Expert series, *Ready-to-Run RPG/400 Techniques* provides a variety of RPG templates, subroutines, and copy modules, sprinkled with evangelical advice, to help you write robust and effective RPG/400 programs. Highlights include string-handling routines, numeric editing routines, date routines, error-handling modules, and tips for using OS/400 APIs with RPG/400. The tested and ready-to-run code building blocks — provided on an accompanying CD — easily snap into existing RPG code and integrate well with new RPG/400 projects. 203 pages.

DDS KEYWORD REFERENCE

By James Coolbaugh

Reach for the *DDS Keyword Reference* when you need quick, at-your-fingertips information about DDS keywords for physical files, logical files, display files, printer files, and ICF files. In this no-nonsense volume, author Jim Coolbaugh gives you all the keywords you'll need, listed alphabetically in five sections. He explains each keyword, providing syntax rules and examples for coding the keyword. The *DDS Keyword Reference*, which is current to V4R3, is a friendly and manageable alternative to IBM's bulky DDS reference manual. 212 pages.

DDS PROGRAMMING FOR DISPLAY & PRINTER FILES, SECOND EDITION

By James Coolbaugh

DDS Programming for Display & Printer Files, Second Edition helps you master DDS and — as a result — improve the quality of your display presentations and your printed jobs. Updated through OS/400 V4R3, the second edition offers a thorough, straightforward explanation of how to use DDS to program display files and printer files. It includes extensive DDS programming examples for CL and RPG that you can put to use immediately because a companion CD includes all the DDS, RPG, and CL source code presented in the book. 429 pages.

Java and the AS/400
Practical Examples Using VisualAge for Java

By Daniel Darnell

This detailed guide takes you through everything you need to know about the AS/400's implementation of Java, including the QShell Interpreter and the Integrated File System (IFS), and development products such as VisualAge for Java (VAJ) and the AS/400 Toolbox for Java. The author provides several small application examples that demonstrate the advantages of Java programming for the AS/400. The companion CD contains all the example code presented in the book and full-version copies of VAJ Professional Edition and the AS/400 Toolbox for Java. 300 pages.

OPNQRYF BY EXAMPLE

By Mike Dawson and Mike Manto

The OPNQRYF (Open Query File) command is the single most dynamic and versatile command on the AS/400. Drawing from real-life, real-job experiences, the authors explain the basics and the intricacies of OPNQRYF with lots of examples to make you productive quickly. An appendix provides the UPDQRYF (Update Query File) command — a powerful addition to AS/400 and System/38 file update capabilities. 216 pages.

SQL/400 BY EXAMPLE

By James Coolbaugh

Designed to help you make the most of SQL/400, *SQL/400 by Example* includes everything from SQL syntax and rules to the specifics of embedding SQL within an RPG program. For novice SQL users, this book features plenty of introductory-level text and examples, including all the features and terminology of SQL/400. For experienced AS/400 programmers, *SQL/400 by Example* offers a number of specific examples that will help you increase your understanding of SQL concepts and improve your programming skills. 204 pages.

We Want Your Response

Mail it ▶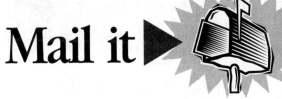

Fax it ▶

Web it ▶

Complete this form to join our network of computer professionals

We will gladly send you a free copy of

❏ *Windows NT Magazine*

❏ *NEWS/400*

❏ *Selling AS/400 Solutions*

❏ *SQL Server Magazine*

❏ *Business Finance*

Name _____
Title _____ Phone _____
Company _____
Address _____
City/State/Zip _____
E-mail _____

Where did you purchase this book?
❏ Trade show   ❏ Computer store   ❏ Internet   ❏ Card deck   ❏ Bookstore
❏ Magazine   ❏ Direct mail catalog or brochure

What new applications do you expect to use during the next year?
_____
_____

How many times this month will you visit a Duke Communications Web site (29th Street Press, NEWS/400, Selling AS/400 Solutions, SQL Server Magazine, Windows NT Magazine, Business Finance)?_____

Please share your reaction to *Essential of Subfile Programming and Advanced Topics in RPG IV* _____
_____
_____

❏ YES! You have my permission to quote my comments in your publications.
(initials) _____

[99SCXBOOK]

Publisher of practical, hands-on technical books for Windows NT and AS/400 computer professionals. Providing help not hype.

COPY THIS PAGE AND MAIL TO
29TH STREET PRESS • 221 EAST 29TH STREET • LOVELAND, CO 80538
OR FAX TO (970) 667-2321
OR RESPOND VIA OUR WEB SITE AT www.29thStreetPress.com

MAKE THE MOST OF YOUR AS/400 WITH NEWSWIRE/400

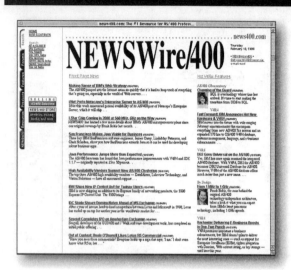

A FREE e-mail newsletter from NEWS/400, the #1 AS/400 magazine worldwide!

Every NEWSWire/400 delivers to your desktop

- Tips & Techniques
- The Latest News from IBM
- Product News
- Industry Updates
- Salary Surveys

Sign up for NEWSWire/400 today & we'll also send you a free sample of NEWS/400, the #1 AS/400 magazine worldwide!

Yes!

☐ I'd like to receive NEWSWire/400 **FREE** via e-mail. Please also send me a sample copy of *NEWS/400* (new subscribers only).

☐ I'd like to receive NEWSWire/400 **FREE** via e-mail. I'd also like to subscribe to *NEWS/400* for $129/year (U.S. only). Please sign me up right away. I understand that I can cancel at any time for a refund.

Copy this page and mail to

**NEWS/400
221 E. 29th St. Loveland,
CO 80538**

**or fax to
(970) 663-4007**

**or subscribe
on the Web at
www.news400store.com**

Name

Title

Company

Address

City/State/Zip

Phone   Fax

E-mail   [99SCDPX]